Radical Externalism

# Radical Externalism

**Honderich's Theory of
Consciousness Discussed**

Edited by
Anthony Freeman

imprint-academic.com

*Copyright © Imprint Academic, 2006*

No part of any contribution may be reproduced in any form without permission, except for the quotation of brief passages in criticism and discussion.

Published in the UK by
Imprint Academic, PO Box 200, Exeter EX5 5YX, UK

Published in the USA by
Imprint Academic, Philosophy Documentation Center
PO Box 7147, Charlottesville, VA 22906-7147, USA

ISBN 184540 068 2
ISBN-13 9781845400682

A CIP catalogue record for this book is available from the British Library and US Library of Congress

# Contents

| | |
|---|---|
| Editorial Preface, *Anthony Freeman* | 1 |

## Target Paper

| | |
|---|---|
| Radical Externalism, *Ted Honderich* | 3 |

## Commentaries and Replies

| | |
|---|---|
| Comment on Radical Externalism, *Harold Brown* | 14 |
| Comment on Ted Honderich's Radical Externalism, *Tim Crane* | 28 |
| Consciousness and Absence, *James Garvey* | 44 |
| Honderich and the Curse of Epiphenomenalism, *Stephen Law* | 61 |
| Radical Externalism or Berkeley Revisited?, *E.J. Lowe* | 78 |
| Some Questions about Radical Externalism, *Derek Matravers* | 95 |
| The Success of Consciousness, *Paul Noordhof* | 109 |
| Consciousness as Existence as a Form of Neutral Monism, *Ingmar Persson* | 128 |
| Radical Internalism, *Stephen Priest* | 147 |
| Consciousness: An Inner View of the Outer World, *Barry C. Smith* | 175 |
| Radical Externalisms, *Paul Snowdon* | 187 |
| Contributors | 213 |
| Index | 216 |

# Anthony Freeman
## *Editorial Preface*

What is it for you to be conscious? To be conscious now, for instance, of the room you are in or the page you are reading? This is the fundamental problem of the Philosophy of Mind and is posed in all its starkness by Ted Honderich in the paper that opens and focuses the discussion presented in this volume.

There has been no shortage of proposed solutions. They run from the materialism of Hobbes and the dualism of Descartes in the seventeenth century, through the empirical ideas of Locke, Berkeley and Hume, to theories of mind–brain identity — or more cautiously of mind–brain correlation — that form the working basis of present-day neuroscience and cognitive science. None of these theories has worked convincingly enough to gain general acceptance, and so the problem of the nature of consciousness has survived them all. The reason, according to Honderich, lies in the persistent and resilient belief of almost all philosophers, and indeed almost all human beings, that consciousness really is *different*.

The theories and attitudes on offer are more alike than is sometimes supposed. They can be divided up into just two large categories of answers to the question of consciousness, labelled by Honderich as *devout physicalism* and *spiritualism*. The first reduces consciousness to no more than the physical, while the second takes it (or part of it at least) out of space and into mystery, the appropriate word even when presented — as it sometimes is — in terms of cool philosophy informed by science.

This second view of the problem of consciousness is the one from which Honderich's new theory of it takes its departure. It is however a point of departure, not a position to be held and defended. The history of the problem is taken to be a kind of proof of the need for something different. So the theory of Radical Externalism, which for a while was called the theory of Consciousness as Existence, is neither devout physicalism nor spiritualism.

It develops from a question and an answer. The question has already been posed: What is it for you to be conscious of the room you're in? The answer given by Honderich himself — an answer that he hopes may get the assent of us his readers — is this: It's for the room somehow to exist. The analysis of perceptual consciousness that is subtly drawn by Honderich out of that answer issues in connected analyses of reflective and affective consciousness. Aiming to do justice to two commonly opposed aspects of this subject, they give a place to the cranialism that the account of perceptual consciousness goes against.

Radical Externalism is committed to the idea that a theory of consciousness should be true to what consciousness actually seems to us to be. But it is owed to more than that. It recommends itself as satisfying a true list of criteria for an adequate theory of consciousness. They include both the subjectivity of consciousness (a criterion that rules out devout physicalism and is an attraction of spiritualism) and also the reality of consciousness and its causal interaction with the physical world (which criteria rule out spiritualism and seem to demand devout physicalism).

At the beginning of this volume, Radical Externalism is set out by Ted Honderich. It is then individually judged, without allegiance or piety, by eleven other strong philosophers. They do not make up a movement, mutual-support network, or cabal, and each of their independently argued verdicts is the subject of a full response by the proponent of Radical Externalism.

Does the problem of the nature of consciousness survive this latest theory? Does the theory survive such sharp and focussed discussion? It is for the reader to judge. In its propounder's view the theory has an essential recommendation: it *is* different from what has gone before it in the history of the philosophy and science of the mind. It is not materialism, spiritualism, identity theory or any other cranialism. It is a response to what can be taken as certain — that it is time for a change.

Ted Honderich

# *Radical Externalism*

If you want a philosophically diligent exposition of a theory, something that has got through review by conventional peers, go elsewhere (Honderich, 2004). If you want an understanding made more immediate by brevity and informality, read on. The theory is a Radical Externalism about the nature of consciousness. If it is not a complete departure from the cranialism of most of the philosophy and science of consciousness, it is a fundamental departure.

You are *seeing this page*. What does that fact come to? What is that state of affairs? The natural answer has a lot in it, about the page as a physical thing, whatever one of those is, and about your retinas and your visual cortex. It also has in it philosophy and science about the relation between a neural process and your consciousness.

So there is more to your seeing the page than your consciousness of it.

Is there some mistake in that remark? Some mistake in saying that your consciousness is only part of the story of you seeing the page? Well, we *can* decide to say that your being conscious of the page *was* all of the fact of your seeing the page as just understood, a fact with your visual cortex in it as a part. But that is a special usage, an extraordinary one. Our ordinary assumption is that your visual cortex was no part of your *being conscious* of whatever it was. That fact about you, that property of you or state of affairs with respect to you had no neurons in it.

Is there anything dubious or maybe uninformed about speaking of your consciousness a minute ago as something that did not have your visual cortex in it? Certainly the verbal practice of a lot of philosophers and scientists of consciousness suggests so (Papineau, 2000; Honderich, 2000). But if there really were something dubious, the whole history of the philosophy of mind would be open to doubt in this preliminary way.

That history has had in it the main proposition that mind and brain — including your mind and brain a minute ago — are two things, this being 'dualism', and also the proposition that they are one thing, in fact the brain, this being 'monism'. In order for it to have been conceptually possible consistently to say they are two things, talk of your consciousness has to be understood as not itself talk of your brain. Also, talk of your consciousness has to be understood as not talk of your brain in order for it to be possible to maintain, as other than a conceptual or logical truth, that your mind really was only one thing with your brain. To which it can be added that the history of the science of consciousness includes much on mind–brain correlation. That too depends on consciousness not having cortex as a part of it.

If we now ask for an explanation of the existence of this standard conception of consciousness, one comes to hand quickly. We ordinarily take it that consciousness is something we *have*. It is because in seeing the page we don't *have* the neurons or whatever that the neurons are not part of the consciousness. Your consciousness, in this understanding of it that is standard and nearly universal, is such that there is nothing in it or to it that you do not *have*.

To this proposition, no doubt, one response will be that it is not clear what it is to *have* something in the sense in question. Somebody will say it's plainly not like having money or an arm or a hope. The rejoinder is that there is nothing clearer to me than what was in my consciousness a minute ago and what was not. I do indeed know what I was seeing, what I was thinking, what I was feeling. My having something in the relevant sense was my doing those things.

Being a difficult philosophical customer, you may say that this is not good enough as a clarification of saying that consciousness is something we have. Well, it has to be admitted that the final answer to the question of what it was for you to have or to experience things or propositions or feelings will be that you were conscious of them, whatever that comes to. We are on the way to an answer to the question.

Our subject right now, however, is whether any answer to which we come will have to be in accord with this datum about consciousness being something we have. One impediment in inquiry, you can think, here or elsewhere, is the idea that we don't know what we haven't got an analysis or decent understanding of. Well, whatever my analytical problems, I know there is past, present and future, and that representations represent, and that effects are not events that might not have happened given everything just as it was. I know too that my consciousness is something that I have. Certainly other pieces of language can be added and they are of some use. Consciousness is present to me, immediate, in no way a matter of inference.

Join me in putting aside, please, talk of the unconscious, the subconscious, lurking or bullied desires unnoticed by their owners, and all that. It preceded Freud, of course, and is entirely independent of his own theories of early sexual desires and what-not. This sort of talk, some of it reasonable, is easily made sense of in terms of brain rather than mind. It is not any kind of consciousness, but rather dispositional beliefs and feelings, which is just to say existing parts of possible causal circumstances, standing parts of possible nomic correlates for ordinary or non-dispositional beliefs and feelings Honderich, 1988; 1990, pp. 86, 92). We can keep confused consciousness, of course, which is just as much consciousness as any other kind.

Come now to the most useful form of the proposition I have been labouring — and, as you will be hearing, not just as an explanation of a conception of consciousness. The most useful form of the proposition that consciousness is something we have is this: with respect to consciousness, *there is no difference between appearance and reality.* With consciousness, what there seems to be is what there is. What there seems to be is all there is. If you want to set out to know the whole nature of your consciousness, not a scintilla left out, let alone a basement, however you subsequently proceed to try to analyse it, just reflect on what it seems to be, tell yourself what you have.

We started, after putting aside your seeing a page, with the property, fact or affairs that was exactly your consciousness of the page. We now have it that a certain question is crucial. What did your consciousness *seem* to consist in? An answer can grow on you fast. It *was for the page to be there*. What your consciousness seemed to consist in was nothing other or more than that. In a better sense of the words than employed by some philosophers, that is what it was like for you to be conscious of the page and that is all that it was like.

It wasn't as if what seemed to be had, or given or on hand, like the page, included something else as well. There wasn't something such that the rest of what was on hand was a *content* — there wasn't a container or vehicle. There wasn't any sign at all of this item raised up into being by ordinary philosophical talk of the contents of consciousness. There wasn't 'the mind' or 'the self', which still turns up in advanced philosophy that does not remember Hume's service in reminding us that we are aware of no such thing. There wasn't a relationship of intentionality, aboutness or directedness in your consciousness of the page. There wasn't an act of affirmation in it as well as the page. No doubt all of that has to do with truths, but not truths about what it seems to be to be conscious of the page you are seeing.

Consciousness is perceptual, reflective or affective — in brief it has to do with seeing, thinking and wanting. We are as good as never engaged in only one of the sorts of things. There are large problems here. One is the understanding of the mixing and melding of the three parts, kinds, sides or whatever of consciousness, of how one contributes to another, even in ordinary seeing and acting.

A further problem, obviously connected, is that of the priority or fundamentality of perceptual as against reflective and affective consciousness. It is clear enough, I take it, that there are relatively pure cases of of perceptual consciousness, whatever has to be said of what is in them, and that maybe one of those was the property, fact or state of affairs that was your being conscious of a page.

That this fact of consciousness necessarily was what it seemed to be, the state of affairs that was *the page's being there*, a state of affairs outside your head, is one of the several most fundamental propositions of the Radical Externalism that is our subject. More fully, to be perceptually conscious is only for an extra-cranial state of affairs to exist — for there to be a spatio-temporal set of things with a dependence on another extra-cranial state of affairs and also on what is in a particular cranium. The page's being there, and more generally *your world of perceptual consciousness* is things being in space and time, with such further properties as colour, and being dependent on a scientific or noumenal world underneath and also dependent on you neurally.

The particular state of affairs in question, and your ongoing world of perceptual consciousness, are different from but also like other states of affairs and worlds. They are different, that is, from other conceptualizations of what there is — where *what there is* is whatever it is to which we bring our perceptual, conceptual, theoretical and other schemes, systems and apparatuses, including our perceptual apparatus.

A world of perceptual consciousness is not the physical world. The physical world, very briefly indeed, consists in two categories: (1) things taking up space and time and also having other properties as standardly or publicly perceived, as distinct from properties dependent on anyone in particular, and (2) things that also take up space and time, are without perceived properties, but stand in causal or other lawlike connection with things in the first category. The physical world then consists in the perceived physical world, including pages, and in what you can call the physical world of science, including atoms — already mentioned as a necessary condition of each world of perceptual consciousness. There is not much of a liberty taken in speaking of there being pages in both a world of perceptual consciousness and in the perceived physical world, and indeed in referring to each of a related pair of things as *a page*.

Radical Externalism is not the externalism of Putnam (1975), to the effect that meaning has a part that is reference-in-the-world, or the externalism of Burge (1979; 1986a,b), to the effect that meaning has a kind of dependency on things in the world. You can object to both (Honderich, 2004, pp. 67–85). The Radical Externalism being contemplated here in one of its three parts is indeed the general proposition that what it is to be perceptually conscious is for a world in a way to exist — i.e. for things to be in space and time with certain properties and for them to have certain necessary conditions. Notice that a clear sense has been given or at least gestured at with respect to talk of the existence. Notice too that there is not much more reason to regard a world of perceptual consciousness as 'mental' than the perceived part of the physical world — both have a dependency on human perception, etc.

Before going on to reflective and affective consciousness, and to argumentation for the whole theory, let us think a little more about perceptual consciousness and what we have already.

Did it occur to you that there might be an old objection to saying that what it seemed to you to be conscious of the page was just that the page was there, and no more than that? Were you tempted to say that the seeming fact was consistent with your in some sense being aware of, your having, no more than a collection of *mental* items — what were first called *ideas* in the history of British empiricism and ended up as *sense-data* or maybe *non-conceptual contents*? That is, did it occur to you that what your consciousness seemed to be might be consistent with the doctrine of phenomenalism or representative perception? As against realism and what is different from realism but closer to realism than phenomenalism, which is Radical Externalism?

Well, I myself can tell the difference between a state of affairs that is the existence of ordinary things and a state of affairs that is the existence of representations of ordinary things. In our lives as they are, there is a good difference between representations, which can be in various ways wrong, and ordinary things, which can't. Seeing isn't like dreaming — seeing doesn't seem to be like dreaming, which truth is unaffected by your having to get out of the dream to know the fact. And if you now say, maybe with traditional phenomenalists, that your perceptual consciousness is a dream that never goes wrong, a dream we never wake up from, is there any distance left between perceptual consciousness as the existence of a world and perceptual consciousness as representations of some world?

There are things to think about there, but not to think about now. So too with the recommendation of Occam's Razor, a principle of simplicity or parsimony in theories, of avoiding the unnecessarily complex — and hence, I think, another recommendation of Radical Externalism. We get rid of something unnecessary. There is another fact about phenomenalism that can be considered more quickly.

There has been one argument for phenomenalism, originally known as the argument from illusion. It comes to the proposition that what we standardly call consciousness of the world might exist without the world, and the person in question couldn't tell the hallucination from a veridical experience. You could have a brain in a vat stimulated so as to produce consciousness indistinguishable from what we call consciousness of a page. And so consciousness of a page is a matter of sense-data or whatever and nothing else.

The worn story depends on something that this Radical Externalism denies. The story depends on the possibility of a causal or lawlike sufficient condition rather than a necessary condition in the brain (Honderich, 1988; 1990, pp. 106–44; 2004, pp. 19–46). According to Radical Externalism, there isn't a sufficient neural condition for perceptual consciousness — whatever is true of reflective and affective consciousness. Much of the history of the philosophy of perception has been resistance to phenomenalism or reluctant and grudging acceptance of it. Think of Ayer (1956). The theory of consciousness we are contemplating has the side-recommendation that it undercuts the only argument for the irritating possibility that it's all a kind of dream.

Now a few words about reflective consciousness, say thinking of home, and affective consciousness, say wanting to be there or intending to get there. As remarked at the beginning, there have been externalisms more radical than the one under consideration, attempts to formulate and sustain a theory of consciousness that takes it out of the cranium in all of its three parts, sides or whatever (Tonneau, 2004; cf. Manzotti, 2006).

The externalism under consideration, the whole thing, does remain true to the proposition that all there is to any consciousness is what is had. The theory also remains true to the proposition that what it is to be conscious in any way is for something to exist in a certain way — hence *Consciousness as Existence* as a name for the theory. Thirdly, therefore, the theory reduces consciousness to things at least close to what other theories and attitudes take to be the contents of consciousness, thereby supposing or implying there is more to it than the contents. But the theory does not take all of consciousness outside the cranium. It does not do so with all of reflective consciousness.

Very briefly, what it seems to be to think of home now is for something to exist that has some of the properties of home. That is what a representation essentially is — something that shares some effects with what is represented. Think of the exclamation 'Fire!', however that may stand as an effect to a previous cause, say fire. Some of these representations *are* external — those in actually written language for a start. These will have the *character*, so to speak, of everything else that makes up someone's perceptual consciousness. We will be coming to that character, partly what will be called *subjectivity*, in a minute or two. But there is also what is rightly called the language of thought (Fodor, 1975). Yours consists in representations internal to you — neural representations. They have a related character.

As for wanting to be at home or intending to get there, and affective consciousness generally, one essential point is that this too is to be understood in terms of the characters of anyone's perceptual and also reflective consciousness. Part of the rest of the story here is that there are values in our perceptual worlds — including scenes in nature, pictures in art galleries, and people who are good-lookers or who care about the hurts of all others. It is very mistaken to suppose that the story of value is a story that does not contains things as real as woods, paintings and people — stuff of perceptual consciousness. More of the story of affective consciousness has to do with bodily sensation before acting or in acting and of course representations of actions.

But leave the subject of reflective and affective consciousness and look at more of what is to be said about and for this Radical Externalism as a whole, and primarily about and for what is primary in it, the account of perceptual consciousness.

You will anticipate, I hope, that it is certainly the determined intention of this Radical Externalism not to be circular. The theory is not and does not include or rest on a non-analysis. It is not the proposition that perceptual consciousness consists in a world's existing *of which there is consciousness or awareness*. Similarly the analysis of reflective consciousness is not the useless line that it consists in representations *of which we are conscious*. So with the analysis of affective consciousness. Rather, Radical Externalism is that the fact of consciousness of the three kinds or whatever is no more than the existence of the three states of affairs — the existence of things with certain dependencies.

Do you say that the proposition that what it is for us to be perceptually conscious is for there to be an external state of affairs is an absurd proposition? Taken in one way, maybe the one that comes to mind first, that is true, but perhaps no skin off the nose of its proponents. The proposition is not conceptual analysis, not a report of ordinary or specialist usage. For such an analysis, for a start, go to the circularities of a good dictionary. You will find consciousness defined as awareness. Or go to ordinary and hesitant beliefs about consciousness, folk-beliefs or images that tend in the direction of what is called Cartesian dualism. Descartes didn't make it up.

Rather, in saying that perceptual consciousness consists in an external state of affairs, what we do is propose what it is reasonable to call conceptual revision or even reconstruction — conceptual revolution if you are being grand (Thagard, 1993) — and what it is also reasonable to call conceptual *correction*. The latter description, implying a mistake in ordinary beliefs and usage, is the important one. It reports the fact that Radical Externalism corrects our concept of perceptual experience so as to bring it into line with what in fact are conceptual commitments of ours that are firmer than the one to Cartesian dualism, better named spiritualism or mentalism.

Radical Externalism so conceived is an exercise in consistency — as always, consistency with something or some things given priority. To speak differently, and to put all of my cards on the table, the proposed Radical Externalism is the only sort of theory that satisfies what are essential criteria for an acceptable theory of the nature of consciousness. If you will put up with my saying so, the criteria have the demands of reality in them.

One of these is that a theory of consciousness must actually be a theory *of consciousness*, not anything else. A second criterion, of which you have also heard, must be truth to the seeming nature of consciousness itself. These two criteria, and what they come to, and the satisfaction of them by Radical Externalism, are perhaps the best introduction to the theory.

We will get to the rest of the criteria, some hardly less important, in a minute. First, consider the matter of the alternatives to radical empiricism, alternative also to be judged by way of the criteria. The argument for Radical Externalism is in a very important part the extent to which the alternatives fail to satisfy the criteria.

Devout physicalism, a true monism, is the belief or perhaps attitude that our consciousness is a fact, property or state of affairs that involves only physical properties in the sense gestured at earlier — and in particular properties in existing and more or less anticipated neuroscience. Devout physicalism, once known as materialism, is thinking of importance on the nature of consciousness in the contemporary philosophy of mind. It includes express denials of consciousness as ordinarily understood, say eliminative materialism, and also analyses of it that purport to be true to the ordinary understanding but fail actually to be so. In my view, functionalism, Dennett and Searle, different as they are, come into the latter category (Honderich, 2004).

What still has the name of dualism, contrary to what is often remarked, is not thinking about consciousness that has been abandoned. In fact, it is in a way the majority view not only in the philosophy of mind and perhaps working neuroscience. I hazard this because it appears certain that a majority of philosophers and scientists are rightly unable to swallow devout physicalism and have nowhere to go but dualism.

In brief, it is is the theory, rightly associated with Descartes, that your consciousness is somehow non-spatial and hence not physical. It is in fact only misleadingly called dualism, mainly because its distinctive nature and its problems are not owed to its asserting that consciousness is other than physical but rather to its asserting that consciousness is out of space and in fact of a mysterious nature. As remarked, it is better named spiritualism or mentalism.

No doubt theories are sometimes destroyed by single counter-examples clearly seen, or by crucial experiments well-conducted. It is my inclination to think this of devout physicalism and spiritualism. Still, others may not be persuaded, and it is proper to have more tests than one for an adequate theory of consciousness. It is also my belief that the alternatives to Radical Externalism are mainly devout physicalism and the spiritualism, and that Radical Externalism, by the criteria for adequacy, is clearly superior. As for the remainder of theories, they are marriages of things close to devout physicalism, and close to spiritualism, and they inherit the fatal personalities of the parties entering into them.

You have heard of two criteria for a theory of consciousness, one being that it must actually be of consciousness as we know we have it, one being truth to appearance. Devout physicalism fails absolutely to satisfy these criteria. Radical Externalism does satisfy them.

A third criterion is that consciousness is somehow subjective. The term has been variously used and abused, but that consciousness has some character that the term points to is indubitable. Devout physicalism allows for no persuasive sense in which consciousness is subjective. Spiritualism in its carry-on about a self or subject or the mind faces overwhelming objections.

For Radical Externalism, perceptual consciousness consists in a state of affairs that not only is partly dependent on one individual, but is also different from related states of affairs dependent on other individuals. It is also different from the state of affairs that is the perceived physical world as well as other states of affairs that are in defined senses objective. If it is a near-physicalism, it does give clear sense to our conviction about subjectivity.

A fourth criterion of adequacy is that a theory of consciousness must make consciousness a reality, which is to say physical or approximate to physical or in some strong sense reducible to the physical. A fifth criterion is that a theory must not make impossible what is actual, which is causal interaction between consciousness and the physical. Spiritualism fails both tests absolutely. Radical Externalism passes them. Those who follow Descartes take consciousness out of space, and therefore postulate causes and effects that are nowhere. That is certainly not so with Radical Externalism.

There are other criteria that can be no more than mentioned. One has to do with the efficacy of consciousness, which is to say the impossibility of epiphenomenalism. Another, of lesser importance, derives from a common uncertainty about whether our consciousness, all of it, is something in our heads.

I leave unconsidered, too, the recommendation of Radical Externalism with respect to the science of consciousness in particular. It saves it from a certain self-doubt, by making *all* of consciousness persuasively understood a subject for science. It also clarifies a long-running uncertainty about the dependency of mind on brain. In proposing a considerable conceptual shift, hopefully a revolution, it can be no stranger to science, certainly not to physics.

Radical Externalism, despite its successes, has its difficulties, more than have been mentioned. Contemplation of them can for the moment be left to others.

## References

Ayer, A J. (1956), *The Problem of Knowledge* (Harmondsworth: Penguin).
Burge, T. (1979), 'Individualism and the mental', *Midwest Studies in Philosophy*, **4**, pp. 73–121.
Burge, T. (1986a), 'Individualism and psychology', *Philosophical Review*, **45**, pp. 3-45.
Burge, T. (1986b), 'Intellectual norms and foundations of mind', *Journal of Philosophy*, **83**, pp. 697–720.
Fodor, J. (1975), *The Language of Thought* (New York: Crowell).
Honderich, T. (1988), *A Theory of Determinism: The Mind, Neuroscience and Life-Hopes* (Oxford: Oxford University Press).

Honderich, T. (1990), *Mind and Brain: A Theory of Determinism, Vol. 1* (Oxford: Oxford University Press).
Honderich, T. (2000), 'Consciousness and inner tubes', *Journal of Consciousness Studies*, **7** (7), pp. 51–62.
Honderich, T. (2004), *On Consciousness* (Edinburgh: Edinburgh University Press).
Manzotti, Riccardo (2006), 'A process-oriented view of conscious perception', *Journal of Consciousness Studies*, **13** (6), pp. 7–41.
Papineau, D. (2000), *Introducing Consciousness* (Cambridge and New York: Icon/Totem Books).
Putnam, H. (1975), 'The meaning of 'Meaning', *Philosophical Papers* (Cambridge: Cambridge University Press).
Thagard, P. (1993), *Conceptual Revolutions* (Princeton: Princeton University Press).
Tonneau, F. (2004), 'Consciousness outside the head', *Behaviour and Philosophy*, **32**, pp. 97–123.

# Harold Brown

# *Comment on Radical Externalism*

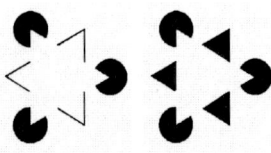

Figure 1

I will begin these comments with perceptual consciousness and focus on a class of persistent visual illusions known as *subjective contours* (see Figure 1). Since I can draw these diagrams myself and tell where my pencil leaves graphite on the paper, it is clear that these contours are not objects in the physical world in the same way as the paper and the graphite. It is this difference that is captured in calling them 'illusions'. Of course, I am not fooled by them and I have no trouble recognizing that they are illusions. The question is whether I *see* them, and the answer to this question depends both on a variety of facts and on how we understand the concept of seeing. Let us consider how Radical Externalism deals with this case.

Professor Honderich writes

> You are *seeing this page*. What does that fact come to? What is that state of affairs? The natural answer has a lot in it, about the page as a physical thing, whatever one of those is, and about your retinas and your visual cortex (Honderich, 2006, p. 3).[1]

This answer applies to the subjective contours since I am aware of them because of the way specific physical things interact with my visual system. Honderich also emphasizes that

> with respect to consciousness, *there is no difference between appearance and reality*. With consciousness, what there seems to be is what there is. What there seems to be is all there is (p. 5).

---

[1] In this commentary all page references are to this target paper unless stated otherwise.

It follows that when I am conscious of the contours they are real. As a result, there is no argument that goes from the contours not being real to the conclusion that I do not see them. A bit later Honderich adds:

> What did your consciousness *seem* to consist in? An answer can grow on you fast. It *was for the page to be there* (p. 5).

Well, the contours are also there: I can describe quite clearly where they appear in space, and even trace them out with my finger. Consider further,

> More fully, to be perceptually conscious is only for an extra-cranial state of affairs to exist — for there to be a spatio-temporal set of things with a dependence on another extra-cranial state of affairs and also on what is in a particular cranium (p. 6).

Subjective contours are located in space and time and depend on other things located in space and time and on what is in my cranium. Still, we must be careful since the contours are located in space and time in a different way from the page and the graphite deposits on which they depend. If I were to close my eyes or look away the page and the graphite would not change, but the subjective contours would cease to exist. The text continues:

> The page's being there, and more generally *your world of perceptual consciousness* is things being in space and time, with such further properties as colour, and being dependent on a scientific or noumenal world underneath and also dependent on you neurally (p. 6).

While most of this holds for subjective contours, they are not coloured — although they can be produced by coloured objects.[2] Does this exclude them from the world of perceptual consciousness? At best they are creatures of a different sort from such other items in this world as the page that Honderich takes to be a paradigmatic instance of its denizens.

Other remarks in Honderich's paper also suggest that subjective contours do not fit into the categorizations provided by Radical Externalism. For example,

> That this fact of consciousness necessarily was what it seemed to be, the state of affairs that was *the page's being there*, a state of affairs outside your head, is one of the several most fundamental propositions of the Radical Externalism that is our subject (p. 6).

Are the contours outside my head? In one sense they are: I can see both the contours and my head in a mirror, and note that the contours

---

[2] Examples can be found on the web, e.g., http://dragon.uml.edu/psych/kaniza.html.

are outside my head; but this, I think, is not the relevant sense. It is more significant that subjective contours depend on what is in my head in way that does not hold for either the page or the graphite. To be sure, if I did not exist with the intra-cranial equipment that I have, the *appearance* of the page and of the rest of the diagram would not exist. But the page and the graphite would still exist while there would be no subjective contours.

Later in the paper Honderich clarifies what he means by 'the physical world'. It consists of two sets of items:

> (1) things taking up space and time and also having other properties as standardly or publicly perceived, as distinct from properties dependent on anyone in particular, and (2) things that also take up space and time, are without perceived properties, but stand in causal or other lawlike connection with things in the first category (p. 6).

The second set comprises atoms and other items postulated by the physical sciences; these do not concern us here. Are subjective contours members of the first set? It would seem that they are since they are located in space and time and do not depend on anyone in particular. They are publically perceived; if this were not the case, we would be unable to discuss them in the way we have been doing. Yet the particular way that subjective contours depend for their existence on features of human perception leaves us with a dilemma. *Either*, subjective contours are not physical objects, from which it follows (for Radical Externalism) that we do not see them. In this case we need additional concepts in order to describe these contours and the mode in which we are aware of them. After all, they have *some* ontological status. They are public items located in space and time and causally dependent on items that clearly are physical objects. *Alternatively*, subjective contours are physical objects. But, again, the way they depend on our perceptual system indicates that they are physical objects of a peculiar kind. The important point for the moment is that it is not clear how subjective contours fit into the conceptual framework of Radical Externalism.

Thus far I have been busily poking a hole in Radical Externalism, but I have been doing so in the service of another of Honderich's themes with which I agree — to a degree. He is quite clear that the argument for Radical Externalism is 'not conceptual analysis, not a report of ordinary or specialist usage'. Instead, Honderich is proposing a

> conceptual revision or even reconstruction — conceptual revolution if you are being grand ... — and what it is also reasonable to call conceptual *correction* (p. 10).

We run into problems in attempting to give an account of perceptual consciousness — and consciousness in general — because the concepts we are using to discuss consciousness are not adequate. Such problems cannot be addressed by unpacking concepts we already have. Rather, to achieve a better understanding of consciousness we must improve our conceptual repertoire. With this I completely agree but I will develop the point in a more radical direction than Honderich does. For, having introduced the option of conceptual revision, he is prepared to pursue it only to a very limited degree. Thus he adds,

> Radical Externalism so conceived is an exercise in consistency — as always, consistency with something or some things given priority (p. 10).

In other words, Honderich does not appear to hold that we may need to introduce a new way of thinking about consciousness that is wholly inconsistent with our current modes of thought about this subject. I want to offer some reasons on behalf of the more radical alternative that we need a more drastic remedy than we are likely to arrive at by seeking consistency with some of our current beliefs that are kept fixed. I will proceed in two steps. First, I will take some examples from the history of physics in order to develop the thesis that inventing the appropriate concepts for dealing with a particular domain is often a central feature of scientific advance. Second, I will consider a case that is more directly pertinent to the theory of consciousness in which we seem to be on the verge of a major conceptual innovation.

The need for new concepts can become apparent for many reasons, including failures of consistency, but I will focus here on situations in which this need becomes apparent because of empirical considerations. One important class of cases arises when a scientist recognizes that well-known phenomena cannot be adequately understood within the limits of available concepts. Consider two of Newton's conceptual innovations. First, Newton introduced the concept of mass as distinct from weight. Mass is an intrinsic property of a physical object that remains the same whatever its location in the world and whatever its state of motion. The familiar phenomenon of weight is reconceived as a relational property: the gravitational force between an object of interest and some other object. In many cases the second object is the planet Earth, but it need not be. With respect to the Earth, my weight changes as my distance from the centre of the earth changes; my weight will also be different if I travel to the moon or another planet. One way of seeing the novelty of this account of weight is to ask how much the Earth weighs. As stated this question is ill formed; we must ask about its weight with respect to some specific object. For example, given Newton's third law, the Earth's weight with respect to me is exactly the same as my weight with respect to the Earth. More generally, every physical object has some weight with respect to every other physical object; any two objects in a pair have the same weight with respect to each other. This, I urge, is a radical departure from ways of thinking about weight that preceded Newton. It replaced those earlier modes of thought because of the role it plays in an account of the behaviour of physical objects that is empirically more adequate than its predecessors.

Second, Newton introduced a concept of acceleration in which changes of speed and changes of direction are instances of the same phenomenon. By way of contrast, Galileo held that motion in a circle at a constant speed is non-accelerated motion (1967, pp. 31–2); Descartes explicitly argued that change of direction and change of speed are different phenomena (2001, pp. 75–6). Descartes' argument is particularly intriguing because it has great intuitive plausibility. He noted that in order to change the direction of a tennis ball I need only change the angle of the racquet, while I must exert a force to change a ball's speed. But intuitive plausibility aside, Newton's approach yields a more empirically adequate account of motion. Consistency with previously available beliefs is quite irrelevant.

Let me add a more recent example, one from special relativity (SR) that is not much discussed in the literature on conceptual change. One of the two main postulates of SR is that no physical motion can exceed the velocity of light in a vacuum (henceforth $c$). Suppose we launch a rocket ship from the earth that achieves a velocity of $.75c$ with respect to our planet. This ship then launches a daughter ship in the same direction that achieves a velocity of $.75c$ with respect to the mother ship. The velocity of the daughter ship with respect to the earth cannot be the sum of these two velocities since that would exceed $c$ (SR deals only with relative velocities). As a result, SR forces us to adopt a new rule for 'adding' velocities — one which ensures that no sequence of summed velocities will ever exceed $c$. Let the two velocities be $u$ and $v$. It follows from the postulates of SR that the combined velocity is $(u+v)/(1+uv/c^2)$.[3] Nothing in everyday thought about velocities or in classical physics suggests this formula; in particular, no preceding views suggest that $c$ appears every time we combine velocities. In Newtonian physics $c$ is just another velocity with no special status. But the massive empirical evidence that supports SR supports the conclusion that this is the way nature combines velocities. Leaving aside

---

[3] This result is derived in Section 5 of Einstein's first relativity paper (1998).

the historical origins of this result, we can describe the situation by noting that there is an unlimited variety of formulas one might propose for combining velocities; which one we should adopt is wholly an empirical matter. Any decision to adopt a particular formula can be challenged as we extend the body of empirical evidence, and this process can lead to beliefs that are wholly inconsistent with previous beliefs on the topic.

In the cases mentioned we can trace systematic relations between the old concepts used to describe an aspect of nature and the newer concepts that replace them. This is important because there must be some degree of continuity in the introduction of new concepts if they are to be understood — although such continuity is by no means incompatible with radical innovation. In the present context it is especially important to be clear that continuity is not the same as consistency. There is a clear contradiction between Galileo's view that circular motion is not accelerated and the Newtonian view that it is. The same holds for Descartes' view that change of direction and change of speed are fundamentally different and Newton's view that they are instances of the same phenomenon. It also holds for the relativistic and Newtonian account of how velocities combine.

Other, more drastic cases, will underline this lack of consistency. At one extreme are situations in which a totally unexpected phenomenon appears. This happened, for example, in the seventeenth century when early microscopists discovered sperm. Sperm had no place in the prevailing view of reproduction and it was a long path requiring many conceptual innovations from such early views as that sperm are parasites of the testes playing no role in reproduction,[4] to the contemporary view that they are packets of DNA carrying a randomly selected half of a male's genetic endowment. The discovery of radioactivity towards the end of the nineteenth century is a more recent example. This discovery played a key role in a deep transformation of our understanding of the physical world. The current view is replete with concepts that would have been unintelligible a century or so ago; examples include quantum tunneling, confined quarks, virtual bosons, and many others. In both of the cases just cited it is possible to trace a series of attempts to understand the new phenomena by massaging available concepts. But while there is considerable continuity

---

[4] See Gasking (1967, p. 54). Farley (1982, p. 43) notes that this view continued into the nineteenth century.

at each step, the path leads us systematically to a way of thinking that has little, if anything, in common with the starting point.[5]

At the opposite extreme we find cases in which specific concepts, and even whole conceptual systems, are dropped from our repertoire. Aristotelian physics is the classic example of the latter sort. Such central concepts of that framework as absolute lightness and the absolute places and natural motions of the elements have long ceased to play any role in physical thought. These concepts will now be found only in the repertoire of those with the relevant historical interests. The key point about this case for present purposes is that the abandonment of this framework did not come about through attempts to improve internal consistency. Aristotelian physics was rejected because of its empirical inadequacies. I am not suggesting that issues of internal consistency never arise; of course they do. But many major innovations in the development of science have been driven by failures to deal adequately with phenomena in the world. These include cases in which the phenomena in question were already familiar, and cases in which they were unanticipated surprises.

With these examples in mind let us ask how such considerations might apply to the study of consciousness. We can begin by noting that some form of mind–body dualism is probably the oldest, deepest strain in our attempts to understand consciousness. As Honderich notes (p. 10), 'Descartes didn't make it up.' But Descartes did give us precise accounts of the nature of mind and matter, and these accounts generated a fundamental problem about how mind and matter interact. This puts dualism seriously at odds with two of Honderich's criteria for a theory of consciousness:

> a theory of consciousness must make consciousness a reality, which is to say physical or approximate to physical or in some strong sense reducible to the physical;

and

> a theory must not make impossible what is actual, which is causal interaction between consciousness and the physical (p. 12).

Note, however, that these criteria were not always apparent to those who sought to understand the place of consciousness in the world. They did not trouble Descartes, Spinoza, or Leibniz, or the occasionalists. Nor did they trouble Locke who held that the ability to understand how mind and matter interact is beyond our capability, and took

---

[5] See Brown (2006) for detailed discussions of these examples, additional examples, and an account of how new concepts are introduced.

this as a permanent limitation on our ability to use ideas, which he held to be our only source of information about the physical world, as a basis for understanding that world (1984, p. 545–6). To be sure, I find these criteria quite congenial and I think that many contemporaries would agree. But I suggest that their current congeniality is itself a result of an historical process which required the introduction of new ways of thinking about the subject.

To a large degree the quest for a non-dualistic way of thinking about consciousness has an empirical basis. Consider pain — often taken as a paradigmatic mental phenomenon. Surely the discovery of anaesthetics enhanced the sense that what is happening in our bodies has a causal impact on what is happening in our minds, although long experience with alcohol and various psychotropic drugs should lead to the same conclusion. There is now also evidence that pain is associated with longer term physical changes in the brain and nervous system. I will note just two examples. First, subjecting new-born rats to painful stimuli seems to change the biology of pain-sensitive neurons in their spinal column (Ruda et al., 2000). A news item in *Science* provides a nice summary of this result:

> painful stimuli delivered to rats shortly after birth permanently rewire the spinal cord circuits that respond to pain. Not only do the circuits contain more axons, but the axons extend to more areas of the spinal cord than they normally would (Helmuth, 2000, p. 521).

Second, people who suffer from chronic back pain seem to lose prefrontal and thalamic gray-matter density (Apkarian *et al.*, 2004). These examples may indicate that pain causes physical changes and thus might provide evidence of a mental phenomenon that has a causal impact on physical phenomena. But there is a possibility that may be even more intriguing: that pain sensation and the attendant physical changes are aspects of a single physical processes. As Hardcastle notes (1999, p. 205),

> How things seem to us is only the tip of the cognitive iceberg and really only gives us the barest of hints about what is occurring in the brain.[6]

Since many of the physical changes associated with pain constitute damage to the organism, it may well be that pain medicine should focus on these processes, not just on alleviating the sensation. This, in turn, suggests a major reconceptualization of what constitutes pain, one that moves away from the common concept of pain as just something we experience and towards a concept that integrates sensation

---

[6] The approach I am suggesting has much in common with Hardcastle's views.

and biology under a single concept. Such a concept would involve a unification of traditional physical and mental phenomenon in a way that is at least analogous to Newton's treatment of acceleration. It is not likely that such a concept will emerge from attempts to improve the consistency of existing ways of thinking about pain, but the only important test of such an approach will be its ability to yield improved empirical adequacy.

At this point we should return to Radical Externalism and tie together the lines of argument I have been developing. I began by discussing subjective contours in order to argue that Radical Externalism, as presented in the present paper, does not provide an adequate conceptual framework for understanding visual perception, which is just one aspect of consciousness. I then moved to Professor Honderich's claim that Radical Externalism is a proposal for conceptual change, not an instance of conceptual analysis. I agreed with this but have been arguing that the kind of conceptual change required for a theory of consciousness is likely to be more radical than anything we can arrive at by seeking to improve the consistency of our available concepts. The systematic scientific study of consciousness is a new endeavour and, as we have found in many other instances in the history of science, the modes of thought that we have inherited from our ancestors are likely to be in need of radical replacement.

## References

Apkarian, A. *et al.* (2004), 'Chronic back pain is associated with decreased prefrontal and thalamic gray matter density', *The Journal of Neuroscience*, **24**, pp. 10410–15.

Brown, H. (2006), *Conceptual Systems* (London: Routledge).

Descartes, R. (2001) *Discourse on Method, Optics, Geometry, and Meteorology*, revised edition, translated by P. Olscamp (Indianapolis: Hackett).

Einstein, Albert (1998), 'On the electrodynamics of moving bodies', in *Einstein's Miraculous Year*, edited by John Statchel (Princeton: Princeton University Press).

Farley, John (1982), *Gametes and Spores: Ideas about Sexual Reproduction, 1750–1914* (Baltimore: Johns Hopkins University Press).

Galileo (1967), *Dialogue Concerning the Two Chief World Systems*, translated by S. Drake (Berkeley: University of California Press).

Gasking, Elizabeth (1967), *Investigations into Generation, 1651–1828* (London: Hutchinson).

Hardcastle, Valerie (1999), *The Myth of Pain* (Cambridge MA and London: MIT Press).

Helmuth, Laura (2000), 'Early insult rewires pain circuits', *Science*, **289**, pp. 521–2.

Honderich, T. (2006), 'Radical externalism', *Journal of Consciousness Studies*, **13** (7–8), pp. 3–13. [This issue]

Locke, John (1984), *An Essay concerning Human Understanding*, ed. P. Nidditch (Oxford: Clarendon Press).

Ruda, M., et al. (2000), 'Altered nociceptive neuronal circuits after neonatal peripheral inflammation', *Science*, **289**, pp. 628–30.

**REPLY TO BROWN BY HONDERICH**

Suppose you get a lead pencil and draw Harold Brown's Figure 1 on a piece of paper. Then, with respect to the part of your figure on the left, you do whatever is necessary — just *what* you do contains the mystery we are concerned with — not to be conscious of the six-pointed star and so on, and instead only to be conscious of one triangle, the one tilted left rather than right. Or, to try to speak just a bit more exactly, you do what is necessary to *attend* to that triangle rather than anything else of which maybe you can be said to be *less* conscious.

The part of your figure on the left, by which I here mean that physical thing consisting of graphite on paper, whatever we say about its role in your attending and consciousness, is not and does not include a triangle. The graphite on paper somehow relevant to something else, your conscious or more conscious triangle, consists only in straight edges of three other shapes and the ends of six lines. Maybe the relevant physical thing also includes blank paper rather than distracting graphite between six points, but still it seems right to say there is no physical triangle. Your conscious or more conscious triangle is therefore called a persistent visual illusion, more particularly a subjective contour.

Your triangle in consciousness may pose a problem for philosophers and scientists who give some simple role to a physical thing in your being conscious. Brown takes it that your triangle is trouble for Radical Externalism. He suggests or implies that it is not clear how the visual illusion fits into Radical Externalism's categorizations and conceptual framework, and hence that the visual illusion cannot be well dealt with by Radical Externalism, and that that framework is not adequate for understanding visual perception.

He offers a string of quotations and considerations in support of these propositions. The quotations and considerations puzzle me a little. His reference to '*the* world of perceptual consciousness' after he gets going (p. 15, my emphasis) does not sound like a reference to one of the many worlds of perceptual consciousness that there are — as many as there are perceivers. His reference makes me wonder if he is really contemplating Radical Externalism in what I am pleased to call its simple beauty. My commenting on his quotations and considerations, or some of them, unconfidently, may lead him and others in that direction.

He starts off by considering a subject larger than Radical Externalism's, which is *seeing*, and in particular whether you *see* the triangle. He reports my incidental sentence on what it is to see something, my summary of seeing naturally understood, as something having a lot in it, including a physical thing and your retinas and your cortex. He says it commits me to saying that you *see* the triangle.

I am not so sure of that since my summary has yet to be filled in. Its reference to a physical thing is a gesture, not an exact specification of a necessity, not a differentiating account of how a physical thing is necessary here as against elsewhere in consciousness. Maybe there is room for decision as well as discovery at this point. My interest of course is in just part of the story of seeing something and the like, the main question of what we call your perceptual consciousness itself consists in.

In connection with the idea that I am committed to saying you see the triangle, we now rightly hear from Brown that Radical Externalism emphasizes that with perceptual consciousness, like the rest of consciousness, there is no difference between appearance and reality. Does it follow for Radical Externalism, as we also hear, that when you are conscious of the triangle it is is real?

Well, the proposition that there is no difference between appearance and reality with this and other consciousness is that there is no more of it than you *have*. That is not in itself enough to decide that the triangle is or is not real in a particular sense — not enough to decide in what sense it is real.

*If* what we have here is *perceptual* consciousness of the triangle, as against reflective consciousness or some sort of extraordinary mixture of reflective with perceptual consciousness, which must be a possibility or indeed a probability, then for Radical Externalism the triangle would indeed exist as part of a world of perceptual consciousness.

It would have be part of what it is tempting to call the fundamental reality of and in our lives, the reality of the world in which we exist — which is to say the one world that there is, that ur-world, conceived as worlds of perceptual consciousness. The physical world, that greatly more theorized thing, derives from and depends on our worlds of perceptual consciousness. But, as I say, maybe your triangle isn't in just perceptual consciousness. Maybe it's a kind of idea, a sort of representation. Then it does indeed have *that* particular reality rather than being just something in a world of perceptual consciousness.

Are we to understand that we already have serious trouble for Radical Externalism in that it doesn't, anyway yet, include a view on the subjective contours — your conscious triangle? these illusions? Are its categorizations and conceptual framework shown to be inadequate by the fact that it doesn't include a settled judgement on this funny phenomenon? Well, I can't see that.

It is more than possible to take the attitude that the theory is OK, anyway for the time being, because it works with standard cases of perceptual, reflective and affective consciousness — seeing pages, thinking of home, wanting to be there. It's not as if its account of your ordinary consciousness of a page in front of you is put in doubt by the funny phenomenon we are considering.

Notice that the situation is quite unlike the situation of argument having to do with total illusions or hallucinations. In *that* situation of argument, because two sorts of experience are indistinguishable, there seems to be reason to abandon a theory about one of them — say the theory that seeing consists in being in some sort of direct and unmediated conscious connection with a certain physical thing.

You certainly don't have identical kinds of experience in ordinarily seeing a page and in being conscious of the funny triangle. You can't make the page go away in the same way, whatever that way is. And of course, most importantly, there is no relevant alternative to your experience of your figure on paper — an experience in which you have the same triangle in your consciousness and the graphite on the paper is, so to speak, just right.

Brown offers other reflections along related lines that also puzzle but do not disturb me. One is about the page *being there*, the next about an extra-cranial sate of affairs, and so on. Given what you have heard about my uncertainty as to where to locate your triangle, in perceptual or in reflective consciousness or wherever, you will know I am also uncertain as to whether to say, for example, your triangle is outside your head. This won't be causing me any lack of sleep for a while.

Let me remark on one other of his reflections. He notes my clarification of what I mean by 'the physical world'. It consists in (1) things taking up space and time and also having other properties as standardly or publicly perceived, as distinct from properties dependent on anyone in particular and (2) things that also take up space and time, are without perceived properties, but stand in causal or other lawlike connection with things in the first category. He goes on to find a dilemma.

He says of your triangle that maybe it is not in the first category — from which, he says, it follows for Radical Externalism that you do not see it. Is the assumption or implication in the first utterance that Radical Externalism says, with respect to your seeing something, that your consciousness consists in the *physical* existence of something? I hope that is not the assumption or implication, since that is certainly false. Is the assumption that for Radical Externalism your consciousness *depends* on the physical existence of something? That is true, and it connects with my bearable problem of whether or not to say that the triangle is a matter of perceptual consciousness.

Brown says that maybe on the other hand your triangle *is* a physical object, but of a peculiar kind given the way it depends on your perceptual system. And, given these two possibilities left open, it is not clear how your triangle fits into the conceptual framework of Radical Externalism.

Well, your experience triangle is definitely not a physical object for Radical Externalism. And I don't really see, as you will anticipate, how, as Brown supposes, he has done much damage. I *agree* that it is not clear how subjective contours fit into the conceptual framework of Radical Externalism. I hope that there is a graduate student somewhere who has liberated himself from the tedious conventions of the current philosophy of mind and will work on the question. I do not agree that a hole has been poked in the boat and that it is taking in water..

To come on to the larger part of Brown's paper, which can be considered more quickly, he completely agrees with the proposition that we need conceptual change, maybe a conceptual revolution, in order to deal with the problem of the nature of consciousness. We need to leave behind conceptions in various mind-brain theories and also in such theories of perception as phenomenalism, realisms, and the disjunctive view.

This is good to hear in a dark age of philosophy. Friends always welcome. But along with the agreement comes what is claimed to be disagreement, about how far we may need to go, or anyway about the nature of the necessary departure from the orthodoxies in the philosophy and science of mind.

This disagreement, real or not, has to do with my remark that Radical Externalism's departure from the orthodoxies is also an exercise in consistency — as always, consistency with something or some things that are given priority. Brown has it that we may need to take up a new way of thinking about consciousness that is wholly *inconsistent* with our current modes of thought on the subject — something more drastic than we are likely to arrive at 'by seeking consistency with some of our current beliefs that are kept fixed'.

He very interestingly lays out conceptual innovations in the history of science. Newton's introduction of mass as against weight, and also his startling concept of acceleration. Special relativity's postulate about no physical motion being faster than light in a vacuum. At least in this last case, a piece of theoretical progress that led to beliefs wholly inconsistent with previous beliefs on the topic. There is yet more inconsistency with the past in the cases of sperm and then DNA and also radioactivity. And in the case of Aristotelian physics, a whole conceptual system was dropped. No continuity even, let alone consistency.

What he says, however, to my mind, is not in conflict with my remark about consistency. As you will see if you look back, that remark was that we need a conception of consciousness that is consistent with something in particular — those special propositions that constitute criteria of any adequate theory of consciousness.

That is a long way from holding that a new theory, Radical Externalism in particular, has to be consistent with the distinctive propositions in preceding theories of consciousness, 'current modes of thought'. It is plainly these that Brown says a new theory may absolutely deny. The criteria of adequately having to do with sticking to the subject of consciousness, going by its seeming nature, its subjectivity, its reality, and its causal connection with physical things, and so on, are very clearly distinguishable from the many previous theories of consciousness that fall under the wide headings of devout physicalism and spiritualism.

Radical Externalism, you can say, departs about as far from those theories, and is as much inconsistent with those theories, as the conceptual revolutions in science departed from and were inconsistent with preceding theories. There is some inventing in it, good or bad. That is not to say that it does not have to worry about being inconsistent with the propositions that are criteria of adequacy for any theory of consciousness. Of course it does.

I doubt that Brown disagrees, really, despite his remark to the effect that there has been change in the history of philosophy, in fact progress, with respect to the criteria for an adequate conception of consciousness. With respect to the progress in terms of criteria, I myself wonder how much it involved new ways of thinking about the subject of consciousness. Was it just actually attending to what we have all known for a long time? Not being pressed or cozened by a philosopher, say Descartes, who couldn't see how to satisfy a criterion in his thinking and so abandoned the criterion rather than the thinking.

I do not see, either, to come to the end of Brown's satisfactorily unconventional piece, that the interesting research on pain does much to make for a real disagreement between us. Anyway so long as it is not taken to put more into our actual consciousness when we are in pain than what we have or feel.

Tim Crane

# Comment on Ted Honderich's *Radical Externalism*

Ted Honderich's theory of *consciousness as existence*, which he here[1] calls *Radical Externalism*, starts with a good phenomenological observation: that perceptual experience appears to involve external things being immediately present to us. As P.F. Strawson once observed, when asked to describe my current perceptual state, it is normally enough simply to describe the things around me (Strawson, 1979, p. 97).

But in my view that does not make the whole theory plausible. There are puzzling questions one can raise about the theory — for example: how can a conscious *desire* for X, or the *imagination* of X simply consist in the *existence* of X 'in a way'? How can this model of consciousness be extended to bodily sensations? What has to exist 'in a way' for a sensation of nausea to exist? But in this brief note I will focus on what are to me three outstanding weaknesses in Honderich's present paper: the formulation of his theory, his treatment of the most obvious problem for the theory, and his criticisms of opposing views.

Radical Externalism is

> the general proposition that what it is to be perceptually conscious is for a world in a way to exist — i.e. for things to be in space and time with certain properties (p. 7).

So to be conscious of reading this page simply is for the page to exist 'in a way', or to 'be there'. Call the state of affairs of the page existing, 'S'. Is the idea that the existence of S *suffices* for you to be conscious of it? Honderich equivocates. At one point he says 'to be perceptually conscious is *only* for an extra-cranial state of affairs to exist' (p. 6; my emphasis). And elsewhere he says that your consciousness of the page

---

[1] Honderich (2006). In this commentary all page references are to this target paper unless stated otherwise.

simply *is* 'for the page to be there'. These remarks imply that the existence of S suffices for consciousness of it. But this is at least puzzling, since it implies that S cannot exist without someone being conscious of it. And surely Honderich himself would reject this Berkeleian consequence.

In other places in his paper, he does reject it:

> your world of perceptual consciousness is things being in space and time ... *dependent* on you neurally.

For you to be conscious, he writes, is

> for there to be a spatio-temporal set of things with a *dependence* on another extra-cranial state of affairs and also on what is in a particular cranium (p. 6; my emphasis).

If we interpret Honderich in what I take to be a charitable way and ignore the remarks quoted in the previous paragraph, then we should interpret him as holding that consciousness actually consists in a *relation of dependence*: your consciousness of S does not consist in the existence of S alone but on the *relation* between S and your brain. Honderich denies that there is relation

> of intentionality, aboutness or directedness in your consciousness of the page (p. 5).

But it follows from the only plausible reading of his view that he thinks consciousness is a relation of some sort.

The idea that mental states are relations to non-mental things is characteristic of many kinds of externalism. Applied to perception, it is the characteristic thesis of the disjunctive view of perceptual experience (Martin, 2004). But Honderich's externalism differs from many contemporary forms of externalism about perception in at least two ways: (i) it denies that the objects of the ordinary physical world are in the world of your perceptual consciousness; (ii) it denies that there can be perceptual consciousness of any kind without a relation to 'extra-cranial' states of affairs. I will take these points in turn.

For a disjunctivist, the ordinary physical page which you see, the same page which exists when you are not looking at it, is a constituent of your perceptual experience. This is because your experience consists in a relation to the page. Honderich denies this, since he says that 'a world of perceptual consciousness is not the physical world'. As we saw, the world of your perceptual consciousness is 'dependent on you neurally', yet nothing in the physical world is dependent on anything neural:

> The physical world, very briefly indeed, consists in two categories: (1) things taking up space and time and also having other properties as standardly or publicly perceived, *as distinct from properties dependent on anyone in particular*, and (2) things that also take up space and time, are without perceived properties, but stand in causal or other lawlike connection with things in the first category. The physical world then consists in the perceived physical world, including pages, and in what you can call the physical world of science, including atoms — already mentioned as a necessary condition of each world of perceptual consciousness. There is not much of a liberty taken in speaking of there being pages in both a world of perceptual consciousness and in the perceived physical world, and indeed in referring to each of a related pair of things as *a page* (pp. 6–7; my emphasis).

The page which is in your perceptual consciousness exists 'in a way' but does not exist in the physical world, since it does not belong to categories (1) or (2). It follows that the page is not the ordinary physical page which exists when you are not perceiving it. This is why Honderich says here that there are two pages, one in the physical world and one in the world of perceptual consciousness.

This consequence is surely bizarre — as bizarre as any of the sense-data views that Honderich ridicules — and may rob the doctrine of Radical Externalism of any of the pre-theoretical plausibility it initially had. Remember that initially what was appealing about the view was how natural it is to think that in perceptual (more properly, visual) experience, the world is simply 'open to view': how things seem to be in your experience is simply how things are with the ordinary mind-independent objects around you. But when Honderich explains what it is for an object of experience to exist 'in a way', he gives up this natural idea. For to exist 'in a way' is to exist in a 'world of perceptual consciousness', in space and time but not in the ordinary physical world.

The upshot is that the objects of experience are physical — because they exist in space and time, and this makes them physical on Honderich's view — but they are not part of the physical world since their existence is dependent on experience. This is the sense I can make of Honderich

> speaking of there being pages in both a world of perceptual consciousness and in the perceived physical world, and indeed in referring to each of a related pair of things as *a page* (p. 7).

The objects of perceptual consciousness correspond to things whose existence is not so dependent — Honderich says the two pages are 'related' — although the nature of this correspondence is not made clear.

What is clear is that it is not the ordinary mind-independent physical page which you see when you see the page. Radical Externalism therefore turns out to be a version of the early twentieth-century sense-data theory which treats experience as a relation to something which is not itself a physical thing, although it inhabits the physical world. It's not essential to the sense-data view that the objects of experience are *mental*; what matters is that their existence is dependent on the existence of an experience; and that's what Honderich thinks. This view is certainly radical, but if I am right it is not new.

This brings me to the second difference between Honderich's view and other forms of externalism about perception — and with it, to my second general point: his treatment of the apparent possibility of consciousness without an existing physical object.

The main *prima facie* difficulty with the claim that perceptual experience is simply a relation to the ordinary mind-independent objects and their properties is this: it seems possible that there could be an experience which subjectively seems exactly the same as a genuine perception, but in which there is no mind-independent object being perceived. If the same state can exist in the absence of some object O then O cannot be essential to that state. Hence experience cannot be a relation after all. This is a version of what has been called the argument from hallucination. Theories of perception respond to it in different ways: sense-data theories respond by saying that the objects of experience are really mind-dependent; intentional theories respond by saying that experience is a representation and therefore not a relation; disjunctive theories respond by saying that the perception and the hallucination do not share a common mental nature. (For a description of this argument and survey of these responses see Crane, 2005). This argument has been the focus of intense debate in the literature in the philosophy of perception of the last ten or fifteen years; and arguably it was the source of the debate about perception in the first fifty years of the twentieth century. The philosophy perception can therefore be seen as the struggle to square the manifest phenomenology of perception with the apparent possibility of hallucination and plausible naturalist metaphysical commitments.

Honderich, by contrast, sees no need to struggle; in one paragraph he seems to dismiss the whole debate. The argument from hallucination, he says,

> depends on the possibility of a causal or lawlike sufficient condition rather than a necessary condition in the brain. According to Radical Externalism, there isn't a sufficient neural condition for perceptual consciousness (p. 8).

Honderich does not say exactly why this undermines the argument given above. Does he have in mind the disjunctivist view that not everything that seems like a perceptual experience is an experience of the same kind? The disjunctivist says that although there can be a sufficient neural condition for a state which *seems like* a state of perceptual consciousness — in the sense that if my retina were stimulated in exactly the same way as it is now but by some cause other than the page, it would *seem to me* exactly as if I were seeing a page — but is not such a state. Does Honderich accept this view? Probably not, since he commits himself earlier in the paper to the claim that 'with consciousness, what there seems to be is what there is' (p. 5). And this plausible claim, of course, is what the disjunctivist denies.

But if he doesn't mean what the disjunctivist means, what can Honderich mean by saying there is no neural sufficient condition for perceptual consciousness? Does he mean that it is *impossible* to stimulate the retina in such a way that produces an experience which seems exactly like an perceptual experience of a page? But how can he know that this is impossible? Asserting its impossibility commits one to the view that what makes a state of perceptual consciousness seem the way it does is either (a) some distal cause upstream of the retinal image which has some way of affecting the causal upshot in the brain without having any effect on the retinal image; or (b) some non-causal condition on a state of mind.

The first reason, (a), goes against what we know about causation. In any case of a causal chain, A–B–C, it is metaphysically possible to 'screen off' A from the effect C, by simply considering C to have been brought about by B instead. The second reason, (b), is tantamount to admitting that perceptual consciousness is not a wholly causal process (according to Valberg, 1992, this is Heidegger's view). Perhaps Honderich has an alternative view of causation in the background; or perhaps he is a closet Heideggerian. But given that he is not a disjunctivist, these seem to be the only options here.

It should be emphasised that the claim that it is possible to produce a hallucination — an experience which seems just like a genuine perception of a mind-independent object O but in the absence of O — by stimulating the retina (e.g.) in exactly the way in which it was stimulated when O is present, does not involve a commitment to phenomenalism, nor to any particular theory of experience, nor to any extreme hypothesis about how the brain works. It is simply a metaphysical possibility which seems to reside in what we already know about experience. So it also should be emphasised that this idea is not, as such, a *denial* of externalism. All externalists in the current debate

# COMMENT ON RADICAL EXTERNALISM 33

— with the exception of a few Wittgensteinians who decline to play this particular language-game — accept the possibility of hallucination in this sense. The question for externalists is not whether hallucinations are possible, but how an externalist should classify them or theorise about this possibility. If Honderich's Radical Externalism simply denies the real possibility of these hallucinations, then he has to take one of the two paths, (a) or (b) above. Both paths are certainly radical, but can there be any future in this kind of radicalism. What does Honderich think can be said in favour of it?

This brings me to my third and final point, concerning Honderich's treatment of other views. His main strategy here is to describe certain criteria which any theory of consciousness has to meet, and then to claim that Radical Externalism satisfies the criteria better than the alternatives:

> the argument for Radical Externalism is in a very important part the extent to which the alternatives fail to satisfy the criteria (p. 10).

Suppose Radical Externalism is really coherent. I myself doubt this, for the reasons given, but let's suppose it for the sake of argument. Then Honderich's strategy here is certainly a good one, so long as he has considered a good range of alternative views.

On this, in my view, he fails badly. He considers only two views: dualism (which for some reason he calls spiritualism or mentalism[2]) and physicalism. Dualism is the Cartesian version of the view according to which consciousness does not exist in space. This doctrine seems to be despatched by stipulation, given what Honderich means by 'physical':

> A fourth criterion of adequacy is that a theory of consciousness must make consciousness a reality, which is to say physical or approximate to physical or in some strong sense reducible to the physical (p. 12).

In other words, in order to be real, something must be physical; in order to be physical, it must exist in space and time; dualism denies that consciousness exists in space; hence dualism denies that consciousness is real. The argument is valid of course; but it must be without force unless it can be shown that any doctrine deserving the name 'dualism' (i.e. any doctrine that treats the mental and the physical as two, not one) *must* say that consciousness is non-spatial. Most forms of dualism around today (e.g. Chalmers, 1996, to pick a prominent

---

[2] Neither of Honderich's terms are very satisfactory, since both 'spiritualism' and 'mentalism' have perfectly clear meanings in and outside philosophy; so I will stick with 'dualism' despite the many things that word has meant.

example) do not say this, and there's no reason why they should. (To be fair, Honderich also attacks dualism on the grounds that it can't handle mental causation. Here he agrees with many materialists, and there is no need to add to the discussion here, except to say there is no knock-down argument against dualism on these grounds.)

Physicalism, on Honderich's view, is the view that

> our consciousness is a fact, property or state of affairs that involves only physical properties in the sense gestured at earlier — and in particular properties in existing and more or less anticipated neuroscience (p. 10).

Honderich insists that he does not mean that this kind of physicalism is eliminative materialism. So it is a theory which says that consciousness exists and only involves neural properties; the best way to understand this is as the identity theory. But now we can see that Honderich's description might mislead: for although the identity theory does say that consciousness is a neural phenomenon, it means by this that certain neural phenomena are also mental or conscious. Identity is a symmetrical relation: if A=B, then B=A. So if consciousness really is neural property P then neural property P is *ipso facto* consciousness. Some of Honderich's criticisms of physicalism fail to fully take on board this feature of the view.

For example, his first criticism is that a theory of consciousness should be precisely that: a theory of consciousness and nothing else. He says that physicalism fails to satisfy this requirement, presumably because it says a theory of consciousness should be a theory of certain neural phenomena. But if consciousness *is* neural property P, then a theory of consciousness *is* a theory of neural property P and nothing else: the objection fails. His second criticism is that physicalism cannot account for how consciousness seems to us. It's not clear why; maybe because consciousness does not *seem* like a brain process. But, to echo Wittgenstein, how would it seem if it *were* a brain process? The objection begs the question. As for the third objection, that physicalism cannot account for the subjectivity of consciousness, this is a familiar objection, and there may be something to it, but since Honderich does not say enough in the article to say what the basis of the objection is, we will have to leave this hanging for the moment.

What should we make of Honderich's Radical Externalism? The contemporary philosophical landscape contains a wide variety of metaphysical views on perception and on the relationship of mind and body. Some are dualist, some are materialist, some claim to be neither. Some are externalist, some are internalist. Instead of indicating that he is aware of this variety and making room cautiously and judiciously for his own view in the crowded landscape of possible views, Honderich seems to me to have decided instead to describe one view which almost no-one holds and to misdescribe a view which many hold, and show how they are incompatible with some of his own rather vague stipulations about the nature of consciousness. It's hard to see how progress can be made by discussing philosophical views in this way. Honderich would have done better to have tried to respond to the obvious problems with Radical Externalism, such as those indicated above, and to take on board discussions of similar problems in the voluminous literature. As it stands, I can see little to recommend Radical Externalism.[3]

## References

Chalmers, David (1996), *The Conscious Mind* (Oxford and New York: Oxford University Press).

Crane, Tim (2005), 'The problem of perception', *Stanford Encylopedia of Philosophy* http://plato.stanford.edu/entries/perception-problem

Honderich, T. (2006), 'Radical externalism', *Journal of Consciousness Studies*, **13** (7–8), pp. 3–13. [This issue]

Martin, M.G.F. (2004), 'The limits of self-awareness', *Philosophical Studies*, **12**, pp. 37–89.

Noë, Alva. and Thompson, Evan (ed. 2002), *Vision and Mind: Selected Readings in the Philosophy of Perception* (Cambridge, MA: MIT Press).

Strawson, P.F. (1979), 'Perception and its objects', in *Perception and Identity: Essays Presented to A.J. Ayer with His Replies*, ed. G. Macdonald (London: Macmillan); Page references to reprint in Noë and Thompson (2002).

Valberg, J.J. (1992), 'The puzzle of experience', in *The Contents of Experience*, ed. Tim Crane (Cambridge: Cambridge University Press).

## REPLY TO CRANE BY HONDERICH

Tim Crane's boisterous and arresting paper has some strong things in it, but not at the beginning.

(1) He says Radical Externalism starts with the good observation that 'perceptual experience appears to involve things being immediately present to us'. No, Radical Externalism does not begin with that vagueness, presumably including some obscure relation of presentness to something or other. It begins from, or anyway rests on, the proposition that perceptual experience appears to include nothing whatever other than an existence of external things.

(2) Nor does Radical Externalism begin from P.F. Strawson, agreeable though it would be to begin from an idea of that prince of English philosophy. Look past Crane's report of Strawson's paragraphs to the paragraphs themselves (Strawson, 1979, pp. 41–7). You will find Strawson assuming and saying that seeing some

---

[3] Thanks to Ted Honderich for being open to frank discussion.

dappled deer includes what he calls a subjective episode, a current visual experience, something that could have occurred without the deer — which subjective thing depends for its description on concepts of physical objects, in this case deer.

With respect to the subjective episode, that piece of perceptual consciousness, despite the point about a dependency on physical objects, nothing whatever is said or implied in the direction of the radical externalist proposition that consciousness of the dappled dear appears to be no more than some or other existence of the deer. On the contrary, what we have suggested in Strawson is an orthodox internalist account of the consciousness, however realist as against phenomenalist.

(3) Crane implies by his scare quotes that it is puzzling that Radical Externalism talks of existence 'in a way'. Well, that way of existence of things with respect to perceptual consciousness is adequately explained, anyway in an initial way. For your world of perceptual consciousness to exist in this way is for there to be things occupying space and time outside your head, with such properties as colour, and dependent on a scientific or noumenal world underneath and also dependent on you neurally.

In its reference to space and time, this conception of existence is close to the most ordinary ones, the most ordinary understandings of the verb 'to be' putting aside its predicative use. Certainly there is not only one way of being in space and time. It is not as if there cannot be different and true characterizations of things all of which take up space and time.

(4) Crane is puzzled particularly about how the imagination of X or a desire for X can consist in the existence of X in a way. On the theory, they don't. What we call being *perceptually* aware of X is indeed X's in a way existing. *Reflective* consciousness of X, at bottom, is the related existence of a representation of X. The *affective* consciousness of desiring X is also something that does not make necessary any existence of X (above, pp. 8–9). Sensations pose no particular difficulty for the theory.

So there is misunderstanding here, as there is elsewhere. If *resistance* to ideas in some special sense, maybe new ideas, had not been so discredited by its home in Freudianism before that came to its end, I might think about misunderstanding owed to it. But there is also the possibility, rather less congenial to me, that I am not among the most clear-headed and clear of philosophers.

(5) The first of three outstanding weaknesses found in Radical Externalism by Crane is the formulation of the theory. This weakness in its first part (partly found by means of taking two expressions of one and the same proposition to be an equivocation) is that

on one reading the theory is Berkeleian. This turns out to be two alleged weaknesses run together — certain things being in space and time with certain properties being held to be sufficient for consciousness of them, and their being there being held to be sufficient for the consciousness. This is taken to be crazy, no doubt, because it makes the existence of *physical* things sufficient for some consciousness, and some consciousness sufficient for the existence of physical things.

But neither proposition is any part of Radical Externalism, which at its centre is about consciousness and worlds of perceptual consciousness, which are not and are no part of the physical world, whatever their dependency on that world. Not to take this in is not to engage with the theory. The theory, further, is perfectly happy to maintain that certain things being in space and time, in the defined way, is logically sufficient for consciousness of them, and vice versa. That more or less *is* the theory. And the two-way proposition is what an ordinary analysis is.

Is a word on the theory's relation to Berkeleian idealism needed here? Well, for Berkeley, as we have heard for a long time, *to be is to be perceived*. For Radical Externalism, *to be perceived is to be In a certain way*, or of course, *to be in a certain way is to be perceived*. But Radical Externalism certainly does not deny the existence of the physical world, and of course has a conception of it as independent of any particular person. Radical Externalism is a long way from philosophical idealism, and in fact further away from it than physicalisms that take the physical world, and arguably too, to be a matter of our *theory*, in fact a theory beginning from worlds of perceptual consciousness.

(6) The first outstanding weakness of theory found by Crane, in its second part, is that Radical Externalism is so formulated that on another reading, in fact not a reading of the same thing in the theory, again produces something like disaster. What leads to disaster this time has to do with the theory's taking your world of perceptual consciousness to be dependent not only on an underlying physical world, but on you neurally. On this charitable reading of Radical Externalism, says Crane, it comes to saying that your being perceptually conscious consists in part in a relation of dependence, which is better than the Berkeleian idea — but there is the awful fact that Radical Externalism specifically denies that there is a relation of intentionality, aboutness or directedness in your consciousness of the page. This is just contradiction.

Indeed the theory does deny any such relation in your consciousness. But taking your world of perceptual consciousness now to be dependent on you neurally is of course *not* to take the relation to be part of the state or event of your being conscious. To say that A is necessary for B, in whatever sense, is not to say that the relation is part of B, let alone that B *is* the relation.

(7) Another part of the first outstanding weakness comes into view when Crane touches on what is called the disjunctive view of perceptual experience. He reports perfectly correctly that on my view your awareness of the page you are looking at — the perceptual consciousness ordinarily described in that way — is not itself a relation to a physical page but rather consists in an existence of something taking up space and time and with certain properties, something not independent of any particular perceiver and so not the physical page. This, he eventually concludes, is surely bizarre. Why is that?

Well, one reason is that being a good student of doctrines of orthodox intentionality, and the proponent of one (Honderich, 2004, pp. 169–71), and not entirely inclined to newer ways of thinking, he is determined to take perceptual experience as including a relation or relations to physical things. He is right in that proposition — *exactly* that proposition — and he is one with Radical Externalism. Your world of perceptual consciousness is in the happily unmysterious relation to you of being dependent on you neurally, and, as reassuringly, dependent on the physical world.

(8) But, he says, in the engaging style of Samuel Johnson, refuting absurdity by common sense, maybe by a kick, here is a man before us who believes in *two* pages. Well, I plead guilty to a little audacity in appropriating a physical-object term for another purpose, but it is for a good purpose. I use it for a near-physical thing.

On the principal and fundamental point, and to become a little Johnsonian myself, who does not believe there is a difference, a lot of difference, between the physical page and what he now perceives — what on my view is the thing that constitutes his perceptual consciousness? Each has properties lacked by the other. There is an awful lot of philosophy on this indubitable difference, most recently labelled by talk of the view from nowhere and the view from here (Nagel, 1986), a little earlier discussed in terms of what was called the construction of the physical world (Ayer, 1973; Honderich, 1991). Earlier than that came British Empiricism. Indeed the difference is in common sense.

I pass over quickly an upshot that is Crane's mistaken line that objects simply being in space and time makes them physical on Honderich's view, and the supposed contradiction deriving from the mistake. No doubt it is time for a concession, however. It is that the relationship or correspondence between a world of perceptual consciousness and the physical world has not been re-explored in

Radical Externalism. That is true. I cannot see that this is much of an objection, or of course that this state of affairs with a new theory is unusual.

(9) In going on about the upshot, Crane slides away from what he has truly reported several times, that the view under discussion takes your world of perceptual consciousness to depend partly on you neurally, your brain. We hear instead that 'it is dependent on experience'. If that were the analysis offered of perceptual consciousness, it would be circular: roughly, experience consists in something dependent on experience. This helps him on to the misunderstanding or anyway contentious understanding of Radical Externalism as again something Berkeleian — version of the early-twentieth-century sense-data theory.

The two theories are alike, of course, in not taking perceptual consciousness to be a relation to a physical object. They are different in that Radical Externalism does not take your being perceptually conscious to include a relation at all — physical, mental or otherwise. They are different, too, and fundamentally, in that it was indeed essential to the sense-data view that so-called objects of experience are somehow *mental*. I have no idea why Crane denies this.That was the unswallowable essence of the view.

With Radical Externalism, the state of affairs that is your perceptual experience of something is is not in any such sense mental. Nor, even, is such a state of affairs in principal private (Honderich, 2004, pp. 137–8, 141) If you and I could become in a way neurally identical, and so on, I could have exactly your experience. It is true that in fact, in this world of neural non-identity, your world of perceptual consciousness when we are together in this room is different from mine. So what? That is a version of what we all believe, isn't it?

(10) Crane now comes to the second outstanding weakness in Radical Externalism, which he takes to be the most obvious problem for the theory, having to do with the apparent possibility of consciousness without an existing physical object. He takes me to task for not turning over dusty and maybe soon to be dusty pages of responses to the argument from illusion. He goes on a good deal about this.

The argument from illusion, as indeed his own paragraphs make pretty clear, depends on the assumption that something in the head with a certain history is sufficient for perceptual awareness of some page, and thereby proceeds to the conclusion that it cannot be that anything external to the head is in any way essential to the experience. Radical Externalism in particular is refuted. Crane elaborates this simple argument himself, if partly by means of notions not clear to me.

Well, if my situation were desperate, and I had no other reply to the argument from illusion, I might still choose a brave course (Honderich, 2004, pp. 122–3, 155–6). Rather than embrace the conclusion of phenomenalism that we are, so to speak, not in touch with external reality, I might regard the argument from illusion as a *reductio ad absurdum*. Certainly there might be hallucinations, but since the argument from them issues in an absurd conclusion, there is something wrong with the argument.

But my situation is not at all desperate, but happy. The argument fails against Radical Externalism, obviously, and, despite Crane's nagging, I do say exactly why. It fails because the theory has it that being perceptually conscious of a page does not have a sufficient condition in my head. No such thing can be produced by cortical stimulation or the like. That is not to say, of course, that the theory denies the possibility of hallucinations. Rather, it comfortably says they must be cases of reflective consciousness — roughly speaking, cases of thinking or imagining something and making the mistake of thinking this is perceptual experience.

While it is true that my study of what is called disjunctivism has not been sufficient, I suppose that Radical Externalism is related to it. That is not to say that it *is* disjunctivism. For a start, it is not a device for dealing with the argument from illusion, but an independently based and independently articulated theory. It has independent strength. It is no fiat or invention, if a clever one, for dealing with an argument that must fail. Its central proposition, that to be perceptually conscious is for something to exist, is certainly not the direct realism or the like that I take it is disjunctivism's account of perception.

Nor does this line of thought conflict with the proposition, a great premise of Radical Externalism, that consciousness is what is *given* to us. If there remains more to say about that, there will be nothing that conflicts with the line of thought.

One other remark. My thanks to Crane for rubbing my nose in the old matter of the argument from illusion. This has led me to see that there was not much force, although some, in an earlier line of thought. that was to the effect that Radical Externalism is a theory of consciousness testable by way of cortical stimulation (Honderich, 2004, pp. 211–14).

(11) The third outstanding weakness found by him in the theory is its criticism of opposing views — which indeed is fundamental in its own recommendation. Here Crane approves of the maybe novel strategy of setting out criteria for a theory of consciousness to

## COMMENT ON RADICAL EXTERNALISM 41

meet, but declares that I fail badly because of not actually considering the opposing views.

He says of Honderich:

> He considers only two views: dualism (which for some reason he calls spiritualism or mentalism) and physicalism. Dualism is the Cartesian version of the view according to which consciousness does not exist in space (p. 33).

Crane would have a little excuse for that judgement in one paragraph of mine in which it is said that the history of the philosophy of mind has had in it the main proposition that mind and brain are two things and also the proposition that they are one thing (p. 4) — he would have a little excuse *if* the paragraph was not followed by several later lines. One, which might have been made plainer, is that dualism has in it a particular kind, one kind among others.

> Or go to ordinary and hesitant beliefs about consciousness, folk-beliefs or images that tend in the direction of what is called Cartesian dualism. Descartes didn't make it up (p. 10).

That dualism is also touched on later, defined as taking consciousness out of space and also making it mysterious, and said for these reasons to be better named as spiritualism or mentalism (p. 10). In the next paragraph, the alternatives to Radical Externalism are said to be mainly the spiritualism and what I call devout physicalism, but are also said to include marriages of things close to the spiritualism and the physicalism.

(12) But enough of this scholarship. Also, let me pass by the schoolmasterly refrain that I should have followed Crane's taxonomic ways, wandered around the contemporary philosophical landscape, and done yet more distinguishing between views — views that share quite general properties that I argue make the views futile. Given my argument about the shared general properties, argument good or bad, there would have been no point at all in that.

(13) No doubt my piece could have been more diligent. It could have been explicit in saying that the philosophical landscape can be said to to contain three species of theories of consciousness, each with subspecies — as, incidentally, the landscape could also be put into different categories or anyway categories under different names.

In the landscape, you can say, there is *dualism*, which makes mind and/or brain two things and includes (d1) spiritualism or mentalism, (d2) theories that make mind and brain into two physical things (e.g. Honderich, 1988; 1990, pp. 87–9; 2004, pp. 100–1, 126), and (d3) Radical Externalism.

There is also *monism*, which makes mind and brain into one thing and includes (m1) the theory that the mind and consciousness have only physical properties, this being traditional materialist monism, and (m2) philosophical idealism and the like, which allows to mind and brain only non-physical and mental properties.

There are also theories, called *marriages* by me, but which might better be called *qualified materialist monism*. These purport to be are somehow physicalistic but add in something somehow on the way to spiritualism or mentalism. An example is (qmm1) the idea that conscious processes are brain processes that have an 'inside' or are in some obscure sense subjective as well as objective.

About this taxonomy for Crane, it is worth remarking that it is like many taxonomies in needing a note or two. Certainly (d3) Radical Externalism, can be both dualistic and also near-physicalist, as it is. Of course the dualism (d2) shares its main character, devout physicalism, with (m1) traditional materialist monism. And, as remarked, (qmm1) qualified materialist monism is an unclear distance away from (m1) traditional materialist monism.

I pass by details of how this deals with several of Crane's strictures, and note only several comparisons.[4]

(14) In the contest between (d3) Radical Externalism and (d1) Cartesian or non-spatial dualism, Radical Externalism wins by making consciousness into a reality that obviously it is, and also in not being vulnerable to the knock-down argument that it makes mind-body interaction hopeless. Radical Externalism wins over (d2) the two-sort devout physicalism partly by making consciousness subjective in a clear and strong sense.

To come on to physicalism, (d2) as remarked is in fact a devout physicalism, sharing that character with (mi) traditional materialist monism. I say, to repeat, that they leave out the known character of consciousness, its subjectivity.

This I express, firmly but not absurdly, by saying that devout physicalism leaves out (c) consciousness, putting only a (np) neural phenomenon in its place. Crane replies, in effect, after reminding me that identity is a symmetrical relation, that devout physicalism doesn't leave out consciousness but just make it into just a neural phenomenon. Indeed it does, as presumably we both agree and can pedantically say. What devout physicalism comes to is that (c)=(np) and thus (np)=(c), and (c) or (np) is only a neural phenomenon. That is exactly what is wrong with theories of devout physicalism and makes them hopeless.

---

[4] For more taxonomy, see Honderich (2004), pp. 205–6 and also 2, 3, 5, 15–16, 19–20, 52–5, 91, 108, 150.

I end there — with the idea about Crane's comment on Radical Externalism that as it stands I can see little to recommend it. Up to you, reader.

**References**

Ayer, A.J. (1973), *The Central Questions of Philosophy* (London: Weidenfeld & Nicholson).
Honderich, T. (1988), *A Theory of Determinism: The Mind, Neuroscience and Life-Hopes* (Oxford: Oxford University Press).
Honderich, T. (1990), *Mind and Brain: A Theory of Determinism, Vol. 1* (Oxford: Oxford University Press).
Honderich, T. (1991), 'Seeing qualia and positing the world', in *A.J. Ayer: Memorial Essays*, ed. A. Phillips Griffiths (Cambridge: Cambridge University Press).
Honderich, T. (2004), *On Consciousness* (Edinburgh: Edinburgh University Press).
Nagel, T. (1986), *The View From Nowhere* (Oxford: Oxford University Press).
Strawson, P.F. (1979), 'Perception and Its objects', in *Perception and Identity*, ed. G.F. Macdonald (London: Macmillan).

James Garvey

# *Consciousness and Absence*

Consciousness as existence or Radical Externalism has a lot to recommend it, and there is much more to it than the abbreviated version presented in this collection. You can find most of it in *On Consciousness* (Honderich, 2004). The arguments for the view consist largely in noticing that the conception of consciousness as existence meets certain criteria of adequacy which other views fail. Quibble about those criteria if you like, but there might be another argument in the book which is just as compelling. The book charts Honderich's thinking about consciousness through the past twenty years or so, and the other argument for consciousness as existence emerges throughout. It is not just the specified criteria of adequacy which get a reader's attention, but a kind of mounting frustration throughout the years, a frustration associated with trying to keep the usual categories of mind and world in view when thinking about the reality of consciousness. The other argument for Radical Externalism is, roughly, that those other categories aren't much help. Everything we have is a kind of mess.

If, like me, you were brought up long after physicalism took hold in the philosophy of mind but just when Jackson, Nagel and others started having second thoughts, the frustration can strike a particular chord. I have no desire to drop perfectly respectable naturalistic commitments, but I can't help thinking that views which are true to them leave out the reality of consciousness. The frustration is just part of the philosophy of mind for some of us. We grew up in the middle of it. So the call for something new is, to put it mildly, something many of us hear quite clearly.

Is Radical Externalism something new? The view isn't reheated Berkeley. Honderich's worlds contain more than just minds and the ideas in them. The view isn't Kant's either. For one thing, Honderich thinks that we can get at the world as it is in itself through theorizing. For another, there is a distinction in Kant, missing in Radical Externalism, between perceptual consciousness and its contents —

another reading of the Refutation of Idealism might be enough to persuade you of this. The view isn't the semantic externalism of Putnam or Burge, as for Radical Externalism it is not just meaning which ain't in the head. The view isn't the extended mind of Chalmers and Clark either, as for Honderich it isn't part of my memory or belief structure that's out there. Radical Externalism really is new, and if something new is needed, maybe this is it.

There are many ways into thinking about consciousness as existence, but I'll take an obvious one. In what follows, we'll wonder a little about what it means to say that a thing exists, think a little more about perceptual consciousness as existence and its two dependencies, and then worry a bit about our consciousness of things which do not exist.

## Existence

It might occur to you to worry more than a bit about an exercise in conceptual correction, as Honderich puts it, which depends on a notoriously difficult concept. Philosophers since Aristotle have had some trouble with the notion of existence. Does that trouble spill into thinking of consciousness as existence?

The trouble I have in mind is owed to reflection on the part of both Hume and Kant. Recall that Hume argues for the claim that every genuine idea is derived from a distinct impression. He puts the problem, as usual, in the form of an apparently inescapable dilemma:

> the idea of existence must either be derived from a distinct impression, conjoined with every perception or object of our thought, or must be the very same with the idea of the perception or object (*Treatise* I.2.vi).

Hume, again as usual, inspects his store of ideas and the impressions he has and concludes that the idea of existence 'is the very same with the idea of what we conceive to be existent.' There is, in other words, no distinct impression of existence conjoined with every experience of something which exists. Existence, he says, makes no addition to the idea of any object. It's empty.

Kant, for once, agrees. Consider this passage:

> By whatever and however many predicates we may think a thing — even if we completely determine it — we do not make the least addition to the thing when we further declare that this thing is ... If we think in a thing every feature of reality except one, the missing reality is not added by my saying that this defective thing exists (*Critique of Pure Reason*, B628).

Being or existence, Kant concludes, is not a genuine predicate. It adds nothing to our conception of something to say that that something exists.

You need not go along with the details of any of this to form a worry about the wisdom of reconstructing a concept of consciousness out of what might turn out to be an empty bag of raw materials. The trouble is not that in saying 'consciousness exists' we say nothing in particular about consciousness, add nothing to our conception of it. The trouble is that Radical Externalism has it that my perceptual consciousness is existence. My consciousness of this page is the page's existing. If Hume and Kant are right, pointing out that the page exists says nothing much. Thinking about consciousness as existence, you might conclude, adds nothing to our concept of consciousness.

Radical Externalism certainly has the resources to deal with this objection. It has a robust conception of existence in it. Here are two expressions of it:

> [T]o be perceptually conscious is only for an extra-cranial state of affairs to exist — for there to be a spatio-temporal set of things with a dependence on another extra-cranial state of affairs and also on what is in a particular cranium.

> The page's being there, and more generally *your world of perceptual consciousness* is things being in space and time, with such further properties as colour, and being dependent on a scientific or noumenal world underneath and also dependent on you neurally (Honderich, 2006, p. 6).

Let's spell out the claims made. Being conscious of the page is the page's existing, being there in a world of perceptual consciousness. The page in my world of perceptual consciousness (i) is in space and time; (ii) has some properties of its own; (iii) depends on another world, the noumenal or scientific world; (iv) depends on me, in particular, my brain. There is more to it, but this is enough. It certainly gets us past the worry that existence adds nothing to our conception of consciousness. It adds a lot, but does it add too much? Does it take us too far in a certain direction? Will we have more than a little trouble when it comes to thinking about our consciousness of things which do not, in some sense, really exist?

## The Double Dependency

The first thing to notice is the double-dependency of my world of perceptual consciousness: it depends on both my brain and the underlying physical world. In what does this dependency consist?

The page in my world of perceptual consciousness depends on me. It would not be there without me. I am a necessary condition of the page's existing. What is it about me? It's my neural events.

> [M]y perceptual consciousness has a dependency on, has a kind of nomically necessary condition in, my own simultaneous neural events (Honderich, 2004, p. 136).[1]

The largest reason for requiring this sort of dependency is that it gives us a distinction between my world of perceptual consciousness and some other worlds.

Try not to get too hung up on talk of various worlds. Honderich argues that there is a good sense in which there is just one world, but there are various conceptions of it. One depends on my world of perceptual consciousness. Another world is the physical world, which consists in perceivable space-time occupants and other things, atoms and whatnot, which stand in nomic relations to those perceivable space-time occupants. A third is the objective world, which consists in things perceivable by more than one person, as well as space-time occupants which exist unperceived. There is also a scientific world, a shaky world of things in current or anticipated science. There is, finally, a noumenal world or world-in-itself — maybe it's what science aims to understand. Obviously there is overlap between the worlds, and the overlap is desirable. It can get you on your way to understanding the connections between consciousness and physical, objective, scientific or noumenal things, connections which are mysterious for other views of consciousness.

The point here is this: of all the worlds, only my world of perceptual consciousness depends on me in the relevant way. This dependency picks out my world of perceptual consciousness from the other worlds. The dependency is required, too, to make some sense of subjectivity, point of view, and so on.

It's not just me that's required for my world of perceptual consciousness. My perceptual consciousness also depends on another world, made up of atoms and whatnot. Which one? Call it the scientific or the noumenal one if you like. What matters is that my world of perceptual consciousness depends on more than what's in my cranium: it depends on extra-cranial events or states of affairs or things. This further dependency is required to ensure that we are dealing with something other than just a mental world, just an interior world.

---

[1] In this commentary all subsequent page references are to *On Consciousness* (Honderich, 2004) unless stated otherwise.

If there were a sufficient neural condition for my perceptual world, then it's hard not to think of that world as consisting of experiences, or mental images, or merely representations, or something else of the interior ilk — something, in other words, which does not exist outside my head. This, it almost goes without saying, would be bad for Radical Externalism. For Radical Externalism, my world of perceptual consciousness is not a merely mental world. You can sit on parts of it. You can't sit on a mental representation.

My world of perceptual consciousness, then, requires both my cranium and bits of the scientific or noumenal world; neither of the pair is alone sufficient for my perceptual consciousness. The necessity of both my neurons and the relevant bit of the world is nomic or lawlike. Probably the necessity depends on causality. However you cash it out, the dependency is double. Without both me and the atoms, no world of perceptual consciousness. You might smell a rat here. We can get at it from several directions.

## Consciousness and Non-existence

Think about illusions, hallucinations, dreams and brains in vats. Philosophers have been thinking about this sort of thing for some time. We have here no flash in the pan — we owe the bent-oar-in-water example to Plato — and such phenomena figure into a lot of arguments for various views having to do with perception, metaphysics, epistemology as well as arguments for various versions of scepticism. Think about illusions for the moment.

Illusions ought to be the easiest of the listed phenomena for Radical Externalism to accommodate. Illusions, unlike the rest on the list, involve seeing something which looks one way but is really another. So at least with illusions the radical externalist can say that both parts of the double dependency are in place, but something has gone wrong with the neural side of things. The difference, in the case of illusions as against hallucinations and the rest, is that there really is something there to be seen, and the trouble is that you are seeing it as it isn't. You are not making an erroneous judgement, exactly, not mistaking a horse for a cow, but actually somehow misperceiving a physical thing.

Look again at the page and stick your finger in your eye just hard enough to double your vision. What just doubled? Traditionally, there is only one answer going. You can say, more than a little preposterously, that the physical page out there in the world of atoms doubled. Or you can say that what doubled was something mental, a representation or image of the page out there in the world. This sort of thinking is probably the main motivation or recommendation for representational realism, phenomenalism and other views in the neighbourhood. What does Radical Externalism say about the doubling?

Part of the strategy is to attack representational realism. The trouble with views which go in for mental representations, Honderich argues, is that they depend on an inference from some premise to the conclusion that there are physical things. The representational realist starts with inner mental images or representations, and argues that our awareness of those plus an inference gets us an indirect awareness of physical objects. But our experience, the phenomenology of perception, has neither the awareness of an inner thing or an inference in it. In defending the theory, the representational realist then has to argue that both the awareness of the inner object and the inference from it to the existence of a corresponding physical object are not conscious. In saying this, Honderich argues, the representative realist takes himself out of the discussion, fails to make his answer an answer to the question about the real nature of consciousness, ends up just putting a spin on some science (pp. 154–6).

There are other objections too or at least methodological considerations which are raised in favour of Radical Externalism. Simplicity and maybe Occam's Razor should point you towards consciousness as existence. It gets rid of more than half the stuff claimed by representational views, namely representations and unconscious inferences (Honderich, 2006, pp. 7–8). It also gets us out of our little mental prisons. We are no longer watching representational television on an inner monitor. When we are conscious of the page, we have the page.

Very well, let's look away from representational realism and have a think about Radical Externalism's take on illusion. Here we certainly can argue that something has gone amiss on the neural end of things, but are we committed to anything untoward? What we have, with the doubling of the page, cannot be just a double image, not if we are taking consciousness as existence seriously. Are we stuck with two things in my world of perceptual consciousness, two objects with properties in space and time? I think maybe we are. But then what is the difference between the page that I had before the doubling and the extra, doubled page I have now? Both depend on me neurally and the relevant part of the physical world; both are in space and time; both have properties. Should we just say that I cannot tell the difference between the two pages, cannot tell which is the page that I had and the new page that I've got? It is an illusion, after all. I'm not supposed to be able to tell the difference.

What I would like, at least, is some way of thinking about the difference, some way of making a distinction. To bother Moore for a moment, I'd like some distinction in my world of perceptual consciousness between objects presented in space and objects to be met with in space, but I don't think we can get it. The robust conception of existence we noticed a moment ago seems to give us too much. It puts the extra page in space and time, gives it a set of properties and dependencies, all pretty much just like the original page. So how am I to think about the illusory page as against the original page in my world of perceptual consciousness, even if we grant that I can't notice a phenomenological difference? If we've dropped images and representations and the like and replaced the lot with propertied objects, do we have the resources to cope with the difference between the page in my world of perceptual consciousness and the extra, illusory page which accompanies it?

The representationalist is stuck with two images, just as the radical externalist is stuck with two objects, but the former can at least say that mental images are the sorts of things which can double in this way. Can propertied objects in space and time double, too?

Turn your attention to the rest of the phenomena on the list: hallucinations, dreams and the experiences of brains in vats. Here we have an immediate problem: we have or might have worlds of perceptual consciousness without half of the dependency relations in place. We have perceptual worlds standing in no relation at all to the objective or noumenal world. We have possible counter-examples to Radical Externalism.

Think about a brain in a vat. Neuroscientists are feeding it electrical impulses or whatever is required to give it the experience of a page, apparently creating a world of perceptual consciousness with no dependency on a page in the noumenal world. Honderich is alive to the difficulty: 'Here, as some have said, is a disaster that finishes off an unlikely idea' (p. 212).

Honderich's response is to deny the possibility of a real, live brain in a vat having the experience of a page when there is no page in sight. The assumption underpinning all thought experiments involving brains in vats is, roughly, that

> there is a neural process that is causally or in some other way nomically *sufficient* for the consciousness. There is a complete causal circumstance, wholly neural, for the consciousness (p. 212).

This is, of course, just what consciousness as existence denies. So Honderich denies the possibility that a brain in a vat could be perceptually conscious. The denial has the virtue of making consciousness as existence testable, Honderich argues. If someone manages to get a perceptually conscious brain in a vat up and running, so much for Radical Externalism.

> You will anticipate that I have to, and happily do, put my money on no brain in a vat ever having perceptual experience just as a result of monkeying around with the brain itself (p. 213).

It would be very good to have done with brains in vats, but I'd like a reason for thinking that they are not empirically possible. I know that Honderich has to deny the possibility of perceptual consciousness without one half of the dependency relations, but it would be good to have something of a story about perception to beef up the denial. It might be that I am just too immersed in something like a causal theory of perception, for what that's worth. It is hard not to think about the causal connections between objects and light waves and retinas and cortices, even if I agree that consciousness isn't all that stuff. It is hard not to think that distal causes in the world set up proximal causes in the brain, which in turn do whatever they do. Why couldn't the causal chain start up proximally or get caused by something causally enough like light waves but different from them to give the brain in the vat the experience of the page? This sounds like a question for neuroscience, and maybe the denial is all we are owed from Radical Externalism.

But then what do we do with hallucinations and dreams? Unlike brains in vats, we cannot deny that such things are possible, and they really do seem like instances in which we have perceptual consciousness with no dependency on an extra-cranial state of affairs. When we dream of a page, as Descartes did, we have a page in a world of perceptual consciousness, but there's no corresponding page in any other world. Someone experiencing a total visual hallucination, say of a pink elephant large enough to occupy her whole visual field, has a world of perceptual consciousness consisting just in a pink elephant, but there's no pink elephant in any other world.

Stop right there. Are instances of total hallucination and dreaming really worlds of perceptual consciousness or just sometimes phenomenologically indistinguishable from such worlds? If these phenomena really are worlds of perceptual consciousness, then we have counter-examples to Radical Externalism's insistence on half of a double dependency. We could lose the dependency or we could say that such things happen in (or are) something other than perceptual consciousness. If we do opt for the claim that hallucinations and dreams are not instances of perceptual consciousness, then we need a way to think about them which fits the rest of the theory. Maybe that way has something to do with a single dependency on a subject neurally.

Do we really want the possibility, though, that there are sorts of mental phenomena, wholly mental phenomena, which smell just like consciousness as existence? Further, when the pink elephant is not the whole of my experience, but just a part of it, just something which wanders into my world of perceptual consciousness, how would we explain the intrusion of this wholly mental thing into a world of propertied, space-time objects?

Let's have one last think about illusions, dreams, hallucinations and brains in vats. We can find a story about illusions in Radical Externalism, but it would be good to have more of one, in particular, one which gives us a way of thinking about the difference between the original page in my world of perceptual consciousness and the illusory page. Maybe we can put brains in vats to one side, and stick with Radical Externalism's denial of their possibility. Still, it would be good to have a little story about proximal causes, but maybe we can leave this to the scientists. Perhaps dreams can be put to one side too, as being instances of something other than perceptual consciousness. With some hallucinations, though, we seem to have something entirely dependent on me, something just mental, intruding on my world of perceptual consciousness. The elephant has only half of the required dependencies.

An earlier version of consciousness as existence countenances the possibility that consciousness has a neural guarantee (p. 137); the later version we have been considering drops this in favour of a dependency on both something in a cranium and something outside a cranium. I wonder if hallucinations might suggest that something in the middle sometimes obtains. Maybe something in between just a neural guarantee and a double dependency would help explain my lingering thoughts about the possibility of brains in vats, too. It might give me a way of thinking about the elephant. I'm just not sure that anything could be in the middle of a single-sided guarantee and a double dependency. Could we have the former for some perceptual consciousness and the latter for the rest? Anyway, we do not have to end up with just a mental world if some of the objects in my world of perceptual consciousness depend only on me neurally, do we?

## Other Experienced Absences

There is one last sort of phenomenon worth considering, one last aspect of perceptual consciousness which might not sit well with the notion of consciousness as existence. Sometimes what I have in my world of perceptual consciousness is clearly something which is not there. When I am looking for my keys, particularly when I am running very late and I'm being told to get a move on, what I see everywhere around me is not the keys. On occasion, this really is just a judgment. You can ring up and ask if so and so is at home. I can look around, think about it, and say that she isn't. You might also ask if the keys are on the table, and I can look and then simply conclude that they aren't. But on other occasions, there is no judgement in play. What I really see is the absence. When your father dies and you pack up his things, you do not see him everywhere.

Think about Sartre's talk of nothingness or absence as something experienced on a par with presence.[2] If you arrange to meet the ever-punctual Pierre at the café, you arrive fifteen minutes late, and Pierre is nowhere to be seen, his absence stands out to you, just as his presence would were he there. It is something you see, something experienced, not something noted or judged. Sometimes what we experience is not the presence of a thing, but the absence of a thing. If perceptual consciousness consists in existence, what sense can be made of experiencing absences?

Although we have been concerned just with perceptual consciousness, Radical Externalism has more in it, namely reflective and affective consciousness, thinking and desiring. Probably something having to do with my thoughts and desires flavours my world of perceptual consciousness. Again Honderich is alive to the theoretical challenges here:

> There are large problems ... One is the understanding of the mixing and melding of the three parts, kinds, sides or whatever of consciousness, of how one contributes to the other, even in ordinary seeing and acting (Honderich, 2006, p. 6).

Does Radical Externalism have the resources to offer an account of the absences we sometimes experience, absences which are not exactly judgments or feelings, but maybe depend on those judgments or feelings?

I at least know a little about how the story cannot go. We sometimes talk of the way the page seems to me, what I take it to be or what I

---

[2] I owe this line of thinking, and whatever understanding of Sartre I have, to Jon Webber.

think it is for. What we cannot have, by Radical Externalism's lights, is the notion that all of this about the page has something to do with content, conceptual or otherwise. Radical Externalism promotes what gets called 'the content of consciousness' to consciousness itself. There is nothing to bring under a concept here, not exactly, anyway. But there at least seems to be plenty of room for some account of what I take the page for in reflective and affective consciousness.

It might be that thoughts along these lines will help Radical Externalism give an account of our experience of these sorts of absences. Of the other things which seem to involve the experience of what does not exist — illusions, hallucinations, dreams and the experiences of brains in vats — I'm a little less sure.

## References

Burge, Tyler (1979), 'Individualism and the mental', *Midwest Studies in Philosophy*, **4**, pp. 73–121.
Honderich, Ted (2004), *On Consciousness* (Edinburgh: Edinburgh University Press).
Honderich, Ted (2006), 'Radical externalism', *Journal of Consciousness Studies*, **13** (7–8), pp. 3–13. [This issue]
Hume, David (1951), *A Treatise of Human Nature*, ed. L.A. Selby-Bigge (Oxford: Oxford University Press).
Jackson, Frank (1982), 'Epiphenomenal qualia', *Philosophical Quarterly*, **32**, pp. 127–36.
Kant, Immanuel (1929), *Critique of Pure Reason*, ed. N. Kemp-Smith (London: Macmillan).
Nagel, Thomas (1979), *Mortal Questions* (Cambridge: Cambridge University Press).
Putnam, Hilary (1975), *Mind, Language and Reality* (Cambridge: Cambridge University Press).
Sartre, Jean-Paul (1969), *Being and Nothingness*, trans. Hazel Barnes (London).

## REPLY TO GARVEY BY HONDERICH

Maybe James Garvey and I desire to about the same extent to persist in respectable naturalist commitments. Maybe we both want to try to understand the particular reality of consciousness by giving up only on the naturalism that is exactly devout physicalism — doctrines to the effect that somebody's being conscious is a matter of only physical facts according to a standard definition. Certainly there is a difference between that physicalism and naturalism in general, which, you may conjecture, is why we have two words.

Naturalism in the relevant sense is a commitment to analysis and explanation by certain properties, most of them in physical science and all of them in science and empirical philosophy. They are properties that do not separate our species from the rest of what exists, do not separate human nature from the rest of nature. If naturalism could do with more definition, is there anything of interest that doesn't?

As for the particular reality of consciousness, we may agree that each of us has a grip or hold on the fact of our own consciousness — and that we have had it since not long after we distinguished milk or mother from just seeing them, thinking of them, or wanting them. Consciousness is a known reality, whatever the difficulties of understanding and analysis.

It is a known reality that results in a certain proposition's being the most resilient in the history of thinking about ourselves — say Hobbes to behaviourism to eliminative materialism to neural functionalism. The proposition is that consciousness, whatever it is, isn't cells — or stuff in fancy physics either, so long as the stuff remains physics, which is to say the part of science actually concerned with only the nature and properties of matter and energy.

Since naturalism is necessary and devout physicalism is impossible, we need some other naturalism.

We can lay out the difference between consciousness and states or processes that are only physical. But we have a conviction of the difference before then, which is important. Does the conviction that when there's somebody in the room there's a non-physical fact in it just beg the question?

You can try that on. But it does so in about the way that the fact that we can indeed see, think and want overcomes us when it first occurs to us — overcomes us in about the way that any clear, large and solid fact or axiom overcomes us until something is produced to put it into question, or, I guess, until it becomes impossible to hope for some understanding of it. If there is no hope of understanding or explaining a thing, very likely, we come to doubt it. As against that, no general habit or authority of a discipline, no imperialism of any science, puts such a thing as the consciousness we know into question.

Such views, as Garvey reports, are certainly not the private property of any one philosopher or scientist. No doubt there is little argument for the truth of certain propositions, including philosophical ones, in majority support. This isn't democracy. There is more argument in the support of some people as against others. Paid philosophers then? Hierarchic democracy? That a large majority of paid philosophers take devout physicalism to be a suspect doctrinalism has this much to be said for it: it is enough to overbear the supposed solidarity of comrades in some of the philosophy of mind, certainly a supposed solidarity made use of by them in philosophical persuasion.

Garvey is right, I trust, in seeing that Radical Externalism, right or wrong, is not the same as any other large thing in the history of philosophy or in subsequent developments. As for its understanding of your perceptual consciousness in terms of only the existence of a world, he articulates and contemplates the objection that rests on the proposition received from Hume and Kant that existence is not a predicate. To the objection he replies that Radical Externalism supplies a robust conception of the existence of the state of affairs that is your awareness of the room you are in — that the state of affairs takes up a certain space and persists for a certain time, has certain properties, and is dependent on a world underneath and on you neurally.

He could have added that saying that something exists, a chair over there or a blackbird on the lawn, is certainly not impugned by the proposition that its existence is not a property of an object like its colour. No well-founded claim as to the existence of something is put in doubt by some philosophical bafflement about ways of existence in general. I suspect myself, incidentally, that what 'existence is not a predicate' comes to, when rescued from some formal logic, is that when you have said all there is to say of the blackbird, including that the is over there on the lawn now, and maybe a bit more about how that comes about, you of course add no more by saying he exists.

To come on to the dependencies of your world of perceptual consciousness, more reasons have been given for its not being a 'mental' world than the one Garvey reports, that is is partly dependent on, indeed bound up with, the physical world underneath. He provides what had not occurred to me, the sharper expression of the point — that if there really were a *sufficient* neural condition of your perceptual world, it would be hard not to think of it as something of the interior ilk.

He then comes to the part of his paper that seemed to me for a bad day to finish off the adventure or Radical Externalism. Aware of a history of argument as old as Plato and as recent as disjunctivism, he distinguishes to great effect four things — illusions, hallucinations, dreams and the conjectured experience of brains in vats.

Illusions, as we say, are cases of seeing something that looks one way but really is another.

> Look at the page and stick your finger in your eye just hard enough to double your vision. What just doubled? (p. 48).

That alarmingly clear-headed and clear question of course is the one that in the past has led in the direction of representational realism and the like — inner mental images, sense data, representations and so on. There can be two of those, as there definitely cannot be two physical objects in question. So the page, also when your finger is not stuck in your eye, is not a physical object.

I certainly persist in maintaining that there are powerful grounds for resisting the sense-data and what-not of our forbears and some of our fellow-workers now. What can be greatly more alarming is that the illusion can look fatal to Radical Externalism, as fatal as to doctrines that perceptual consciousness itself is a mysterious relation to a physical object.

> What we have, with the doubling of the page, cannot be just a double image, not if we are taking consciousness as existence seriously. Are we stuck with two things in my world of perceptual consciousness, two objects with properties in space and time? I think maybe we are (p. 49).

If nothing specific could be laid out against this supposed outcome, it might be that philosophical stubbornness would sustain me, a stubbornness not devoid of reason, and akin to the stubbornness of disjunctivism in going on saying that two indistinguishable experiences, one of them an hallucination, are different. Speaking for Radical Externalism, you *can* remain impressed by a theory of perceptual consciousness that works better than any other theory when you are not sticking your finger in your eye. Remember the criteria for an adequate theory of consciousness and how it can be argued that they select Radical Externalism and nothing else.

It is not as if one strong counter-example exactly stated is the sum total of our knowedge and judgement. There *is* the strength of the proposition that consciousness is what we *have*, and that what I have in ordinarily seeing a page is bloody definitely not an inner picture of a page and also a page — or just an inner picture. You can take the line, obviously, that our ordinary seeing is a whole pile of counter-example or better than that against a denial of Radical Externalism. What we have, then, is a choice between conflicting counter-examples or better. The situation isn't the easy one in logic where 'All x is f' runs up against an x that isn't f.

If this sort of fortitude is possible in reply to Garvey's doubling of the page, it is fortunate that there *is* something else better to say. You can take the view that more has to be put into the theory of Radical Externalism — and that it can be. If this is a concession about the past, so be it.

Garvey remarks, again correctly, that in the case of the finger in the eye and the resulting illusion, something has gone wrong or amiss not with respect to the dependency of the experience on the physical world underneath, but rather with the neural end of things — in which he presumably includes or to which presumably he adds the perceptual apparatus of the person in question. That is a thought that can go a lot further, lead to another thought.

Suppose some advanced neuroscientific tinkering with my retinas and/or cortex has the effect that whenever there is a photo of Blair in front of me, the forehead has a label on it, 'Sincere Guy'. And maybe there is a dead Iraqi in the photo as well. Maybe a lot more than one. Does Radical Externalism commit us to saying that my experience consists in a world of perceptual consciousness? I propose that it does not.

For a world of perceptual consciousness, there has to be not only a dependency on the person, but *the right kind of dependency*. As soon as that is said, it is as obvious as Davidson's (1980) proposition that a desire to act in a certain way has to cause a movement in the right way for it to be true that the movement is an intentional action. There isn't an intentional action if the desire so shamed the man that in a bodily spasm he somehow did what he had wanted to do.

In short, the story of neural and perceptual dependency of a world of perceptual consciousness has to be enlarged, and it perfectly reasonably can be. There will be the upshot that the experience resulting from sticking your finger in your eye is not a world of perceptual consciousness or not just such a world and in particular not such a world with two pages in it.

Should we go on to say the experience goes into the category of reflective consciousness? Well, that would be less wrong. But not persuasive, certainly not persuasive until more is said. It may be that the finger in the eye and the doubled page are best responded to, in Radical Externalism, by in effect replacing the three parts, sides or sort of elements of consciousness with more than three. The illusion will not turn up in the category of perceptual consciousness, or standard perceptual consciousness, in this new classification, or of course in standard reflective consciousness.

Certainly this enlargement of Radical Externalism would take work. There is a whole subject under the label 'the right kind of dependency on the neural and perceptual end of things'. It may well have in it, with respect to visual worlds of perceptual consciousness, the worlds that are dependent on other senses, including touch. There is work to be done on the puzzlement in thinking, so to speak, of new mixed worlds.

Do you suppose there is some arbitrariness in the first step, taking your ordinarily seeing the page to include a world of perceptual consciousness and what we call seeing the page doubled, as a result of a finger in an eye, as not including a world of perceptual consciousness? Well, what is arbitrary in general is what is not based on reason, but on random choice or unargued fiat or something of the sort. The prospect now in view for Radical Externalism is not likely to be arbitrary. You have heard some anticipations of reasons for the prospect, not excluding more categories of consciousness.

One last reflection here. Seeing depends on eyes, you say. We all know that. We know something about the standard operation of retinas, rods and cones and so on. Suppose someone produces a case, in thought or in reality, where the only changes are large ones inside somebody's eyes, which eyes stay where they are. She now has what we would call experience of what is not in front of her but behind her head. Is our conception of seeing such that she sees what is behind her head? Not in my book. Not without taking a funny decision about an ordinary concept, that of seeing. Isn't there a good lesson here about worlds of perceptual consciousness? For seeing you need the right kind of dependence on eyes.

To come on quickly to the experience of brains in vats, Garvey correctly reports that such a brain, on my view, is not having that sort of consciousness that is perceptual consciousness. That seems to me a pretty comfortable position. What is not so comfortable is the need for another concession. Maybe there was something in the proud hope that Radical Externalism could be open to empirical test. What seems more defensible is just the position that the theory gives argued grounds for a distinction — the distinction according to which there can be no world of perceptual consciousness in the case of the brain in the vat or an hallucination, but something else. That there is consciousness is certainly not to be denied. There may be more to be said about all this, but not now.

To come on to hallucinations and dreams, Garvey contemplates for a paragraph that they are instances of perceptual consciousness. My view, given the dependencies proposition in Radical Externalism, is that hallucinations and dreams cannot involve worlds of perceptual consciousness. Different accounts have to be given of them, very possibly a further enlargement of Radical Externalism. We do have a basis in that theory, don't we? What is on offer is not the thin stuff of direct realism, what Ayer (1940) with reason called naive realism, and then the taking of a stance against the upshot of a counter-example.

Leaving aside a bit more of Garvey's reflections, there is the final proposition that in pretty ordinary perceptual consciousness, I can really see an *absence*, say of my keys. Sartre is prayed in aid here. And there is the resulting question about Radical Externalism. If perceptual consciousness consists in existence, what sense can be made of experiencing these absences?

The line of thought is inventive, not more of the same. It is also inventive of Garvey to think of the possibility of trying to deal with the phenomenon by means of affective consciousness in particular — in a word, desiring. It needs to be kept in mind, of course, that the lightly sketched accounts of affective and reflective consciousness in Radical Externalism definitely do not require, in worlds of perceptual consciousness or anywhere, the existence of things desires and the like or thought of and the like.

There is also room for speculation owing something to past philosophy on the subject of negative facts — about an absence of X amounting to a presence of something else, but I leave this out, and end with a thought like one or two others you have heard. It is that if Radical Externalism is OK except for a puzzle about dealing with absences, it is pretty much OK.

My hope, pretty confident, is that the theory survives or can come to survive this and the preceding effective questions, but that one in particular, about sticking your finger in your eye, calls out for what is possible, a larger theory, whether or not of my own devising. It will be true to what we have — consciousness as it seems to be, existing things inside and outside the head, no funny relationships or containers in it, satisfaction of criteria of adequacy.

## References

Ayer, A.J. (1940), *The Foundations of Empirical Knowledge* (London: Macmillan).
Davidson, D. (1980), *Essays on Actions and Events* (Oxford: Clarendon Press).

Stephen Law

# *Honderich and the Curse of Epiphenomenalism*

In 'Radical Externalism'[1] Ted Honderich offers an ingenious and radical new solution to the problem of consciousness — a solution that promises, among other things, to do justice to two important features of consciousness — to both its subjectivity *and* its causal efficacy.

According to Honderich, the main alternatives to his own Radical Externalism are certain forms of dualism, or, as he puts it, 'spiritualism', and 'devout physicalism'. Honderich's central argument for Radical Externalism is that it succeeds in respecting those features of consciousness to which these two main alternatives fail to do justice. It is, therefore, the superior theory.

But is Radical Externalism superior? Does it have this advantage over its two main rivals?

I don't believe it does. The central argument of this paper is that Radical Externalism falls foul of much the same kinds of problems concerning causal interaction that plague spiritualism. Indeed, ironically, it turns out that Radical Externalism is vulnerable to a similar objection to that which Honderich himself cleverly levelled again Anomalous Monism almost a quarter century ago.

But before we get to that objection, let's begin by briefly outlining what Honderich takes to be the two main alternatives to his own theory — spiritualism and devout materialism — and examining their alleged failings.

### Devout Physicalism and the Problem of Subjectivity

By devout materialism Honderich means:

---

[1] Honderich (2006). In this commentary all page references are to this target paper unless stated otherwise.

the belief or perhaps attitude that our consciousness is a fact, property or state of affairs that involves only physical properties ... and in particular properties in existing and more or less anticipated neuroscience (pp. 10–11).

The devout materialist either identifies mental properties with physical properties, or else eliminates them altogether (as in eliminative materialism).

So what's wrong with devout physicalism? Honderich maintains it fails, among other things, to do justice to the *subjectivity* of consciousness. We're all familiar with the kind of thought experiments involving black and white rooms, fool's pain, homunculi-headed robots and so on to which Honderich is perhaps alluding when he says

[n]o doubt theories are sometimes destroyed by single counter-examples clearly seen, or by crucial experiments well-conducted. It is my inclination to think this of devout physicalism ... (p. 11).

It's certainly a perennial complaint that these various kinds of materialisms somehow fail fully to allow for the subjective quality of conscious experience.

## Spiritualism and the Problem of Causal Interaction

Which brings us to what Honderich believes is the other main alternative to his own theory — spiritualism. What characterizes the dualist or spiritualist position, he says, is a commitment to the non-spatiality of consciousness. Spiritualism, says Honderich, is

the theory, rightly associated with Descartes, that your consciousness is somehow non-spatial and hence not physical. It is in fact only misleadingly called dualism, mainly because its distinctive nature and its problems are not owed to its asserting that consciousness is other than physical but rather to its asserting that consciousness is out of space and in fact of a mysterious nature (p. 11).

The problems that plague spiritualism, says Honderich, include the problem of causal interaction. Descartes famously attempts to place the locus of interaction between the mental and the physical realm in the pineal gland. But of course it remains blankly mysterious how this interaction might take place. How can something that is not anywhere causally impinge upon a spatio-temporally extended, physical object?

And so it seems that spiritualism also fails a key test of adequacy, in this case, the requirement that any adequate theory of consciousness

must not make impossible what is actual, which is causal interaction between consciousness and the physical (p. 12).

So we appear to face an intractable dilemma so far as consciousness is concerned. We can either favour some form of devout physicalism, but then we fail to do justice to the subjectivity of consciousness. Or we can embrace some variety of spiritualism, in which case we run into the problem of causal interaction — indeed, we may find ourselves unable to prevent a slide into epiphenomenalism (or occasionalism or pre-established harmony theory, or whatever).

I'm sure many philosophers of mind would acknowledge that we do at least face *something* like the dilemma that Honderich presents us with. Indeed, finding a way out of this sort of dilemma has surely been one of the main preoccupations of philosophers of mind for the last couple of decades.

The question is: does Honderich's new alternative — his third way, as it were — actually allow us to resolve the dilemma? Does it really let us do justice to both of these features of consciousness: to both its subjectivity *and* its causal efficacy?

It's immediately obvious that we might attempt to mount an attack on Radical Externalism from at least one of two directions. First, we might argue that, actually, like devout materialism, Radical Externalism fails to do justice to the subjectivity of consciousness. Or we might try to show that, like spiritualism, Radical Externalism faces problems in allowing for causal interaction. Or we might do both these things.

While I suspect Radical Externalism probably does face problems with respect to subjectivity (see the end of this paper), *it's on problems with causal interaction that I'll focus here*. As Honderich's case for Radical Externalism is that it avoids those problems that respectively plague spiritualism and devout materialism, establishing that Radical Externalism does indeed run straight into much the same old problems regarding causal interaction as does spiritualism would suffice seriously to undercut his case.

## Radical Externalism

Let me briefly sketch out both what I take Radical Externalism to be, and how I believe Honderich supposes it allows us to resolve the dilemma outlined above.

At the heart of Radical Externalism lies something Honderich calls *worlds of perceptual consciousness*. One important feature of a world of perceptual consciousness is that it is not located 'in the head' (not *at all*, in fact, unless e.g. you happen to be looking at your own brain). It encompasses the same tracts of space that those objects of which you are perceptually aware occupy. Hence the 'Radical Externalism'.

And yet, despite being spatially extended, a world of perceptual consciousness is also supposed to be subjective.

In what sense subjective? Well, a world of perceptual consciousness is something you *have*. Our worlds of perceptual consciousness are numerically distinct. You have yours. I have mine. When you and I simultaneously look at an orange placed on a table in front of us, our worlds of perceptual consciousness may spatially overlap. But still, while we may be conscious of the same orange, there are nevertheless two worlds of perceptual consciousness involved here, not one. Each subject has *their own* world of perceptual consciousness.

A corollary of this is that a world of perceptual consciousness is only immediately accessible to its owner. A world of perceptual consciousness is, in this sense, a *private* world. This kind of privacy is of course commonly supposed to be one of the hallmarks of the subjective (yet note that we are still dealing with a radical form of externalism here — we're not talking about inner Cartesian theatres, or anything like that).

There's at least one further way in which a world of perceptual consciousness would seem to qualify as subjective. A world of perceptual consciousness is subjective in that

> [w]ith consciousness, what there seems to be is what there is. What there seems to be is all there is (p. 5).

This, I take it, is the familiar claim that while I might be mistaken about there actually being an orange on the table in front of me, I can't be mistaken about the fact that that is how things subjectively *seem* to me. Within a world of perceptual consciousness, appearance is king. You can't, as it were, have *fool's x*, where *x* is something that features within your world of perceptual consciousness.

## Resolving the Dilemma

How, then, does the introduction of worlds of perceptual consciousness allow us to resolve the dilemma sketched out earlier? How does it succeed in doing justice both to the subjectivity of consciousness and its causal efficacy?

Let's start with subjectivity. That Honderich's worlds of perceptual consciousness do at least do justice to the subjectivity of consciousness might seem obvious. They make perceptual consciousness something you *have*, and they also respect the fact that the illusion/reality distinction collapses when it comes to conscious experience. They are also private. So perhaps the subjectivity of consciousness is indeed taken care of.

But what of causal interaction between the mental and the physical? How do they allow for that? Well, remember that, according to Honderich, the problem spiritualism faces concerning causal interaction is simply this: how can something that is *non-spatial* causally impinge upon the physical? Honderich's worlds of perceptual experience do indeed appear to sidestep this problem, for the simply reason that they *are* spatial.

So it might seem that Honderich's Radical Externalism does indeed allow us to do justice to both the subjectivity of consciousness and its causal efficacy. A pretty neat trick, if successful.

Unfortunately, I don't believe it is successful, as I'll now try to explain. In particular, some very serious problems concerning causal interaction appear to remain.

Honderich outlines *one* problem about causal efficacy facing spiritualism — the problem of how the non-spatial might causally impinge on the physical. And perhaps Radical Externalism does succeed in sidestepping *that* problem. The problem is that that is not the only problem. In fact, spiritualism faces far more serious difficulties concerning causal interaction, including the kind of difficulty that Honderich earlier raised for anomalous monism.

The problem for Honderich, as I'll try to show below, is that *Radical Externalism faces much the same kind of difficulty concerning causal interaction.*

## Honderich's Attack on Anomalous Monism

Let's begin by briefly reminding ourselves of Honderich's own earlier attack on Davidson's anomalous monism (Honderich, 1982). Anomalous monism itself arose in part out of a problem concerning the causal efficacy of the mental. According to Davidson, there can be a causal relationship between events only if they fall under some law. But there are no psychophysical laws. So how then can mental events cause physical events?

Davidson's solution is to point out that laws relate events only under some description or other. A token mental event $a$ can cause a physical event $b$ if $a$ is also a physical event. For then $a$ and $b$ can both fall under some physical description and so some physical law. But because there are no *psycho*-physical laws — no laws under which mental events *described as mental* cause physical events, so there can be no possibility of a *type*-identity between mental and physical events.

So Davidson's anomalous monism claims that token mental events are token physical events. But it seems that these token events have two quite distinct sorts of property: mental properties and physical properties. The mental properties of an event are neither identical with nor reducible to its physical properties. So it appears that anomalous monism is still committed to a *form* of dualism — namely, a form of *property* dualism.

Which brings me to Honderich's attack on anomalous monism. Back in 1982, Honderich cleverly pointed out that while Davidson does indeed allow mental events to have causal efficacy, it seems that epiphenomenalism still threatens. The problem is that while anomalous monism may allow mental events to have causal clout, *it's not in virtue of their mental properties that they have such clout.* You could entirely strip away the mental properties of an event, and its physical efficacy would remain undiminished. But, as Honderich puts it, it's surely mental events *as mental* that have causal efficacy. Honderich concludes that Davidson thus fails to do justice to one of our fundamental intuitions about the mental. Surely the mental properties of events *are* causally relevant. Anomalous monism makes them epiphenomenal. So anomalous monism won't do.

## Why Non-Spatiality Is *Not* the Only, Or the Most Serious, Problem Concerning Causal Efficacy Facing Spiritualisms

Honderich's argument against anomalous monism is neat, clear, and I believe ultimately telling. But notice that it *has nothing to do with the non-spatiality of the mental.* (Indeed, notice that it's not even clear that anomalous monism makes mental properties non-spatial. If physical events are spatially located, and physical events have mental properties, then why aren't mental properties also spatially located?) Indeed, surely the Really Big Problem about the causal efficacy of the mental so far as dualism more generally is concerned is *not* that it makes the mental non-spatial (for, as I say, it's not clear property dualism has to make the mental non-spatial, and in any case we might question whether the concept of cause requires both a cause and its effect to be spatially located).[2] In fact, what more often than not tends to force modern dualists in the direction of epiphenomenalism are not worries about the non-spatiality of the mental role so much as worries

---

[2] After all, there are many who would at least allow action at a distance, and if we allow that, then allowing non-spatial causes is perhaps not such a great further leap.

about the absence of psycho-physical laws and/or worries about the causal closure of the physical — in particular, the worry that if every physical event has a sufficient physical condition, then the mental ends up being causally locked out of the physical domain. As I say, this sort of worry about causal interaction is quite independent of any worries generated by the alleged non-spatiality of the mental.

But then a problem for Radical Externalism is this. Maybe it does sidestep *one* of the problems for spiritualism concerning causal interaction. By making worlds of perceptual consciousness spatial Honderich does perhaps avoid the problem of explaining how the non-spatial might impinge on the physical (though I have my doubts even about this: even if I acknowledge that a 'phantom' pain produced by a severed limb is spatially located [in thin air], that, by itself, still leaves it blankly mysterious how this pain might have any causal impact on the physical). But *that is not the only problem dualism faces so far as causal interaction is concerned.* Indeed, it may yet turn out that Radical Externalism is vulnerable to some of the other classic problems.

In fact it seems to me that Radical Externalism *is* vulnerable. For much the same kind of argument that Honderich wields against anomalous monism can be used against his own Radical Externalism.

Let's return to worlds of perceptual consciousness. They are supposed to solve the problem of causal efficacy by making consciousness spatial. Non-spatiality is supposedly what leads spiritualisms into trouble with causal efficacy. So that trouble is sidestepped.

Well, yes, *that* trouble is avoided, but the other problems remain. Worlds of perceptual consciousness may be spatially extended. But Honderich makes clear that they are nevertheless numerically distinct worlds. Nor are they identical with the physical world (or, I take it, any part of it). But then *what difference can they make, causally speaking, so far as what goes on in the physical world is concerned?* After all, if we removed these worlds of perceptual consciousness, the physical world would remain, and everything, presumably, would continue on in it exactly as before. So *why aren't worlds of perceptual consciousness epiphenomenal?*

In particular, if we can explain everything that happens physically entirely by reference to the physical, without our making any reference to worlds of perceptual consciousness or whatever goes on in them *at all*, then aren't worlds of perceptual consciousness epiphenomenal?

## A Reply

To this, the reply may be that, while a world of perceptual consciousness may not be identical with the physical world or any part of it, *it can nevertheless include physical objects.* I am currently conscious of this book. Therefore this very book constitutes a part of my world of perceptual consciousness. As the book is a physical object, it can have physical effects. But then, as my world of perceptual consciousness *includes* the book, *so it too is able to have physical effects.*

This surely won't do. Suppose this book tips over and knocks over a vase. The book tipping over causes the vase to smash. And the book tipping is part of my world of perceptual consciousness. So is this an example of my world of perceptual consciousness having a physical effect? That's an odd-sounding conclusion to draw, to say the least. But even if it did follow, it remains true to say that *featuring in my world of perceptual consciousness has nothing to do with the book's causal efficacy.* Had my world of perceptual consciousness been removed, the causal sequence that was played out in front of me — the book tipping resulting in the vase smashing — would still have been the same. We might put it like this. The event of the book's tipping may have a certain *mental property* — the property of falling within my world of perceptual consciousness. But *this mental property of the event is causally irrelevant to how things play out physically.* The book would have done what it did anyway, whether or not it happened to feature within my world of perceptual consciousness.

Of course, Honderich rightly points out that a world of perceptual consciousness is causally dependent upon what's going on physically. It exists in part as a result of what's going on neurologically. But of course this doesn't make worlds of perceptual consciousness any less epiphenomenal. Honderich allows physical properties can have effects on consciousness. The difficulty is in explaining how consciousness is to have any physical effects. It does seem as if God could have made a physically identical world, but without including any worlds of perceptual consciousness at all. They add nothing so for as how things play out physically is concerned.

But if Radical Externalism falls foul of these same classic difficulties concerning the causal efficacy of the mental, then it seems it has no very substantial advantage over the various spiritualisms to which Honderich thinks it should be preferred.

## Does Radical Externalism do Justice to Subjectivity?

I'll finish by briefly turning to the other horn of the dilemma about consciousness — of how we are to do justice to the subjectivity of consciousness. This is something Honderich claims 'devout physicalisms' fail to do. But does his own Radical Externalism fare any better?

Part of my difficulty here is in identifying precisely what worlds of perceptual consciousness are supposed to include. The suggestion seems to be that they can include real physical objects, as opposed to mere subjective surrogates for them. Suppose, for example, that you are conscious of this page. Honderich asks:

> What did your consciousness *seem* to consist in? An answer can grow on you fast. It *was for the page to be there*. What your consciousness seemed to consist in was nothing other or more than that. In a better sense of the words than employed by some philosophers, that is what it was like for you to be conscious of the page and that is all that it was like (p. 5).

The idea seems to be that your consciousness of the page is neither more nor less than for the page itself to exist. Well, actually, that's obviously false, as the page can exist without you being conscious of it. It's not entirely clear what Honderich is after, here. But it does at least seem that he wants to make the *physical object itself* feature in your consciousness. He wants to include *it* (and not just some mental surrogate for it) in your world of perceptual consciousness.

But earlier we noted that one of the criteria Honderich thinks any adequate theory of consciousness should meet is to do justice to the thought that when it comes to the realm of consciousness, the illusion/reality distinction collapses. You can be mistaken about what's objectively there, but not about what's subjectively there.

But then an obvious question arises — if real physical objects can crop up in all their objective glory within worlds of perceptual consciousness (as opposed to mere subjective surrogates — seemings, sense- data, ideas, or whatever) why doesn't that make possible exactly the distinction between illusion and reality Honderich wants to avoid?

Perhaps it doesn't, but I don't yet see why it doesn't. After all, it may seem to me like there's a book in my world of perceptual consciousness, but as a matter of fact there isn't. I'm hallucinating. So I'm mistaken about what there is in my world of perceptual consciousness.

In a nutshell, the problem is this. It seems Honderich wants to include real physical objects within worlds of perceptual consciousness. But by including them, worlds of perceptual consciousness no longer appear to be the infallibly given worlds it seems he requires them to be if his theory is to satisfy his own criterion concerning illusion/reality.

## Conclusion

In the preceding section, I raised a worry about how Radical Externalism is supposed to explain what Honderich suggests any adequate theory of consciousness should explain: namely the absence of an illusion/reality distinction within the realm of consciousness. Perhaps Radical Externalism can explain this, though I don't yet see how.

This is merely a worry, however. Perhaps my inability to see how Radical Externalism explains this is down to my not having fully understood it. It seems to me that the more substantial difficulty facing Radical Externalism concerns causal interaction. Perhaps Honderich has solved one of the problems that plagued at least some spiritualisms concerning causal interaction. But in my view the most serious difficulties concerning causal interaction are just as much difficulties for Radical Externalism as they are for spiritualism. So, as it stands, Radical Externalism seems to me to have no very substantial advantage over spiritualism.

Like Honderich, I'm not keen on 'spiritualism' or 'devout physicalism'. I am persuaded that we probably should be looking for a much more radical solution. Honderich's Radical Externalism is bold, imaginative and, I suspect, a very significant step in the right direction. But I am not persuaded that, as it stands, Radical Externalism really does solve the causal interaction problem, as Honderich claims. Not as it stands.

## References

Honderich, Ted (1982), 'The argument for anomalous monism', *Analysis*, **16**, pp. 59–64.

Honderich, Ted (2006), 'Radical externalism', *Journal of Consciousness Studies*, **13** (7–8), pp. 3–13. [This issue]

## REPLY TO LAW BY HONDERICH

Stephen Law in his independent and properly tough-minded piece begins by agreeing, I take it, that devout physicalism — consciousness itself is nothing but physical — can give no adequate account of what has long been called the subjectivity of consciousness, no account of the fact that your consciousness is not a thing, property, fact or state of affairs about you like your location, DNA, weight, synapses or the like.

He depends for his agreement, more than I do, on philosophical thought-experiments about black and white rooms, fool's pain and homunculi-headed robots. If the thought-experiments can seem crucial, I prefer the means or policy of mental realism that lies behind them, and on which they depend — contemplating your own consciousness directly, which you can certainly do, rather than allowing yourself to be distracted by more tractable but different subjects.

However, he may contribute to the high cause of Radical Externalism by seeing that it recognizes two simple facets of of the large fact of subjectivity that have been overlooked or not enough emphasized by me. One is the facet that when you and I, as we ordinarily say, see the orange on the table, my consciousness is a different thing from yours in that, whatever the explanation of this, your consciousness precisely does not have in it a funny relation to one thing, a single physical object that is *also* on the other end of my relation and thus is common to us both. In place of that, there are two distinct worlds of perceptual consciousness.

The other facet of the large fact of subjectivity is that your consciousness is indeed something you *have*, that there is no more to your consciousness than there seems to be — which truths, however, are a little more intimately related than Law conveys by separating them in his list. This facet, again, is its being totally *present*, so different from your location, DNA, weight, synapses or the like, to say nothing of the rest of the physical world.

These facets of the subjectivity of consciousness he adds in privacy, useful but to my mind not so large or deep a thing as sometimes supposed. At least there is no conceptual or logical barrier to my having consciousness the very same as yours, and knowing I have. There is the remote possibility that with with some technical help, now science fiction, our successors might be able to have identical worlds for a minute or two, each of us having a perfect counterpart of the other's.

As against his positive contributions, Law does not make so explicit what can seem to be the principal facet of subjectivity — that your being perceptually conscious is subjective in exactly the sense that it is *different*. A world of perceptual consciousness is different from the physical world, or an objective world in a defined sense, or the world of things already admitted to current science or likely to be admitted soon. These are indeed views from nowhere, standardized possessions of no one in particular. So too, despite the remote possibility just mentioned, your world of perceptual consciousness is different from anyone else's world of perceptual consciousness.

Such a world, then, is subjective in clear and unelusive ways. We have no need of half-ideas or fleeting images of a subject or self, or a container or private theatre, or the interdependent existence of two items that cannot be got into focus, or some inner fact of awareness, let alone a supposedly two-term relation in perceptual consciousness that can relate somewhere within consciousness to nothing at all on the other end (Honderich, 2004). Further, and of course necessarily, the clear account of subjectivity with worlds of perceptual consciousness is a means to clear accounts with what they enter into, which is reflective consciousness and affective consciousness.

Law does not object to the broad division of almost all other theories of consciousness into devout physicalism and the particular dualism that is spiritualism. He is sure , too, that many philosophers of mind acknowledge the resulting dilemma or something like it having to do with no real subjectivity or no mental or conscious efficacy. How could they fail to? He supposes, more particularly than I have, and probably rightly, that it is exactly the different conceptions of subjectivity in spiritualist accounts of consciousness that are said to make it impossible for those accounts to explain or even make conceivable causal interaction between and the mental or conscious realm and the physical realm. But, he says, the pretty neat trick of Radical Externalism, giving an account of subjectivity that escapes the failure of devout physicalism in that respect and yet allows for the causal efficacy of perceptual, reflective and affective consciousness — mainly but not only making your perceptual consciousness into an external world of perceptual consciousness — this a trick that isn't successful. He will return in a more critical spirit to the subjectivity in Radical Externalism, but he first gives two reasons for his disappointment in connection with the argument about causal interaction, in fact reasons for thinking the dilemma collapses because spiritualism is OK.

The first reason is more hesitant. It is that it is or may be mistaken to require of causes and effects that they be things in space — and hence that it is or may be mistaken to suppose that spiritualism's conscious states and events cannot be causes of physical effects. It may be OK to say of something that is nowhere that it can causally impinge on a spatio-temporally extended, physical object, and so Radical Externalism has no advantage over spiritualism.

He makes several remarks in this direction, the first being a question. Suppose what we call a mental event is claimed to be an event with both physical and mental properties, as in the property-dualism that is Donald Davidson's Anomalous Monism. Suppose events that are physical, and hence these, are spatially located. Then why aren't the mental properties of Davidson's events also spatially related?

The short answer is that you could try to say that, given some new and very different idea of mental properties, but spiritualism just says otherwise. Whatever was Davidson's account of mentality, if any, as distinct from a failing logico-linguistic criterion for picking out certain statements (Honderich, 2004, pp. 5–18), it is spiritualism that is now our subject. The tradition of spiritualism, in pursuit of subjectivity, as is undisputed, takes mental events out of space. That Davidson's uncompleted dualism, indeed a dualism that could fall back into devout physicalism despite having a suspicion of rarefied spiritualism about it, does not clearly face the problem of causal interaction is no premise whatever for supposing that spiritualistic dualism escapes the problem.

In the aid of that dualism, or anyway in aid of objecting to my claim of Radical Externalism's superiority, Law also asks a more general question. It is whether the concept of a cause requires both a cause and its effect to be things in space. I have to admit that it has not seemed to me a question worth asking, for several reasons.

The main one is that causation, exactly that, is a relation between events or happenings — other talk of causes and effects as ordinary things like matches or stuff like snow, or facts and the like, and whatever else, reduces quickly to talk of events in a general sense. And an event of this kind, to be brief, is or is close to an ordinary thing in space having a property for a time. This truth about our concept of an event, I take it, is what rules out numbers, propositions and other abstract objects from the category of causes and effects. Also spatial points and locations, and no doubt some other items, some of which turn up in interpretations of Quantum Theory.

Would a more developed answer to the question of whether causes and effects are necessarily in space require argument about the nature of space? Deciding between Newton, Leibniz, Kant and others? Would it require separating causes from other sorts of supposed explanations — say Aristotle's final causes? Would an answer require a certain amount of physics, and engaging with space-time? And time itself — temporal properties and temporal relations? Even going back to action at a distance? And something on phantom limbs?

I doubt it, but cannot rule it out, and so end here with the admission that I have not tried to satisfy a philosopher who actually supposes that causes and effects are not events. More work for somebody?

Law's second and more confident reason for supposing that Radical Externalism is in trouble about causal interaction is also approached by way of Anomalous Monism. Davidson's account of mind and brain, although evidently a kind of dualism, was also true to its name in being to the effect that mind and brain are one thing in some sense or other. the account was derived from three claims or principles, the first two being truistic in different ways. These were that (1) there are causal connections between mental or conscious events and physical events, (2) where there are causal connections between events there are lawlike or necessary connections between them, and, pretty amazingly, (3) there are no such lawlike connections between mental and physical events.

Davidson's very neat escape from the inconsistent triad, by saying that it must be that mental events *as physical* are connected to physical events, immediately gives him the doctrine that mind and brain are in some sense one thing. The doctrine is also a dualism of properties, of course, as Law too remarks. It was to Davidson's credit that if he did not dispel uncertainty about the tendency of his doctrine, he did disdain what he called 'nothing-but' materialism, the utterance that the mind is nothing but the brain, a paradigmatic expression of devout physicalism.

His argument for Anomalous Monism, in my view and Law's, failed partly because of a truistic claim of mine. It is (4) that where events are cause and effect in virtue of only some of their properties, they are of course in lawlike connection in virtue of those properties. If it is the mass of the thing that is causal with respect to something else, and not is being purple, then the lawlike connection and of course the law or the statement of lawlike connection are in terms of its mass, not its colour.

Davidson's own denial (3) of the possibility of psychophysical lawlike connection rules out of the possibility that one of his events of consciousness is causal in terms of its being mental as against physical. Further, with respect to what then obviously has to be the causally efficacious property of a mental event, its physical property, this in no way depends on the event's mental property. There is no lawlike connection, remember, between mental and physical properties, in particular no connection whereby a mental property is nomically necessary to a physical property, including in the case where they are properties of the same event.

So, to come to the conclusion of this refutation of Anomalous Monism, the doctrine is an epiphenomenalism, an unbelievable denial of the efficacy of consciousness (Honderich, 1982; 2003; 2004). Law notes that the refutation does not depend at all on any idea that the mental properties, whatever they are, are made not spatial. He proposes the irony that Radical Externalism suffers the same awful fate, to my mind suffers as good as a reductio ad absurdum.

What has pushed modern dualists into epiphenomenalism, he says, is indeed a belief or inclination in the direction of the absence of psychophysical laws and/or the causal closure of the physical. The latter is the proposition that every physical event has a causally sufficient or causally necessitating condition that is physical. Thus, he says, the mental ends up being locked out of the physical domain. Epiphenomenalism.

And what of Radical Externalism?

> Worlds of perceptual consciousness may be spatially extended. But Honderich makes clear that they are nevertheless numerically distinct worlds. Nor are they identical with the physical world (or, I take it, any part of it). But then *what difference can they make, causally speaking, so far as what goes on in the physical world is concerned?* After all, if we removed these worlds of perceptual consciousness, the physical world would remain, and everything, presumably, would continue on in it exactly as before. So *why aren't worlds of perceptual consciousness epiphenomenal?* (p. 67).

One answer is that those lines by Law are a non-sequitur. It does not follow, from the premise of the numerical distinctness of worlds, in particular a world of perceptual consciousness and the physical world, that there are not lawlike connections between them. It does not follow from the premise that the one world there is, as we all recognize, can be categorized in different ways, that things in one cannot be necessary conditions of things in the other. Radical Externalism differs from Anomalous Monism, first of all, in that Radical Externalism does not deny but rather *embraces* psychophysical lawlike connection in general. In the two propositions of dependency, it already asserts such connections.

According to them, each of the physical world and you neurally is necessary to your world of perceptual consciousness, the two being sufficient. Therefore it follows that without your world of perceptual consciousness, there could not be the conjunction of exactly the physical world outside of you and also you neurally. So it is exactly part of Radical Externalism that it is not true that if we removed worlds of perceptual consciousness from the scene, the whole physical world would be as it was and everything would continue exactly as before.

Of course these necessity relations having to do with general connections between consciousness and the world, are not the specific ones relevant to the matter of epiphenomenalism. Those are between worlds of perceptual consciousness, as well as other consciousness, and our physical actions and their effects. There is no obstacle whatever in Radical Externalism to the needed relations of necessary connection.

As for the causal closure of the physical, dignified by that mere piece of talk, *of course* it is denied by Radical Externalism. The remarkable doctrine that every physical event has a causally sufficient condition that is physical *is* among other things the absurdity that the movements of my fingers in writing these lines would have happened without my thoughts ordinarily conceived, my reflective consciousness ordinarily conceived. The proposition of causal closure with respect to all physical events has epiphenomenalism in it, and most certainly it is denied by Radical Externalism.

Law's reflections go off the rails at the end of his piece, in the third and second last sections, when he contemplates a very different reply on my part to his objection about epiphenomenalism.

> To this, the reply may be that, while a world of perceptual consciousness may not be identical with the physical world or any part of it, it can nevertheless include physical objects (p. 68).

That is certainly not the theory in question. A world of perceptual consciousness is indeed not identical with the physical world or any part of it. I find it hard to think of why Law supposes that does not entail that a world of perceptual consciousness does not include physical objects. In any case, this is fundamental to the theory.

His supposition that a world of perceptual consciousness includes physical objects plays another role in the second last section of his paper. If there are physical objects in worlds of perceptual consciousness, these worlds can't be subjective in the ways they were supposed to be. Indeed so, I reply. That is why there are not physical objects included in them.

He also supposes that if there are physical objects in world of perceptual consciousness, and worlds of perceptual consciousness are what perceptual consciousness consists in, then physical objects depend for these existence on your consciousness of them. They also depend on your neurally. Indeed so. That is another good reason why there are no physical objects in worlds of perceptual consciousness, whatever the relations of those worlds to the physical world.

I conjecture that Law's surprising thoughts at the end of his paper have to do with a state of incredulousness on his part. Maybe it comes into view most clearly, although I find him a little hard to follow, when he thinks about seeing a book tip over and so knock over a vase — thinks about his world of perceptual consciousness in which there are events that can be so described. There is also the physical world to consider, in which related events occur.

Putting aside his remarks about causal closure, already considered, his lines suggest he cannot bring himself to believe that worlds of perceptual consciousness could conceivably be in causal connection with the physical world.

> Suppose this book tips over and knocks over a vase. The book tipping over causes the vase to smash. And the book tipping is part of my world of perceptual consciousness. So it this an example of my world of perceptual consciousness having a physical effect? That's an odd-sounding conclusion to draw, to say the least (p. 68).

Well, I admit that there is room and need for development of Radical Externalism with respect to the relation between the tipping in a world of perceptual consciousness and the tipping in the physical world. Some of my *interworld relations*, to give them that large name, need thinking about. But how much more difficulty will there be in thinking of them than in thinking of relations between, say, the world of football and the world of money? Or a world specified in terms of colour and a world not so specified? What difference in kind is there in thinking about the three sets of relations?

That there is room and need for work does not lead me near to conceding in advance that the conception of a world of perceptual consciousness cannot be in causal connection with things in the physical world, say arm movements — as things within a world of perceptual consciousness can be in causal connection, or things within the physical world. The room and need for more thinking does not lead me near to conceding, either, to stick to the present subject, that worlds of perceptual consciousness are not satisfactorily subjective.

Some say it may be a strength of a theory that it is fertile, that it makes possible and gives rise to more reflection.

### References

Honderich, T. (1982), 'The argument for anomalous monism', *Analysis*, **16**, pp. 59–64.

Honderich, T. (2003), 'The argument for anomalous monism', 'Anomalous monism: Reply to Smith', and 'Smith and the champion of mauve', all in *Mental Causation and the Philosophy of Mind*, ed. N. Campbell (New York: Broadview Press, 2003).

Honderich, T. (2004), *On Consciousness* (Edinburgh: Edinburgh University Press).

E.J. Lowe

# *Radical Externalism or Berkeley Revisited?*

Ted Honderich's 'Radical Externalism'[1] concerning the nature of consciousness is a refreshing, and in many ways very appealing, approach to a long-standing and seemingly intractable philosophical conundrum. Although I sympathize with many of his motivations in advancing the theory and share his hostility for certain alternative approaches that are currently popular, I will serve him better by playing devil's advocate than by simply recording my points of agreement with him. If his theory is a good one, it should be able to stand up to the strongest criticisms that we can muster against it. I shall do my best to articulate some of those criticisms as forcefully as I can.

Honderich begins his account with what he calls a 'datum' about consciousness: that consciousness is *something we have*. If this is just another way of saying that *all of us are — at least sometimes — conscious*, then I have no quarrel with it. But I have an uneasy suspicion that it amounts to more than just that: that it involves a potentially problematic *reification* of consciousness. There have been past philosophers who have illicitly reified consciousness, treating it as some mysterious kind of *thing* or *stuff*, either located inside our heads or, even more mysteriously, somehow outside of space altogether. Honderich is, of course, emphatically opposed to such views. But I suspect that it would be no less of an illicit reification to regard consciousness as something — some *thing* or *things* — located *outside* our heads. And yet this is what Honderich himself seems to do.

A crucial claim, which seems to have axiomatic status for Honderich, is that 'with respect to consciousness, *there is no difference between appearance and reality*'. By appealing to this principle, he seeks to justify his view that whatever consciousness *seems* to consist in, it

---

[1] Honderich (2006). In this commentary all page references are to this target paper unless stated otherwise.

*does* consist in. I shall not question the principle here — not that I think that it is perfectly unquestionable. However, I do wonder whether Honderich applies it correctly in generating his theory. Let us see how he applies it in the case that he uses for illustration — our perceptual consciousness of the page now before us. He asks: what does our consciousness in this case *seem* to consist in? And he answers: it seems to consist in *the page's being there* (p. 6). Ergo, applying the principle, our consciousness of the page just *is* the page's being there ('in a way', at least). And the page, of course, is something 'extra-cranial' — literally located *outside* our head. But this argument has the air of sleight of hand about it. Here is another way of construing the application of the principle concerning appearance and reality to the case of perceiving the page. In normal circumstances, when I perceive the page, my consciousness is such that the page *seems to me to be there*. Since, 'with respect to consciousness, there is no difference between appearance and reality' (p. 5), what I may conclude is that there is no difference between the page's *really* seeming to me to be there and its merely *appearing* or *seeming* to seem to me to be there — that's all. Construed in this way, the principle doesn't license any very exciting ontological conclusion: it doesn't license any inference of the form 'Consciousness *seems* to be *F*, therefore consciousness *is F*', but only a conclusion of the form 'Consciousness that something seems to be *F* is identical with consciousness that something *seems* to seem to be *F*'. I venture to suggest that what philosophers have traditionally meant by the principle that Honderich invokes is much closer to what I have just implied than it is to Honderich's reading of it. Thus, it is something like my interpretation of the principle that is traditionally taken to rule out the possibility of our being mistaken about what we *seem* to be perceiving: for, according to that interpretation, it makes no sense to suppose that it only *seems* to us that we seem to perceive an *F*, when *really* what we seem to perceive is a *G*.

This last point merits, perhaps, a little elaboration. Traditionally, philosophers have contended that we can be mistaken about what it is that we *are* perceiving, but not about what it is that we *seem* to be perceiving: for instance, that we may be mistaken in thinking that what we are perceiving is a bent stick, when in fact what we are perceiving is a straight stick, but that we can't be mistaken in thinking that what we *seem* to be perceiving is a bent stick. It is *this* sort of contention that I take to be implied by the appearance-and-reality principle as it is traditionally interpreted, not the sort of contention that Honderich attempts to support by appeal to the principle. In short, I think that whereas philosophers have traditionally construed the principle as having only *epistemic* import, Honderich turns it into one with distinctively *ontological* import. Consequently, the unwary reader who accepts the principle as traditionally interpreted, but fails to spot the new gloss that Honderich gives it, may be too readily persuaded to swallow the rather startling conclusion that Honderich seeks to derive from it.

But let me move on. Honderich wants to maintain that *all there is* to my perceptual consciousness of the page is *the page's being there*. More particularly, he wants to deny that the page's being there is just the 'content' of a state in my mind or head which serves as the 'container' or 'vehicle' of this content (p. 5). His point is that my consciousness of the page just doesn't *seem* to be like that — it doesn't seem to involve anything more than the page's being there. Other philosophers have noted this and sometimes make the point by saying that perceptual consciousness seems to be completely 'transparent' or 'diaphanous': in perception, we seem simply to be directly confronted by certain objects, such as the page before us, without the presence of any *medium* through which they are presented to us. However, that such a 'medium' doesn't *seem* to be present doesn't necessarily mean that it *isn't* present, *contra* Honderich's version of the appearance-and-reality principle — as the following example may help to convince us. We are, I take it, all familiar with the experience of being completely absorbed by a drama played out on a television screen or at the cinema. In such a state of absorption, we are entirely oblivious to the patterns of light and colour flickering across the screen, because we are attending intently to the dramatic goings-on that are being depicted. If we do turn our attention to the screen itself, we lose all sense of the reality of the dramatic events that formerly engaged our rapt attention. Clearly, however, the patterns of light and colour *were still there on the screen* while we were attending to the drama, even though we were oblivious of them at the time — and if they had not been, we would have been unable to attend to the drama. Why should not matters be the same with perceptual consciousness quite generally? All of us, it may be suggested, are *able* to attend to features of our perceptual consciousness which stand to the objects of perception in a relation analogous to that between the pattern of light and colours on the cinema screen and the dramatic scenes depicted there. If we fail to do so most or even all of the time, that should be unsurprising. It is not clear to me that anything that Honderich says refutes this suggestion or reveals any incoherence in it. This is not to say that I necessarily want to endorse the suggestion myself, just that I don't think that it can be dismissed as easily as Honderich seems to think it can.

Now I want to focus on a key implication of Honderich's doctrine of Radical Externalism — an implication which makes his choice of the epithet 'externalism' to describe his position distinctly contentious, in my view. According to Honderich, as we have seen, my consciousness of the page is just a matter of *the page's being there*. The implication, of course, is that when I *cease* to be conscious of the page, the page *ceases* to be there. This conclusion seems inescapable, given the supposed identity between my consciousness of the page and the page's being there: for, given this identity, when my consciousness of the page ceases to exist (when, for instance, I close my eyes or turn away), the state of affairs in which this consciousness supposedly consists — to wit, the page's being there — likewise ceases to exist. In short, for objects like this page, *esse est percipi*. It turns out, or so it would seem, that Honderich's 'extra-cranial' objects of perception are very much like Berkeley's *ideas*. Of course, Honderich himself explicitly repudiates 'what were first called *ideas* in the history of British empiricism and ended up as *sense-data*' (p. 7), so that what I have just alleged may seem entirely inapposite. I don't think so. For Berkeley notoriously contended that *he* was defending common-sense realism against the kind of indirect or representative realism that he found in the writings of Locke. He emphasized that he was not trying to turn *things into ideas* but, rather, *ideas into things* — thereby reversing what he saw as the sceptical direction of empiricist thought in the hands of materialists like Locke (see Berkeley, 1975, p. 193). It seems to me that, at least in some respects, Honderich is in the same direct realist tradition as Berkeley.

In what sense is Honderich a 'radical externalist', in view of what I have just said? Certainly, he wants to say that the objects of perception, such as the page that I now perceive, are 'extra-cranial' and located in space at some distance from the perceiver's head. And yet, as we have just seen, he is committed to saying that this page is something that will cease to exist once I cease to perceive it. The pages that other people perceive are not strictly identical with the one that I perceive, since they depend for their existence on those other perceivers, just as this one depends for its existence on me. But now we have to ask: what exactly is the nature of the *space* that this page occupies? Is it strictly identical with the space that is occupied by the pages perceived by other people? Indeed, is it strictly identical with the 'physical' space that is occupied, according to Honderich, by various imperceptible *atoms*, upon which (he thinks) the perceptible pages also partly depend for their existence? (In this respect, of course, Honderich is no latterday Berkeley, since Berkeley rejected altogether the existence of imperceptible matter.) From what Honderich says, it would seem that he thinks that there is just *one* space in which all these things — both those that depend for their existence on perceivers and those that don't — are housed. But can he offer any compelling argument for believing that this must be so? Berkeley thought that there was no good reason to identify *visual* space with *tactile* space. Does Honderich have any good reason to identify the perceptual spaces of different perceivers and all of these with the space occupied by imperceptible physical objects such as atoms? What he *says* is that

> The page's being there, and more generally *your world of perceptual consciousness*, is things being in space and time, with such further properties as colour, and being dependent on a scientific or noumenal world underneath and also dependent on you neurally (p. 6).

And what this *suggests* is that, in his view, there is just one 'space and time', or space–time. But what isn't clear is what entitles him to this assumption. After all, he goes on to assert that 'A world of perceptual consciousness is not the physical world': so why should a *space* of perceptual consciousness be *physical* space?

If Honderich cannot make good the claim that objects in a world of perceptual consciousness occupy literally the same space as the physical atoms posited by science, then his 'externalism' is misleadingly named, it seems to me. If all it amounts to, when we say that the perceived page is 'extra-cranial', is that it lies at some distance in my perceptual space from the place occupied by my *perceived* head, without any implication that either the perceived page or the perceived head are themselves located in the physical space occupied by atoms and other such physical objects studied by scientists, then Honderich's 'externalism' is quite unlike that of those modern self-styled externalists who claim that the objects of thought and perception simply *are* complex aggregates of atoms situated in physical space. These latter theorists certainly *don't* want to maintain that the objects of perceptual consciousness *depend for their existence* upon perceivers and, indeed, would describe as *internalist* any theory that did maintain that. Part of the problem here is that the internal–external distinction is ambiguous. On the one hand, it may be interpreted in *spatial* terms — and, in these terms, what is 'external' is quite literally located 'outside the head', i.e., is 'extra-cranial'. On the other hand, it may be interpreted in terms of *dependence* — and, in these terms, what is 'external' is what exists independently of, or 'outside', consciousness. According to Honderich, the page that I perceive is external in the sense of being 'extra-cranial'. But it also seems *not* to be external, inasmuch as it would not exist if I were not perceiving it: for its *being there*, according to Honderich, just *is* my consciousness of it. By emphasizing the 'extra-cranial' character of the page, Honderich seems to be endorsing a full-blooded direct realism. But once we take into account the consciousness-dependence of the page according to his view of it, the air of realism seems to dissipate, just as it does with Berkeley's protestation that he is defending common sense.

An important aspect of Honderich's argumentative strategy is to suggest that his 'Radical Externalism' is manifestly superior to the alternative positions available — taking these to be, on the one side, out-and-out physicalism and, on the other, some sort of phenomenalism or — worst of all, it seems — dualism ('better named spiritualism or mentalism'). But I think that Honderich weakens the case for his own position by characterizing some of the opposing views uncharitably and even, at times, unfairly. He suggests, for instance, that phenomenalists must believe in 'sense-data' and that the 'argument from illusion' can only be construed as aiming — and failing — to support that belief. But it is possible to endorse the view that — as Honderich puts it — there is 'a sufficient neural condition for perceptual consciousness' without contending that the immediate objects of perceptual consciousness are 'sense-data'. Consider the proposition whose truth Honderich denies in this connection:

> You could have a brain in a vat stimulated so as to produce consciousness indistinguishable from what we call consciousness of a page (p. 8).

Someone who believes this to be true needn't contend that what the brain would be conscious of would be a sense-datum or mental image of a page. More generally: it is not necessary to contend that hallucinatory experiences are experiences *of* anything at all, in the sense that there are certain objects of which the persons undergoing such experiences are conscious — objects that are not 'extra-cranial' but somehow either inside their brains or not located in space at all. For it is perfectly possible to characterize hallucinations as experiences which merely *seem* to the persons undergoing them to be perceptions of objects — perceptions, that is, of ordinary 'extra-cranial' objects such as pages — even though, in such cases, not only are no such objects there to be perceived but *nothing else* is perceived either. A case of *seeming to perceive* a page doesn't have to be taken to be a case of perceiving *a seeming page* — a mental image of a page, say.

But what of the proposition itself — that consciousness indistinguishable from consciousness of a page could be produced by suitably stimulating a brain, in the absence of a real, 'extra-cranial' page? Honderich is clear that his Radical Externalism must deny the truth of this proposition — not, it seems, on purely logical, conceptual or more generally purely *a priori* grounds, because he seems to concede that the question of its truth or falsehood is an empirical matter. That being so, Radical Externalism has made itself a hostage to fortune and a rather perilous one at that, it seems to me. For the empirical evidence thus far available doesn't look favourable to it. We don't need to go to the length of creating and experimenting upon brains in vats to see this. There is plenty of already existing evidence which suggests that a sufficient means of producing a conscious visual experience as of seeing a page is to arrange for the wavefronts of light impinging upon a person's retinas to replicate those that would impinge upon them if the light came from a source illuminating a page placed in front of the person's eyes. This, indeed, is precisely how holograms work. Other evidence that points in the same direction is provided by 'virtual reality goggles', which give those wearing them a quite compelling sense of being visually conscious of a real external environment. No doubt such devices are not yet capable of producing conscious experiences absolutely indistinguishable from those typically enjoyed by the unaided senses in normal, everyday perception. But it would be a rash philosopher who put money on this *never* being achieved. Honderich is to be commended for his candour when he affirms that

> According to Radical Externalism, there isn't a sufficient neural condition for perceptual consciousness (p. 8).

Unfortunately, there not only seems to be no *a priori* reason to think that Radical Externalism is correct in this regard, but also the empirical evidence already available points strongly in the other direction.

Could it be that part of the appeal of Radical Externalism for Honderich is that it seems to provide an escape from *scepticism* concerning 'the external world'? I strongly suspect that that is so. Honderich, I suspect, concurs with the many philosophers over the ages who have blamed scepticism on a supposedly mistaken 'indirect' theory of perception — the sort of theory that maintains that our conscious engagement with our physical environment is always mediated by mental states whose intrinsic nature is such that those very same states *could* exist even in the absence of such an environment. I confess, however, that I have never really understood why scepticism should be blamed on any particular theory of perception, nor how by advocating another theory of perception we could somehow hope to evade the sceptic. For the sceptic simply trades on the inescapable fallibility of all human cognition. The proper response to the sceptic is not to try to evade or undercut the doubts that he seeks to sow, by endeavouring to render his very attempt to raise those doubts incapable of articulation. Whatever account of human knowledge and its sources in perception and reason we try to give, it must be one that acknowledges our thoroughgoing fallibility. The sceptic only presents a challenge to those who mistakenly claim certainty for anything within the scope of human knowledge. We defeat him not by trying to prove that something is, after all, known with certainty, but only by refusing to play his game and acknowledging the true lesson that he has for us. This is that knowledge of what is real can only be had at the expense of foregoing any claim to certainty with regard to what we know at any given time. To allow that my current consciousness *could* be indistinguishable from the consciousness of a suitably stimulated brain in a vat is not in any manner to concede, in all seriousness, that I might well *be* a brain in a vat. I do not have the slightest reason to take the latter hypothesis seriously. In particular, the mere fact that I cannot *rule it out* with absolutely certainty is not even the slightest reason to suppose that it is *true*. No doubt much more can and should be said on this and related matters concerning scepticism. The main point that I would insist upon at present is that we cannot hope to defeat the sceptic by changing our theory of perception. Apart from anything else, the sceptic will simply point out that a theory of perception is indeed just that — a *theory* — and, as such, as fallible as any other claim to knowledge that we may make.

I said earlier that I felt that Honderich is unfair to some of his opponents' views. His characterization of dualism, in particular, is something of a parody. As Honderich has it, the dualist maintains that 'consciousness is somehow non-spatial and hence not physical'. He alleges that 'its problems are ... owed ... to its asserting that consciousness is out of space and in fact of a mysterious nature' (p. 11). Setting aside the historical Descartes, whose views on these matters are all too often pronounced upon without any attempt to refer to solid textual evidence, I venture to say, as a self-confessed latterday dualist, that I have not the slightest inclination to say that consciousness is 'non-spatial', save in the following completely innocuous sense. Consciousness, I consider, is not a *stuff* of any space-occupying kind, in the way that gold and water, for example, are. But, equally, it is not any kind of *non*-space-occupying stuff. Indeed, I don't really understand what a non-space-occupying stuff could possibly be. Consciousness, I consider, is not any kind of thing or stuff at all. Rather than saying, with Honderich, that consciousness is 'something we have', I just want to say that all of us are, at various times, *conscious*. *We* are 'things', in a very broad sense of 'thing', and *we* occupy space. The reason why it doesn't make sense, in my view, to ask *where* our consciousness is is just that this question involves a category mistake, by treating 'our consciousness' as if it were some thing or stuff which, like us, is capable of having a spatial location. It makes just as little sense, I suggest, to ask *where* our weight or our height is. I am here, sitting in this chair, but my weight and my height aren't sitting in this chair. The *only* sense in which a location can be attributed to my weight and my height is via *me*: it is just the sense in which they are *my* weight and *my* height, and *I* am sitting in this chair.

I can't resist responding to another jibe that Honderich directs at dualism, or 'spiritualism' as he scornfully describes it, when he asserts that 'Spiritualism in its carry-on about a self or subject or the mind faces overwhelming objections' (p. 11). Of course, if the 'self' or 'subject' or 'mind' is supposed to be some sort of immaterial and spatially unlocated thing or stuff — a 'spirit' — it may indeed face overwhelming objections. But I take it that any sensible view of the self holds that selves are no different from persons and that persons are incontestably subjects of experience. In this sense, *I* am a 'self', as is any other human person. And that I exist and have thoughts and experiences is quite as much a 'datum' as Honderich's 'datum' that 'consciousness is something we have'. Indeed, I don't really know what to make of Honderich's 'datum' other than to interpret it as a slightly misleading way of saying that *we exist and have thoughts and experiences*. As for *what* we are, I am strongly inclined to think that we are not simply identical with our biological bodies, nor with any particular part of them, such as our brains (see Lowe, 1996, ch. 2). But that by no means commits me to saying that we don't possess spatial locations and spatial properties, such as height. In short, there are varieties of 'dualism' which do not even remotely resemble the unfriendly caricature of it that Honderich presents.

Towards the end of his paper, Honderich mentions certain *criteria* which he thinks a theory of consciousness must satisfy, contending that Radical Externalism alone plausibly does so. For reasons just adumbrated, I don't accept his contention that dualism — properly conceived — cannot accommodate the *subjectivity* of consciousness, because I don't accept his criticisms of the dualist conception of the self as a subject of consciousness. Honderich himself, I note, makes no attempt to offer a positive account of what *he* takes 'us' to be, so it seems to me that his account of the subjectivity of consciousness in terms of its (partial) *dependence upon us* is rather thin as it stands.

However, a more serious difficulty, it seems to me, arises for Honderich in respect of his *fifth* criterion. This is that

> a theory [of consciousness] must not make impossible what is actual, which is causal interaction between consciousness and the physical (p. 12).

He contends that dualism (or 'spiritualism') fails this test, whereas Radical Externalism passes it. Why does he think that dualism fails it? Because

> [t]hose who follow Descartes take consciousness out of space, and therefore postulate causes and effects that are nowhere (p. 12).

I have already explained why I think that this charge rests upon a caricature of dualism. A dualist can maintain that *I* am located in space and that there is no more problem about 'locating' my consciousness than there is about locating my weight and my height, which no one denies are capable of 'causal interaction with the physical'. But Honderich's theory, by contrast, does face a difficulty in this regard. For remember that I raised earlier the following question, apropos of Honderich's claim that my consciousness of the page just is the page's being there. Is the *perceptual space* of the perceived page identical with the *physical space* in which the atoms studied by the physicists are located? Nothing in Honderich's theory, as far as I can see, explains why it has to be. But if it isn't — if each person's perceptual space is distinct from everyone else's, and all of them are distinct from the physical space of imperceptible atoms — then it is *Honderich* who has a problem of causal interaction on his hands. The problem now is not how things that *aren't* in space can causally interact with things that *are*, but how things that are in *different* spaces can interact with each other. If this problem can't be solved by Honderich's theory, then Radical Externalism can't achieve what he claims for it at the very end of his paper, namely, 'making *all* of consciousness persuasively understood a subject for science' (p. 12).

## References

Berkeley, G. (1975), *Philosophical Works, Including the Works on Vision*, ed. M.R. Ayers (London: Dent).
Honderich, T. (2006), 'Radical externalism', *Journal of Consciousness Studies*, **13** (7–8), pp. 3–13. [This issue]
Lowe, E.J. (1996), *Subjects of Experience* (Cambridge: Cambridge University Press).

## REPLY TO LOWE BY HONDERICH

Jonathan Lowe does not dispute what he calls the principle that with respect to consciousness there is no difference between appearance and reality. But, he says, as devil's advocate, there is an air of sleight of hand in using it to pass from the proposition

- Your perceptual consciousness of this page seems to consist in an existing of the page

to the proposition

- Your perceptual consciousness of this page does really consist in this existing of the page.

But what he finds in the argument is not so much dexterity or cunning that issues in mistake, deception or bafflement but rather plain mistake. The mistake, or anyway unnecessary choice, is the first proposition. He has an alternative, which is

- Your perceptual consciousness of this page seems to consist in a seeming existing of the the page.

From this different proposition about seeming seeming, all that follows is

- Your consciousness is the page's really seeming to be existing.

As he remarks, we in a way stay with epistemology here rather than ontology — stay at the level of thoughts and the like rather than what they are about. Certainly there is a lot of difference between 'If it seems to be an F, it is' and 'If it seems to be an F, that's what it seems to be'.

What is it for something to seem to be an F? Let me speculate a bit. There is something that somehow leads to the proposition that it is an F. But you wouldn't just say that it seems to be an F rather than that it is an F if there wasn't also something or other that makes it unsettled whether it is an F. Let me call these items the positive ground and the negative or uncertain ground for the thing being an F.

In general, what is it for something to *seem to seem* to be an F? Well, I guess it is for there to be a prior positive ground and a prior negative or uncertain ground for a later positive ground and a later negative or uncertain ground for the thing's being an F. Rather a mouthful, but there it is.

If that is right, and something like it is surely right, you were certainly mistaken if you thought that what we call your awareness of the page was pretty simple. Lowe is asking you to discern quite a lot more in it. I can't discern it all myself, in my case. That four-part story is a lot richer than my experience. Are you aware of all that stuff when you see the page? No, you're not. This seems a pretty good start on a reply to our devil's advocate.

But maybe you can succeed in doubting that general analysis of propositions about seeming — in terms of a positive and another ground. That won't stop you from just saying about your consciousness what was assumed in the first proposal above, about seeming rather than seeming seeming — that with consciousness what seems to be the case really is the case. As can rather grandly be said, you can go from epistemology to ontology. Your perceptual consciousness of the page is what it seems to be. Or, to retreat to the proposition that is pretty essential to Radical Externalism and also solid as a rock,

- Your consciousness of the page can't have in it what it does not appear to have in it.

If this isn't what philosophers have traditionally meant by a principle of theirs about the impossibility of mistake, so what? Your consciousness isn't their property. And as for passing from epistemology to ontology, you can say that is the very point of the proposition and that you are in a lot of very good philosophical company. Indeed philosophers have not often done epistemology for its own sake.

Having made those two remarks, I feel an urge to confession. It is that it may possibly have been misleading of me to talk of your being conscious of the page as *seeming* to be such and such — thereby allowing that in what we call your being aware of the page you not only have some positive ground for this being an existing of the page but also some ground for at least uncertainty. On reflection, anyway, that is not the fact of my perceptual life, and it is unlikely to be yours. If we really are to do phenomenology, by which I mean description of all and nothing more than all of a thing, and certainly there is reason to do phenomenology with consciousness, what it is to be conscious of the page is to given nothing but an existing of the page — certainly no ground at all for doubting the thing.

Of course, you might have been reading Locke or Ayer or one their current residuary legatees, and been taken aback by the argument from illusion. But *that* supposed ground for a certain scepticism about an experience is definitely no part whatever of the experience. I don't see an additional line on the page saying 'Don't trust your experience absolutely — worry a bit philosophically'. And it's the experience that has been and is our subject matter right now, not an argument or theory by somebody else or ourself on some other occasion.

It was misleading, then, to talk of your being conscious of the page as *seeming* to be only an existing of the page (p. 5). It was better to propose what preceded this, which was the proposition that what you *have* in the episode, what is *given* or what is *presented*, is only an existing of the page. Are those metaphors? I guess so. Better a decent metaphor than many a literal thing. It's not as if the line of life that is thinking about consciousness is so full of literal general truths that we can ignore a guiding metaphor. And, of course, you can expect a metaphor to issue in or get translated into something literal — in this case a theory, Radical Externalism.

Against my saying that in being aware of the page what you have is only an existing in a way of the page, Lowe asks if this comes to saying, just, that you were conscious of the page. Not surprisingly, he agrees with *that*. Surprisingly, however, all that he has against my proposition about what you have in the episode, putting aside his alternative idea about seeming seeming and some traditional philosophizing, is that it leads on to a potentially problematic *reification* of consciousness. He allows that Radical Externalism does not make consciousness into a thing or stuff in a head, or a thing or a stuff absurdly somehow nowhere, but suspects that the theory does make consciousness into a thing or things outside a head.

Well, what any theory of consciousness is best described as concerned with is the question of *what it is for something to be conscious*. That invites, rightly, an answer that identify a property, fact or state of affairs with respect to the thing. Radical Externalism identifies what it is to be perceptually conscious as a certain extra-cranial state of affairs. That isn't to make consciousness a thing in an ordinary sense of the word, of course.

Lowe perhaps half-suggests that there is some *general* failing in taking consciousness to be a state of affairs with things in it. He perhaps half-suggests some antecedent general argument for seeing that this sort of answer is a mistake. As against, of course, particular arguments against Radical Externalism. He does not let us know what that general argument is. Could there be such a thing? Don't all theories of consciousness deal in a property, fact or state of affairs?

I leave the subject of what you *have* in seeing the page, the givenness, presentedness or immediacy — and the matter of reification — with an uneasy awareness that somebody needs to do some more thinking about the givenness or the like, maybe you. Let me remark again only that the fact in question, as I take it to be, is not clearly or even half-clearly the traditional philosopher's proposition that we can be mistaken about what we *are* perceiving but not what we *seem* to be perceiving. *Having* comes before thinking about, judging, inferring and so on — a lot of what happens in that part or side of consciousness that is its reflective side. So *having* comes before mistakes can or cannot happen. It's prior. It's all of the *data*, not what happens when you start think about it. There is no thinking about it that can make it less than all the data, deprive us of a hold on what was not there and what was.

Lowe moves on to the point that other philosophers have said that perceptual consciousness is transparent or diaphanous, where that means we are confronted by certain objects, without the presence of any medium through which they are presented to us. I'm sure that these philosophers weren't Radical Externalists, and I'm pretty sure they weren't on the way to being such — did they talk about the content of consciousness, thereby distinguishing it from something else in consciousness?

But the main point to be made here has to do with Lowe's reinstatement of the medium.

> ... that such a 'medium' doesn't *seem* to be present doesn't necessarily mean that it *isn't* present, *contra* Honderich's version of the appearance-and-reality principle ... (p. 80).

Rather, the medium could be what is called present but not attended to, like the light and colour flickering across the television screen when we are attending to the news from Iraq or the play.

Well, I contentedly deny that there is a parallel with and within consciousness. Of course there is a lot of neural explanation of your being perceptually conscious, a lot of stuff analogous to the light and colour on the screen, but being conscious of the page isn't also being conscious of something called a medium. You can't *attend* to a medium either. You can try to think about your consciousness, of course, but that is not to succeed in noticing something extra when or after you're seeing the news. I'm glad the devil's advocate, when he takes off his horns, doesn't necessarily want to endorse the suggestion himself. It is in fact a case of that old bad habit mentioned elsewhere in his piece, a category mistake — putting a relation between me and somethings into the category of things in my consciousness.

I can be about as quick with the objection, heard of before now, that Radical Externalism is reheated Berkeley. The first reply is that the theory is indeed that what it is for your to be perceptually conscious is really for things to be in space and time outside your head. I'm sure Berkeley didn't say or commit himself to that. But if he did, then of course he has been monstrously misunderstood by an awful lot of philosophers, including Lowe, and I am delighted to welcome him to a happy band of brothers and sisters.

To which Lowe replies that I allow that a world of perceptual consciousness ceases to exist when you cease to be conscious in a certain way. I do indeed allow that, and positively *want* the proposition in the interest of providing my fellow-workers with a further facet of the large fact of subjectivity.

Does this response make a world of perceptual consciousness very much like Berkeley's *ideas*, or *sense-data*? There seems to me a pretty good answer to that. Go back to the physical world, or rather the perceived part of it — the chairs as against the atoms. In the absence of perceivers, after the cataclysm, or if it ever happens that we're *all* asleep, it won't exist. It doesn't have in it what is dependent on bats. It is tied to the existence of observers in general, whatever difficulties there are with the fact.

In what sense does that demote the perceived physical world into being a 'mental' world? Well, I accept, without a lot of strain, that my world of perceptual consciousness at the moment is 'mental' in a similar or related way (2004, p. 135–43). I can live with that. In short, there is a lesser truth related to *esse est percipi* for each of the perceived physical world and a world of perceptual consciousness — both related to *esse est percipi* despite differences between them.

Moreover, that your world of perceptual consciousness can rightly be said only to be similar or related to the perceived world in the given way, and also in other ways, is not a weakness of Radical Externalism. It is in fact part of a strength. We know about the strength or at any rate the ambition of each of spiritualism and devout physicalism — one in catering for subjectivity and one in catering for causal interaction. In order really to satisfy those two criteria, it will of course be true that Radical Externalism is in a way similar to but definitely not identical with each of the alternatives.

Lowe presses his case about reheated Berkeley by asking what space it is that is occupied by things in a world of perceptual consciousness. He supposes, rightly, that the best answer is the space of the perceived and the unperceived physical world. However, it puzzles me he seems to want an argument for this proposition or assumption. He gives no reason for thinking this cannot be part of Radical Externalism. This space turns up in a lot of worlds, including the world of science, which is not actually identical with the physical world — and also the worlds of fashion
and football.

Certainly there are problems about the nature of space and space–time. But what is the problem about the proposition that when, as we ordinarily say, you and I see the plume poppy in the flower bed, my consciousness consists in things of a kind and yours does, and they are in the same space as physical objects? And hence that there is this fundamental difference between Radical Externalism and Berkeley's idealism?

Nor is the fact of the *dependence* partly on a perceiver of a world of perception consciousness enough to make the name 'externalism' misleading. For a start, however some theorists have used a term, one thing does not become *internal* to another in an ordinary sense or in any other significant way, by being dependent on it — think of more or less any effect and its preceding causal circumstance. It seems to me remarkable to suppose that a dependence of a thing on something else, maybe a pile of coal on the mining industry, dissipates the air of realism of the thing. I take it there is some misunderstanding between Lowe and me.

Do I also weaken the case for the theory by uncharitable or unfair characterizations of alternative views? Should more time have been spent distinguishing the various items that philosophers have brought into the world as objects of perception as a result of the argument from illusion? Why should that have been done when the point of importance, given my argumentative strategy, was simply the undisputed one that the new objects of perception shared a non-realist character? If somebody says all conservatives are generous, and I think I can show that general proposition is false, do I also have to spend time distinguishing among conservatives? As for my usages, say 'spiritualism', they are defined. And there is a lot to be said, I think, for something less than piety in approaching covertly persisting orthodoxies.

Lowe is on better ground, indeed strong ground, when he objects to my views that Radical Externalism's view of perceptual consciousness faces only or exactly the possibility of future empirical refutation by stimulation of the brain in the vat. While some more might be said of that, it is simplest to concede that we can see *now* on logical grounds or the like that if a brain in a vat comes to be perceptually conscious — anyway of the wrong scene — then Radical Externalism fails. Fortunately I do not even have to think about taking back something else more important — that it is also possible now for Radical Externalism to describe the case in terms of other than perceptual consciousness, and to do so for good reason.

Leaving aside the diagnosis of Radical Externalism as providing an escape from scepticism, and coming on to my supposed unfairness in characterizing dualism, I must defy my devil's advocate and plead not guilty, indeed not in sight of guilty. Except perhaps in giving too brisk a summary of a theory at the beginning of this book, and in particular too brisk a summary of alternatives to it.

If you will put up with my cavilling in self-defence, however, here are some passages from that summary. The first is about the history of the philosophy of mind.

> That history has had in it the main proposition that mind and brain — including your mind and brain a minute ago — are two things, this being 'dualism' ... (p. 4)

The second passage is about something else, 'what still has the name of dualism'. It is Cartesian dualism, as is said, which takes consciousness out of space and is better named spiritualism or mentalism. Unfortunately for me, it is also referred to as just 'dualism'.

Putting aside the cavilling, it remains my position, as you have heard in an earlier reply, that the principal alternatives to Radical Externalism are devout physicalisms, some of which can be argued to be dualisms in the generic sense, and the specific dualism that is spiritualism, of which no doubt there are species (pp. 40–42). To these alternatives, as you know, Radical Externalism is in my book superior.

Lowe comes in the end not to be devil's advocate, but advocate of himself, perfectly properly. His book *Subjects of Experience* is now on my reading list, but for the meanwhile I must go on his lines above.

> ... selves are no different from persons and ... persons are incontestably subjects of experience. ... As for *what* we are, ... we are not simply identical with our biological bodies, nor with any particular part of them, such as our brains ... (p. 86).

Until I learn some more, I shall be unhappy in the view that this *is* a spiritualism in my sense. What is said about it in order to reduce its mystery is that these *subjects* are in some relation to biological bodies, and bodies have spatial properties. With respect — I do mean respect — that seems to go nowhere towards making these subjects either spatial or unmysterious. They're not *at all* like weight or height. Descartes himself, after all, had his notorious egos in some or other relation with our spatial bodies.

But read Lowe's book. In the meantime, don't suppose, to come to the end of his comments above, that it is in fact Radical Externalism that has a problem with causal interaction in connection with perceptual consciousness. Worlds of perceptual consciousness are unlike *subjects*. They not only in real space in virtue of, and only to the extent of, being in some elusive relation to something that really is.

Derek Matravers

# *Some Questions About Radical Externalism*

It is hard not to sympathise with Professor Honderich's starting point. It is easy to feel pessimistic about philosophy's ability to throw light on the nature of consciousness. What, then, to do? One option is to persist with the various current approaches. It is clear that Honderich thinks this would be akin to putting more effort into trying to work out the temporal priority of the chicken and the egg. The thought of the orthodox is that an account of consciousness is going to be either fundamentally materialist or fundamentally dualist. The first of these is untenable as consciousness has other or more than neural properties. The second is untenable for various reasons, Honderich's favoured one being that it renders consciousness as out of space and of a mysterious nature. A second option would be to follow Colin McGinn's lead, and think that the problem is of such a nature that it is necessarily unsolvable (McGinn, 1989).

Alternatively, we should be more radical and think creatively, not necessarily respecting our current conceptual boundaries between the mental and the physical, the inside and the outside. The solution, Honderich says, lies in the thought that 'my consciousness now consists in the existence of a world' (Honderich, 2004, p. 130).[1] I shall say a little about what I understand by this claim, by raising what I take to be three obvious questions, looking at Honderich's answers them, and inviting some further clarification. Throughout I will address only the question of perceptual consciousness.

The first question is that we seem to have an understanding of *a* world out there, in which there are causal relations between objects in virtue of them having certain properties, which is, to put it bluntly, not a matter of our consciousness. That world does not depend upon the

---

[1] In this commentary all page references are to Honderich (2004) unless stated otherwise.

perceiving subject, our consciousness does depend upon the perceiving subject, so how can some such world be our consciousness? Honderich considers and answers this question.

In addition to my 'world of perceptual consciousness' (WPC), there are 'three larger worlds', which do not depend for their existence on the subject. There is 'the physical world':

> This is the world ... that is spatio-temporal and has perceived properties or is spatio-temporal and is in nomic connection with things that have perceived properties.

There is 'the objective world':

> It has in it things perceivable by more than one person, and perceivable by more than one sense, and such as also to exist unperceived.

There is 'the world of things in current or anticipated science', which, Honderich says,

> is an indeterminate world to say the least.

These are not three ontologically independent worlds, but rather three different conceptions of but one world (pp. 135–6). I am not sure quite what this latter claim amounts to — a worry to which I return below.

Having introduced these conceptions, Honderich faces the question of how they are related. One obvious thought is that WPCs are ways that the physical world appears to us: that is, the unperceived part of the physical world cause certain things to happen in our heads such that our environment appears a certain way to us in our experience. However, this does nothing to explain consciousness — rather, it presupposes it. This is clearly not Honderich's view (it is not radical). Furthermore, he distinguishes between the perceived part of the physical world and my WPC. The 'signal difference', according to Honderich, is that 'the perceived part of the physical world has no dependency on a *particular* subject' (p. 143). However, it does depend on some subject or other: 'it is not there when we are *all* asleep, and parts of it are not there when they are in *nobody's* experience' (p. 142).

Consider the situation of the first person to wake up and, so to speak, smell the coffee. Before they did so there were elements of the unperceived physical world floating around (coffee molecules), which, when they encounter the sense apparatus of our lone waker bring into existence something perceived: the smell of coffee. The bits of the perceived part of the physical world that are brought into existence (the look of the walls, the smell of the coffee) have exactly the same content as the WPC of the lone waker. Are they identical? No, because different conditionals are true of each of them: if the waker falls asleep, his WPC will cease to exist but the perceived part of the physical world will not (provided, by then, someone else has woken up).

If we persist, however, in examining the situation of the lone waker before he is joined by a second we can see that the difference between his WPC and the perceived physical world cannot be only the truth (or not) of conditionals. Honderich maintains that his WPC *resembles* the perceived parts of the physical world. Furthermore, it is not that the WPC contains representations of the physical world, but the WPC contains objects (chairs) which resemble objects in the physical world (chairs). Perhaps the lone waker thinks that the chair in his WPC would resemble the perceived chair from a number of possible points of view. However, that does not seem to amount to more than the thought that one's current view of the chair is only one of a number of possible views of the chair. I must confess to being unsure of what the two objects, both bought into existence by the lone waker, are.

Do we need this conception of there being a perceived part of the physical world, dependent on no particular subject? There seems an alternative: that we have a conception of the physical world simpliciter which brings about, for each of us, a WPC when we turn out senses towards it. In postulating the perceived part of the physical world, Honderich seems to want us to have some idea that the physical world's appearance is somehow there, manifest, even when it is not manifest to us (provided it is manifest to someone). One reason might be because we want to make sense of an analogue of John Campbell's 'modal datum'; that 'objects might have been coloured exactly as they are even had there been no sentient life' (Campbell, 1993, p. 181).

I say 'an analogue' because, as we saw above, Honderich rejects that datum as it stands. He might want to provide substance to the thought that objects are exhibiting the appearance they exhibit when I am looking at them, even when I am not looking at them, provided that someone else is. However, that thought seems (to say the least) baroque, and it is not clear why one would want to try to save it. It is true that we need a way of describing perceived objects from no particular point of view; that is, one that is neutral between particular WPCs. However, that would not introduce new sorts of object (perceptible chairs) that are independent of WPCs.

Let us look at the broader picture. Our WPCs do not contain representations of chairs; they contain chairs ('You can sit on things in this world', p. 139). The resemblance with part of the physical world makes it the case that my WPC 'is an articulated and relatively rich conception ... an articulated state of affairs' (p. 144). It is perhaps this need for articulation that is the rationale for postulating the perceived part of the physical world. However, I am not sure we need to do this in order to make this claim. Consider the following paragraph:

> The principal role of the unperceived part of the physical world as we have understood it is to do some explaining with respect to the perceived part. That is also the principal role of the world indicated by science. We carry over this idea, of course to our world-in-itself [the world of particles in fields of force]. What we then get is that my world of perceptual consciousness, while having a dependency on my neural events, also has a dependency on the world-in-itself. The world-in-itself, we can say, if obscurely, is somehow constitutive of my world of perceptual consciousness (p. 140).

The view here seems to be that the world as it really is (particles in fields of force) is a cause of changes in my neural system, on which my WPC depends. Thus, it would seem, the WPC will have articulated structure written into it by the nature of its causes.

Despite the difficulty in seeing how Honderich justifies his reification of the perceived physical world, it does have an important (if to me, obscure) place in his overall theory. The danger, in thinking about these matters, is to slip back into old habits of taking there to be a world out there of particles in fields of force (the world-in-itself) which cause changes in our neural system, which manifests itself in our awareness of our environment (the previous paragraph is an instance of this). However, as Honderich would point out, that is hardly an account of consciousness: what exactly is 'an awareness of our environment'?

Instead, Honderich offers something like the following: the world-in-itself causes changes in our neural system and something happens — a WPC comes into existence. The world appears a certain way to me. Why is this not merely an appearance (a mental world)? Because part of its content is things that resemble the perceivable aspect of the physical world: it is 'spatial, temporal and has chairs in it' (p. 144). The worry I have been pressing is that this radical conclusion only follows with some quite robust notion of the perceived physical world, and I am not sure that Honderich is entitled to that.

One final niggle on this question. When introducing the different worlds above, I said that Honderich did not claim all his various worlds existed, but rather that they were different ways in which a single world could be conceived. So when Honderich says 'for something to be conscious is for a world to exist' (p. 145), this should be synonymous with 'for something to be conscious is for the world to be conceived in a certain way'. However, Honderich thinks that his discussion concerns matters ontological (WPCs are epistemically and conceptually prior to all other worlds, and perhaps ontologically as well, Honderich, p. 145). It would be interesting to learn more about the relation between conceiving of things as being one way or another and how this affects or changes the ontology of the things conceived.

The second of my two questions concerns the transparency of consciousness. Honderich would like to drop locutions such as 'we are conscious of the table' in favour of our consciousness of the table being a way of the table existing. It is the fact that consciousness seems transparent, that whenever we focus on our consciousness of objects, all we seem to get are objects, that does much to motivate Honderich's view. In 'Radical Externalism', we get this.

> What did your consciousness *seem* to consist in? An answer can grow on you fast. It *was for the page to be there*. What your consciousness seemed to consist in was nothing other or more than that. In a better sense of the words than employed by some philosophers, that is what it was like for you to be conscious of the page and that is all that it was like (Honderich, 2006, p. 5).

This view has led Honderich (in his book) all the way to denying the intentionality of perceptual consciousness; there is no split between our consciousness and the content of our consciousness; all we have is the world to be there.

> ... when I am aware of this room now, what is within my consciousness, so to speak, is *the room* — and no other relevant thing. Seeing isn't always seeing double. Seeing isn't seeing by way of using some conscious means to the end, having some image or idea or whatever else. There's no picture or word or the like in the story of my perceptual consciousness now. It's not as if I'm aware of living my life as a life doing something like watching television (p. 165).

However plausible this seems at first pass, it seems to me to leave out an important facet of our pre-philosophical thinking about consciousness. Although we do not have a constant awareness of a mechanism through which we access the world, our grasp of consciousness is of more than what in the old way of talking we would call the content of consciousness. We can perform a simple experiment: press your eyeball with your finger and your mental images (so to speak) of the objects around you double. (This 'experiment' was first described to me twenty years ago by Mark Sainsbury, although I cannot recall what was being discussed at the time). Here is one way of describing what is going on. At the time you are doing this, the way your experience represents the world as being is that there are two pens in front of you (or one rather weird and discontinuous pen).

However, this does not cause us to believe that there are two pens in front of us; rather, we take ourselves to be representing the world inaccurately. That is, we take our consciousness to be misrepresenting our immediate environment. Consciousness is not always transparent; at any time if we were to press our eyeball we would be conscious of being conscious of the world, and not just of the world. The truth of this conditional is part of our concept of consciousness, so even when we are just seeing the pen we are aware that we could make our consciousness if not opaque, than at least translucent to us. If this is true, then one of the key motivations Honderich has for his account disappears.

Finally, my third question concerns the extent to which this theory is explanatory. Honderich is ambitious: he wants to analyse consciousness in terms of something else. He is critical of attempts (if they are attempts) to give an account of consciousness in terms of locutions such as 'what it is like to be' something. As he points out, 'the *analysandum* is right there in each of the *analysans*' (p. 131). Honderich's theory looks, prima facie, to escape this by explaining one thing (consciousness) in terms of another (the existence of the world). Let us walk through the steps one more time to see where the burden of the explanation lies. Our destination is the claim that 'the difference between me now and a chair in this room ... is that for me a world exists, and for the chair a world does not exist' (p. 130).

There is a 'world-in-itself' (the world of particles in fields of force) and 'there is a causal circumstance for my neural event in which the world-in-itself plays at least a large part' (p. 140). A WPC depends in part upon these neural events. It would be good to know what else is in the causal circumstance that is not part of the world-in-itself. Two things suggest themselves: first, properties of the perceived part of the physical world and second, properties of my WPC. There are two worries with these suggestions. First, the same as that expressed above, namely, that the different 'worlds' were supposed to be different conceptualisations of a single world and whether or not something is a cause does not, surely, depend upon how we conceive it. Second, such properties are supposed to be the effect of the interaction of the world in itself on our neural events, and an effect cannot be its own cause.

This is important because of what we found puzzling about consciousness in the first place. That we have neural properties and the chair is not yet a problem. We simply have different physical properties — albeit of vastly different complexity. The world-in-itself causes changes in us and also in the chair, but with very different results. In our case what happens is that a WPC is brought into existence ('My neural events are a kind of sufficient condition for my world', p. 141). By why? What is so special about some physical properties (neural events) that they can bring worlds into existence but other physical properties (being made of wood) cannot?

Honderich might reply here that he is not primarily interested in the question of how consciousness is caused, but rather in what it is. This may be a fair point, however it is part of the nature of WPCs that they can be brought into existence by neural events and not other sorts of physical property, and it is this that is giving me difficulty.

I suppose that if there is a question arising from this, it is the nature of Honderich's ambition for an account of consciousness. He complains that functionalism and other materialist approaches 'leave something out' (p. 128). The alternative Honderich provides is that particles in fields of force cause changes in neural events which, in conjunction with something else not yet specified, cause the existence of WPCs. To claim that there is something amiss here, that there is a whiff of the *analysandum* being part of the *analysans*, might be to demand the impossible.

Thinking there is a problem with consciousness arises from combining several different thoughts: that only the physical is ontologically respectable; that consciousness exists; that consciousness is over and above the physical; that any attempt to produce consciousness solely from the physical is doomed to failure. To make progress, one or more of these has to go: the claim that no physical accounts are possible and that no non-physical accounts are respectable leaves us nowhere to turn.

What about the account in terms of consciousness as existence? How do we get from neural events to the existence of a world? Given the above, there has to be some weirdness in an account, otherwise it will be doomed to failure. However, as philosophers it is a funny position to find ourselves in adjudicating between competing weirdnesses (cf. pp. 214–17).

Honderich is an adventurous and resourceful philosopher. His account, as he has argued, has many advantages, not being one of the standard accounts principal among them (p. 127). This point needs to be taken seriously: it does seem that progress will be made only with some radical change in direction. The fault might be in me, but I am not sure I have yet fully understood the direction which Honderich wants us to take.

## References

Campbell, J. (1993), 'A simple view of colour', in *Readings on Colour: Volume 1*, ed. A. Byrne and D. Hilbert (Cambridge, MA: MIT Press).
Honderich, T. (2004), *On Consciousness* (Edinburgh: Edinburgh University Press).
Honderich, T. (2006), 'Radical externalism', *Journal of Consciousness Studies*, **13** (7–8), pp. 3–13. [This issue]
McGinn, C. (1989), 'Can we solve the mind–body problem?', in *Modern Philosophy of Mind*, ed. W. Lyons (London: Everyman).

## REPLY TO MATRAVERS BY HONDERICH

Derek Matravers begins his open-minded and contemplative inquiry by identifying options for the philosophy of mind now. The two general ones considered by the orthodox, as he says with reason, are ploughing on with materialism and trying to do some ploughing with spiritualism. He is another of us, as I cannot resist noting, who takes those two general characterizations of most thinking on the mind to be correct and useful.

A third option is the idea that the problem of consciousness is necessarily unsolvable, as argued in some pages by Colin McGinn (1989). Well, it is hard for me to think of known pages weaker in the logic of philosophy. James Garvey, of whom you know, lays out McGinn's failure to make rudimentary distinctions necessary to his argument (Garvey, 1997). They are distinctions of a kind fundamental to good philosophy and too often lacking in the science and particularly the psychology of consciousness. Also, pages devoted to proving we can never solve the mind–body problem have the absurdity of having to be considered, anyway for a minute or two, as advice to the human race to give up one of its three or four most compelling intellectual problems.

Matravers's fourth option, Radical Externalism, is simply and truly characterized by him in a way that instructed this exponent of the theory — it is thinking that does not necessarily respect our current conceptual categories of the mental and the physical, the inside and the outside.

The theory is indeed at bottom that my perceptual consciousness consists in the existence of a world. Matravers begins his discussion of the theory by safely assuming there is a world out there,, with objects in causal relations in it, which world does not depend on us at all. Does a very first question arise, then, I take him to ask, of whether it can reasonably be supposed there are also worlds that do depend partly on us, worlds in which our perceptual consciousness consists?

He surveys the theory's different worlds more independent of us and worries about speaking of these in terms of conceptions of but one world — a worry to which he will return. Before then he notes the matter of relations between these more independent worlds and worlds of perceptual consciousness.

He rightly puts aside an idea of a world of perceptual consciousness that would do no explaining but merely make for a circular account of consciousness. He goes on to consider the relation of a world of perceptual consciousness to the perceived part of the physical world. He rightly remarks, after the slip of saying they have the same content, that they differ in more ways than one, and that a WPC can be said to resemble the perceived part of the physical world.

A main thought in these paragraphs is a kind of suspicion of a theory with various kinds of coffee and chairs in it, somehow related by resemblance. The suspicion goes with the question of whether the subject-matter of Radical Externalism is worlds or just conceptions of a world.

He then asks if we can improve the theory by leaving out the perceived physical world? Do we need instead only a physical world simpliciter and our worlds of perceptual consciousness? Despite a certain motivation related to one of John Campbell's, is it necessary to preserve the idea of things of a certain colour or other appearance existing *if* somebody or other is aware of them, otherwise not?

> ... that thought seems (to say the least) baroque, and it is not clear why one would want to try to save it. It is true that we need a way of describing perceived objects from no particular point of view; that is, one that is neutral between particular WPCs. However, that would not introduce news sorts of object (perceptible chairs) that are independent of WPCs (p. 97).

Let me try to deal with this sequence of speculations and propositions. An early one was whether there is any point in talking of different worlds rather than just conceptions of one world — in effect whether the stock-in-trade of Radical Externalism is worth offering for consideration.

Well, if you start at the beginning, or one beginning, as a result of realizing that all there is to your perceptual consciousness is what is given to you, and thus ask the question of what *is* given to you, you get what there is every reason to call a world — things in space and time, with properties, in causal relations. You don't get a conception of a world. That is indubitable.

A conception of a world is exactly what I get when I sit here, maybe with my eyes shut, and tell myself to think of conceptions of a world — concepts, general ideas, images or what-not. Certainly I can tell the difference between a state of affairs of things somehow in space and time and an idea of it and them.

We need to remember there is a big difference between perceptual and reflective consciousness, and between each of them and affective consciousness. The differences are important. A decent theory of consciousness will not only deal with what is given to us in consciousness, but will also really respect differences in what is given, give different accounts of the three different sorts of things. That is another test of a good theory.

But to stop straying to that wider subject, I do indeed want to maintain that the world given to me now as I look down at the back courtyard of this house is also defensibly said to be the one world there is conceived in a certain way — the one world partially and uniquely related to me now. There is no contradiction between those two descriptions, none whatever. Realities, to put the point rhetorically, are something like *choices from reality*. That does not make them into concepts or whatever. Something picked out by me as my Land Rover or the automobile industry or a lovely part of Somerset doesn't become just an idea by being picked out.

And, to revert to Matravers's very first question, yes, there does seem to me reason indeed to think there are worlds dependent on each of us in addition to a world or worlds independent of us. Why not? One good reason that you should be able to keep in mind right now is that you get a different theory of perceptual consciousness thereby, the one we are considering, something whose need is more or less granted by Matravers.

He comes back to the matter of worlds as against conceptions of worlds later and his lines can best be noticed now.

> ... Honderich did not claim all his various worlds existed, but rather that they were different ways in which a single world could be conceived. So when Honderich says 'for something to be conscious is for a world to exist' (p. 145), this should be synonymous with 'for something to be conscious is for the world to be conceived in a certain way' (p. 98).

Certainly not. No synonymy at all. As you will expect, reader, we Radical Externalists say instead, thereby also avoiding the disaster of circularity, that 'for something to be conscious is for a world to exist' is to say 'for something to be conscious is for a world conceived in a certain way to exist'.

Come back now to where we were and the suspicion of various kinds of coffee and chairs. It seems we need reminding, say, of physical and other science, or just physical science. Coffee and chairs turn up differently categorized in physics, chemistry, botany and so on. The chair in physics is different from the chair in chemistry. If you say this sort of thing is OK with science but not with philosophical categories, you will need to supply some general principle of difference. Let's have it, please.

I wonder myself if suspicion of the worlds of Radical Externalism and things in them is partly owed to other and totally different talk of worlds in philosophy. Philosophy admittedly has a past and an all too recent history of extravagant ontological talk, of course including unnecessary talk of possible worlds (Honderich, 1988). None of that is any part of Radical Externalism.

What of the idea of just leaving out the perceived physical world and making do with just a physical world simpliciter and worlds of perceptual experience? This seems not to be an idea with a lot of point. The perceived physical world has long been distinguished, and certainly *can* be distinguished from other things. And you do indeed make an advance, as it seems to me, and as Matravers implies himself, by making use of the idea in our different theory of perceptual consciousness. It's far from being an idea that does no work. For a start, it is essential to dealing with the sort of confusion or resolution of thinking that a world of perceptual consciousness is just somehow mental.

Nor, so far as I can see, does the quoted passage about baroqueness do much damage. If you accept just the bottom idea of British Empiricism and a good deal of other philosophy, and of course the science of sense perception, you certainly accept an idea that assigns to the perceived physical world a dependency on all of us, a dependency of public objects. Clearly they need to be distinguished from worlds of perceptual consciousness. And, to continue a refrain, they are distinguished in a needed and good theoretical cause — the cause of the theory that is our subject-matter.

Also with respect to the quoted passage, I doubt that Matravers can have it both that we need a description of perceived objects from *no* point of view and that this is not to introduce objects independent of worlds of perceptual consciousness. The objective world as specified by him cannot be any particular world of perceptual consciousness. Are we failing to understand one another here?

Let us now go forward from his paragraph on the baroque, to what he calls the broader picture — and maybe to some more failing in mutual understanding.

Radical Externalism has in it that my world of perceptual consciousness depends on the physical world below and also me neurally. It has not been my idea, as I think Matravers supposes, that the physical world below contributes only via my neurons. It is not clear to me why he takes a world of perceptual consciousness to depend on the perceived physical world — and raises a question about the latter's being up to the job, its robustness.

As you have heard already, it does not seem to me that the following paragraph, already quoted from and considered, about worlds and conceptions of worlds, does not do much damage to Radical Externalism. It is also clear, as Matravers perhaps suggests in a line about conceiving affecting ontology, that there is room for more thinking in Radical Externalism about the conceptualization of reality, conceptual schemes.

Matravers's second main concern in his paper has to do with what he calls the transparency of consciousness, what you have heard of from me in terms of what is *given* in perceptual consciousness — nothing more than a world. He remarks, rightly, that Radical Externalism denies that your consciousness of the room includes something in addition to a room, which is a relation to it or anyway something more than what other theories of consciousness call its content.

We return to James Garvey's telling us to stick a finger in an eye (p. 48), apparently an instruction used in the past by the excellent Mark Sainsbury.

> ... press your eyeball with your finger and your mental images (so to speak) of the objects around you double. ... Here is one way of describing what is going on. At the time you are doing this, the way your experience represents the world as being is that there are two pens in front of you (or one rather weird and discontinuous pen) (pp. 99–100).

A first thing to be noticed in these very lines is a proposition for the most part assented to by Matravers. It is that what we get when we press an eyeball is two pens or something weird, *not* something in addition to two pens or something weird, *not* a representation, *not* a funny relation, *not* a container or vehicle for a content, not 'the mind'. *Not* what Matravers in one sentence slips into including in our experience when he says that we are 'conscious of being conscious of the world, and not just of the world' (p. 100).

So the eyeball experiment in itself does not at all support the idea that all we get in perceptual consciousness is more than what is given to us. Suppose you are as impressed as you ought to be by the thought that everything that there is in your consciousness, everything *of* your consciousness, is given to you. And now you press your eyeball. You thereby get not the slightest reason to put into consciousness a relation, container or whatever. In the experiment you just get the two pens or the weird pen.

You may want to say something, of course. Matravers does say or imply it when he strays from what he assents to for the most part. He says that pressing your eyeball may provide another facet to thinking about consciousness, alter your thinking about consciousness, lead you to a conclusion about our concept of consciousness. More precisely, you may be persuaded by the argument from illusion that what you have, here and in all perception of the world, is some interior item, a representation or whatever.

Yes, you may think that — people do make what from the point of view of Radical Externalism and realist theories of perception and disjunctivism is a mistake. But it is a very good idea to keep clear to yourself that you are *not* depending there on something being given to you in consciousness in addition to the two pens or the weird pen. The test of what is given in consciousness, you may also think, must carry the day over what is a piece of invention owed to an extraordinary case.

As for the rest of my response to the experiment, you have heard it already. Almost always when we say or are inclined to say we see things or otherwise perceive them, what it is for us to be conscious is for there to be a world of perceptual consciousness. Sometimes, however, as in the case of a finger in the eye, what it is for us to be conscious is instead to be described at least partly in terms of reflective consciousness. Or, better, what we need to do is think about such cases by way of more categories than just those of perceptual and reflective consciousness. This we can do without coming near to giving up the principal propositions of Radical Externalism. Maybe we can get some help from disjunctivism. Certainly, according to a summary or two if it, it can get some help from us.

Matravers's third concern, of which I do not follow some phases, has to do with whether Radical Externalism is a truly explanatory theory or just circular. On the face of it, it *is* explanatory — your being conscious of the pen is not 'explained' as your being *aware* of the existence of the pen or anything along those lines. But could it be, not that there is circularity, but that there is the blunder of a world of perceptual consciousness being part of the explanation of itself? A response is that I certainly do not say and have not contemplated *that*, and have no need to do so.

In passing, with respect to the sentence in my book 'My neural events are a kind of sufficient condition of my world', I note that Matravers has not noted a footnote attached to it. The sentence from a paper should have been replaced by something better. Radical Externalism does indeed abandon a lot of philosophy, including something expounded and defended by me, the Union Theory of mind and brain (Honderich, 1988; 1990; 2004, pp. 47–85).

Another remark in passing. As Matravers more or less allows, I do not have a need to explain how some physical facts — neural ones — are different from others and thus can contribute to their being worlds of perceptual consciousness. Neuroscience is doing that. It is possible to hope that it will do it still better with the aid of a clarified logic about consciousness. That logic puts no limit at all on its ambition.

On the main point in Matravers's third concern, it doesn't seem to me that in Radical Externalism there is even a whiff of the *analysandum* being part of the the *analysans*. You don't get such a whiff, so far as I can sense, from the explanation of how WPCs come about. So the theory has a necessary virtue not had by all theories, most obviously some that try to explain consciousness in terms of intentionality where that is a relation to 'the mind'.

Finally, does a theory of consciousness that escapes the disasters of the old ones have to be weird? It certainly has to be really different. And you can get used to Radical Externalism. Your can also agree with Matravers and me and a lot of philosophers and scientists that it is time for a change.

## References

Garvey, James, 1997, 'What does McGinn think we cannot know?', *Analysis*, **57** (3), pp. 196–201

Honderich, Ted (1988), *A Theory of Determinism: The Mind, Neuroscience and Life Hopes* (Oxford: Oxford University Press).

Honderich, T. (1990), *Mind and Brain: A Theory of Determinism, Vol. 1* (Oxford: Oxford University Press).

Honderich, T. (2004), *On Consciousness* (Edinburgh: Edinburgh University Press).

McGinn, Colin (1989), 'Can we solve the mind–body problem?', in *Modern Philosophy of Mind*, ed. W. Lyons( London, Everyman).

Paul Noordhof

# The Success of Consciousness

According to Honderich's stimulating and provocative theory of consciousness, consciousness, or more precisely, perceptual consciousness is the existence of a world (sometimes Honderich talks of it 'consisting in' a world (Honderich, 2004, p. 130).[1] The world in question is the world of chairs, tables, socks and shoes, trees and leopards and the like. Honderich, like other philosophers contemplating the contents of perceptual experience, is struck by the fact that its proper characterisation seems to involve no intrusion of qualia, sense data or other phenomenological items especially tailor made to characterise it. Instead, the content of perceptual experience seems properly characterised in terms of objects and properties in the world of the kinds listed above.

Some philosophers take this observation to support a certain view of perceptual experience: *Disjunctivism* (of the Naïve Realist kind — qualification omitted hereafter). According to such philosophers, perceptual experiences are not a common kind of mental state but involve at least two distinct kinds. There are the mental states which involve the world appearing to the subject of experience and there are those which involve mere appearance. Such philosophers do not suppose the observation supports a complete theory of perceptual consciousness. Other philosophers take the observation to reveal the representational character of phenomenology. According to these, *Representationalists*, to first approximation, there are no phenomenal differences without representational differences, that is, differences in what is represented about the world (where 'the world' may include facts about our own mental lives). One way of assessing the force of Honderich's theory is to consider the motivation for developing the observation in the way that Honderich prefers against these two alternatives and, in the case of the first, a more ambitious development of

---

[1] In this commentary all page references are to Honderich (2004) unless stated otherwise.

it. This will be the subject matter of the first two sections of the paper. In the third section, I will consider whether Honderich's theory performs well with regard to what he considers a crucial feature of perceptual states, namely that they have causal consequences for our behaviour. In the fourth section, I will discuss Honderich's approach to reflective consciousness and argue that it contains an important insight that representationalists should use to answer a substantial objection against their position — one pressed by Honderich. I close with a brief discussion of the impact of hallucinations on Honderich's theory.

## Disjunctivism

Disjunctivists take Honderich's observation that, when we are perceptually conscious of something, there exists a world, to describe a necessary condition for perceptual consciousness, that is, the distinctive mental state characterised by the first disjunct of their approach: perception. It provides no particular illumination of the nature of consciousness but simply a statement of what the *content* of perceptual consciousness must be like. Honderich's theory of perceptual consciousness is an attempt to develop a theory of perceptual consciousness which takes the phenomenology of perceptual consciousness seriously. The deciding point, between disjunctivism and Honderich's theory, might seem to be — from Honderich's perspective — whether disjunctivism or Honderich's theory best captures this phenomenology. When we are perceptually experiencing a world, do we experience the world as dependent upon ourselves (in particular, according to Honderich, our neural properties), do we experience it as mentally or neurally independent, or is the phenomenological content of our perceptual experiences neutral over these two?

If either the first or third answer is correct, then there is no reason why Honderich should not appeal to the phenomenology of perceptual consciousness to justify his starting point. Unfortunately, the most plausible answer is the second. When we are perceptually conscious of the world, it is presented to us as independent of the perceptual experience we have of it. Our perceptual experience of the world as independent might turn out to be mistaken, or indeed, difficult to justify on reflection. There is also a nice question of what is required of a subject to be able to experience perceptually the world in this way. Nevertheless, phenomenologically speaking it seems to be the case and Honderich takes it that this fact should be determinative of how we develop a theory of perceptual consciousness (pp. 133, 183; Honderich, 2006, p. 5).

In which case, it might be productive to see whether a development of the disjunctivist's approach to perceptual experience may provide an account of perceptual consciousness. At one point, Honderich expresses his position in the following fashion: a subject is perceptually conscious if and only if there exists a world *for the subject* ('*for me* a world exists', p. 130, my italics). We might agree with that and emphasise that the world which exists for a subject is just a part of the subject/neurally independent spatiotemporal world — viz. that part of which the subject is currently aware.

Honderich rejects a theory of exactly this type (pp. 133–4, 154, 184). His concern is that such a theory would not be sufficiently illuminating. It seems to involve the claim that S is perceptually *conscious* if and only if S is *aware* of a world i.e. some portion of the objective spatiotemporal world. If awareness is nothing but consciousness, the worry goes, little advance is made. All the work is being done by awareness in selecting from the complete subject/neural independent spatio-temporal world, that part which is for the subject. Put baldly like that, it is hard not to agree with Honderich.

However, the dismissal is rather too swift. Proponents of a disjunctivist account of consciousness may distinguish between two types of theories of consciousness: the first characterises what must be the case for there to be consciousness and the second characterises the way in which this is done. They may identify a product/process ambiguity which serves to obscure these two roles since, obviously, one way to characterise the process involved is in terms of its results. Thus, they will go on, what there must be for perceptual consciousness to be present is a *process of awareness* which makes a portion of the subject, or the neurally independent spatiotemporal world, *for the subject*. This account is not unilluminating since it rules out the possibility of perceptual consciousness without presentation and it talks of a process of awareness whose proper characterisation need not ultimately involve the very terms Honderich uses to characterise perceptual consciousness. Of course, Honderich and others would press: Exactly what is this process of awareness? How are we to characterise it? Indeed, the sceptic may insist that once we have made this distinction to characterise perceptual consciousness in the way that we have done and say no more about the process of awareness is to leave what is of most importance out of the theory of consciousness.

One response to this scepticism is to insist that philosophy cannot do everything. It can identify the necessary conditions for perceptual consciousness to be present but at a certain point — in the characterisation of the process of awareness say — there is nothing more that philosophy can do and we must look to science to take over. I think that this would be an overly defeatist response on behalf of the philosopher. I'll explain why in the next section. In this one, I want to explore whether Honderich's own development of the idea of consciousness as existence avoids simply characterising a certain kind of thing as consciousness-conferring and hoping that science may fill in the details. It seems to me that the answer is no.

As I have already indicated, the crucial difference between the theory just sketched and Honderich's own theory is that the existence of a world (which, according to Honderich, *is* perceptual consciousness) is dependent upon the neural properties of a particular subject (pp. 136, 154). Strikingly, Honderich's explanation of perceptual consciousness is — in terms of its explanation of the *consciousness* bit — no different from one which might have been offered by sense datum theorists.

It would be quite compatible with their approach to suppose that the presence of sense data or qualia is nomically dependent upon a subject's neural properties. Then, for such theorists by analogy, perceptual consciousness is the existence of sense data or qualia. A natural objection to make against the sense data or qualia theory is that we have here no explanation of consciousness but rather something which presupposes an explanation of it in order to make sense of qualia or sense data. These are understood to be things of which we could not fail to be aware. But what exactly is it to be a thing like that?

Precisely the same objection may be raised against Honderich's theory. The objects of his perceptual world also seem to require characterisation in terms of the impossibility of failure of awareness. Of course, Honderich has other reasons to reject sense datum or qualia theories of perceptual consciousness. I don't want to disagree with him about their force. However, it appears he has no objection to the *structure* of the theory that such a sense datum theorist would provide, namely in terms of neurally dependent objects, even if he differs over what these are.

Honderich's answer to this concern seems to be that all he has suggested is that the perceptual world *nomically depends* upon certain neural properties in a particular subject (pp. 157–8, 161). Here we have no appeal to objects or properties which cannot exist without consciousness of them. Put baldly like that, though, we have the possibility of consciousness without a subject. If it is the perceptual objects which are consciousness, then it should be possible for these objects to occur in a world with slightly different laws without any subjects or neural properties at all. Consciousness is not, contrary to advertisement, different from the objective spatiotemporal world. It is simply that part of the objective spatiotemporal world that displays a dual nomological dependency.

To avoid this consequence, we might make a slight adjustment to Honderich's theory. Human subjects have neural properties and, in addition, intrinsic properties which are nomically dependent upon them. Suppose further that the spatiotemporal objects in the world may also be characterised in terms of their relation to these intrinsic properties. For instance, a chair may exist without the intrinsic properties of the brain. However, the chair-as-cause-of-intrinsic-property-$I_1$ could not exist without the presence of $I_1$ while being only nomologically dependent on neural properties. Specify the intrinsic properties of the brain with the right degree of complexity — so that they would not be present without the brain being conscious — and there is no prospect of consciousness without subjects.

With or without this adjustment, there is an obvious worry about Honderich's approach. With the adjustment, we may note that there are many objects we might define as a result of many different intrinsic properties nomically dependent upon neural properties. Not all of them constitute perceptual consciousness. So the question is: which do? In terms of the unadjusted theory, there are many objects we may specify in terms of a nomological dependency upon neural properties prior to conscious processing and also dependent upon the environment. What's special about those objects which constitute perceptual consciousness? Is Honderich able to say anything more than that they are the consciousness-conferring ones?

Perhaps Honderich will say: we can start by putting it like that but we will be able to give another specification of these properties which don't use these terms. It's not immediately obvious what this will be since shape, colour and other sensory properties aren't naturally thought of as properties whose existence depends upon the current existence of certain neural properties. In any case, the proponent of the disjunctivist account of perceptual consciousness will have the same expectation to be able to characterise the awareness-conferring process independently. Both have this gap in their accounts which, if Honderich is right, should not figure in the full philosophical theory of consciousness.

## Representationalism

Honderich's fundamental reason for rejecting representationalist accounts of consciousness seems to be that he sees nothing clear in the notion of intentionality when applied to perceptual consciousness.

He offers a different bundle of reasons for each putative account of intentionality but a key consideration, which he keeps coming back to, is that an (allegedly) definitive characteristic of intentionality is the impossibility of existential generalisation for subject terms and yet intentionality is taken to be a relation (pp. 164, 167–8, 173, 177). Here is Honderich at his most trenchant on the issue:

> It is no good tripping lightly past the so-called 'problem' of a non- existent term of a relation. This is in fact a simple contradiction. The relation of representation or whatever is indeed presented as a relation. What we are thus offered is a nonsense — the nonsense of the possibility of a dyadic relation with one term, the nonsense of a relation between a something and a nothing (p. 168).

Two points are relevant here. First, not all representations have a meaning independent of the existence of the items they signify. Demonstratives and indexicals are examples. So it is open to representationalists about perceptual consciousness to claim that the kind of representations involved are of a similar character. The meaning of these representations will involve a relation. The meaning of other terms — for instance, a fountain of youth — may involve relations to the constituents e.g. fountains or youths — but nothing which is a relation to the whole putatively non-existent entity: the fountain of youth. What relations are required and whether the relations must be to those entities which currently exist or existed in the past are nice issues which seem not to be dealt with by a simple argument to the effect that there is no relation which may hold between a representation and a *currently* non-existent thing it represents.

Second, Honderich himself provides a non-relational account of (derived?) intentionality when he turns to talk of reflective consciousness. He claims that representations are representations because they share to some extent the causal role of that which they represent (p. 193). If that's right, then I presume that representations of different things have different causal roles. Does Honderich assert this and yet deny that the causal roles of these representations serve to determine what is represented by the representations? If not, then presumably this will allow a relation to hold between the representation and what is represented in cases where what is represented does exist and, when it does not, we correctly characterise what is represented in terms of this nonexistent thing because the representation has the causal role that thing would have if it were to exist (cf. p. 171).

If representationalism is still a viable prospect, then it enables us to say something more about the process of awareness specified in the previous section. Part of its characterisation, we can now see, will be that it has states with representational properties explaining why a particular part of the objective spatio-temporal world is the object of awareness. Just saying this, of course, does not complete the story. We need to consider whether non-conscious representational states are possible and what distinguishes between conscious presentational states like perceptions and conscious non-presentational but representational states such as beliefs and thoughts. In the present paper, I shall offer nothing on the first question partly because, to do so, would be to take us too far away from the detail of Honderich's work. On the second question, in the section after next I shall make a suggestion drawn from an observation by Honderich.

## Mental Efficacy

Honderich holds that his theory of perceptual consciousness as existence can allow for the efficacy of the mental. His line is that since perceptual consciousness is the existence of spatiotemporal objects, albeit neurally dependent, and the latter are efficacious, perceptual consciousness is efficacious (pp. 152–4, 218–19). He writes

> consciousness as existence, particularly in connection with perceptual consciousness, makes epiphenomenalism the mad proposition that the external world, so to speak, is causally inefficacious with respect to consciousness (pp. 218–19).

It is questionable whether Honderich is entitled to this conclusion.

At least two puzzles arise in Honderich's picture. The first concerns the relationship between the objects of a subject's perceptual world and spatiotemporal objects of science (hereafter, objective spatio-temporal objects). These objects are not identical since the objective spatiotemporal objects can exist independent of a particular subject's neural properties whereas the perceptual objects cannot. Perceptual objects seem to have all the properties of objective spatiotemporal objects, apart from these objects' objectivity, with additional neurally dependent essential properties.

If that's right, then a version of a familiar concern arises. Just as we might ask whether it was in virtue of the mental or non-mental physical properties of mental events that they were causes of behaviour, so we might ask whether it is the perceptual objects or the objective spatiotemporal objects that are efficacious. Or, alternatively, without making the options mutually exclusive, whether the objects are efficacious in virtue of being perceptual objects or in virtue of simply being spatiotemporal objects. I see no reason to believe that any significant efficacy attaches to an object such as a chair in virtue of it being a perceptual object. Its spatiotemporal properties will be responsible for its effects on the neural properties of a subject. Those of its properties which are dependent on a particular subject's neural properties will not be causes of these neural properties. The neurally dependent properties will be constitutively related to the intrinsic non-neural properties which, in turn, are nomically dependent upon the neural properties.

Now it may be that there is an answer to this worry but until we are clearer about the connection between perceptual objects and spatiotemporal objects and how the efficacy of the properties of one may imply the efficacy of the properties of other, Honderich's theory has at least as many difficulties as alternative more standard accounts. Indeed, his position may be in worse shape. This brings me to the second puzzle.

It is not enough that consciousness is granted an efficacy. It must have the right efficacy. Nobody would suppose the horrors of epiphenomenalism avoided if we had a theory which made consciousness irrelevant to behaviour and other mental states and yet relevant to the flaring of sunspots. Of course, things aren't as bad as that for Honderich's theory! However, it is not clear how Honderich's theory makes consciousness a cause of a subject's behaviour. Unlike the objective spatiotemporal objects, Honderich takes the perceptual objects to be nomically dependent upon a subject's neural properties. The perceptual objects are not, themselves, causes of the instantiation of these neural properties. It is plausible that we behave in the way we do because of the instantiation of neural and perhaps other intrinsic properties of the brain. In which case, how do perceptual objects — those objects which are consciousness according to Honderich — cause behaviour?

## Reflective Consciousness and Presentation

According to Honderich, reflective consciousness is the existence of representations rather than the existence of a perceptual world. So, as I have already noted, it appears that Honderich does not reject the possibility of representations nor, indeed, intentionality (p. 196). His earlier argument against the very coherence of intentionality must have an answer (p. 168). What he is left with is the claim that, while it might be appropriate to appeal to intentionality in order to understand reflective consciousness, it is inappropriate for the proper understanding of perceptual consciousness.

We have already seen that one reason for arriving at this view – namely that perceptual consciousness cannot concern something which does not exist — is ill founded (p. 165). There are representations that only have significance if they have referents e.g. demonstratives and indexicals. A second reason, though, is rather more promising. It is the claim that there is a significant phenomenal difference between belief, say, and perception. The latter involves presentation of objects whereas the former does not (p. 165).

In fact, Honderich's contrast of reflective consciousness with perceptual consciousness suggests a solution to the representationalist's difficulty. Honderich argues that reflective consciousness is just the existence of representations. These characterise the content of our reflectively conscious states in much the same way as perceptual objects in Honderich's sense capture the content of our perceptually conscious states. Representationalists should agree about this characterisation of the phenomenal character of conscious belief. We are conscious of the representation properties of the belief rather than what is represented by the belief e.g. the images and sentences we entertain in thinking this or that. Thus, when we consciously judge or think that p, although p might be the proper specification of the content of the state, the object of consciousness is not what is represented — that p — but rather the representational properties of the state — the properties doing the representing.

Representationalists should just insist that in the case of perceptual consciousness matters are quite different. Perceptual states present the world *in virtue of* their representational properties. By this, I do not mean that they are intermediaries any more than experiences are intermediaries when we experience the world. The 'in virtue of' characterisation does not always serve to introduce an intermediary as opposed to, in this case, enabling us to talk of features of an experience which make it the kind of experience it is. The simple thought is that a state's representational properties may determine the content of consciousness in two ways: either by what they represent or by being the object of consciousness. Recognising this provides representationalists with the resources to distinguish between the phenomenal content of perception and belief.

## Concluding Remarks

It is the fate of stimulating, provocative and paradigm-shifting theories to be criticised. This fate has not escaped Honderich's theory in the present paper — where normal philosophy (presumably an accompaniment of normal science) has asserted itself. I have argued that, in phenomenological terms, Honderich's theory is less well supported than a disjunctivist alternative. I have developed this disjunctivist alternative within a representationalist framework and explained how Honderich's attack on intentionality must founder, even by his own lights, given his later willingness to understand reflective consciousness intentionally (Honderich, 2004, p. 196). Finally, I have explained how representationalists can capture the difference between perception and belief which was the other source of support for Honderich's position. The last two points don't show that Honderich's theory is mistaken but just question its motivation. The first point, together with the problems relating to mental causation, provide some grounds for questioning Honderich's approach.

A final reason for caution stems from test cases involving hallucinations or brains in vats. Honderich rejects the latter as a problem. He considers it a recommendation of his theory that it puts forward a testable hypothesis that might — though he suggests it will not — be refuted if brains in vats correctly take themselves to be perceptually conscious (pp. 154–6). Brains in vats, of course, are hard to produce and so actual verification of Honderich's claims here are some way off. Realistic hallucinations as a result of drug taking are not. They exist, subjects are awake during them, and it seems to them that certain items exist in the world. What does Honderich say about this type of case?

It seems to me that the only thing he can say about them is that these subjects are mistaken about the phenomenology of their mental lives. They take it that there is the existence of a world but in fact there isn't. Perhaps the subjects aren't conscious at all or perhaps they are reflectively conscious. What he cannot say is that reflective consciousness supplies the very same phenomenology (albeit in a different manner) on pain of undermining his grounds for supposing that perceptual consciousness is the existence of a world in the first place. However, if he does claim that subjects are mistaken about their phenomenology, then he opens up a gap which he rejected in his initial characterisation of perceptual consciousness as the existence of a world. He writes

> there is every reason for taking the seeming nature of all consciousness simply to be its very nature, the full reality of it (p. 183).

The appearance-reality distinction does not apply to consciousness it seems. But if we can be mistaken over whether a particular phenomenology involves the existence of a world, then there is a distinction between the appearance of consciousness and its reality.

The plausibility of Honderich's theory stems from the fact that it states the success conditions of consciousness. Honderich is right that when we are perceptually conscious it seems to us that there is a world. That's what perceptual consciousness must provide us with if it is to count as perceptual consciousness of some kind or another. However, Honderich's attempt to derive a substantive theory of consciousness from it is problematic if the reasons given above are sound.

## References

Honderich, Ted (2004), *On Consciousness* (Edinburgh: Edinburgh University Press).
Honderich, T. (2006), 'Radical externalism', *Journal of Consciousness Studies*, **13** (7–8), pp. 3–13. [This issue]

## REPLY TO NOORDHOF BY HONDERICH

Doubt does not arise in my mind about whether Paul Noordhof's paper is a good one. But I have found it hard to get a hold of all of it. Maybe the reason is a common one — another philosopher's immersion in a local doctrine or doctrines and hence a use of labels, abbreviations and styles familiar to a group of comrades but not the rest of us, or not yet the rest of us. Does a disbelief in anything else go along with this immersion, indeed an attempt to reform anything else into something akin to local doctrine?

If, reader, you take those opening remarks as intended to convey a certain superiority, your impression should be affected by also hearing that I am aware that the labels, abbreviations and styles of Radical Externalism are not exactly a philosophical *lingua franca*. Rather, my remarks are meant to explain why it seems best in what follows to make my way through Noordhof's paper in a pedestrian way, registering some items as they come into view, rather than attempting an overview of the geography, let alone a geology.

He says in his first paragraph that for Radical Externalism the proper characterization of what it is for something to be perceptually conscious is for a world to exist. The world in question, he then says, is the world of chairs, tables, socks and shoes, tree and leopards and the like. It is natural to take him to be referring to just the physical world. Well, as you will know from earlier pieces in this book, that is definitely *not* the world in which my perceptual consciousness is said to consist by Radical Externalism.

In a word, the theory is a kind of near-physicalism, not devout physicalism. Also, it is not any theory that somehow makes the physical world what is called the *content* of perceptual consciousness, which consciousness also has something else in it. Radical Externalism intrudes into consciousness no phenomenological items, these at least typified by sense data or by qualia as sometimes understood. And, as perhaps needs to be added, Radical Externalism intrudes into perceptual consciousness nothing else in addition to a world either — of which, more in a minute or two.

Whatever characterization or observation of or about worlds or content supports whatever theory, it is perhaps implied by Noordhof in his second paragraph, and subsequently that the complete theory of Radical Externalism is supported or motivated only or principally by the proposition about what is given in consciousness. That is not the case at all. What is given in consciousness is part of the best introduction to the theory and one strong argument for it, but not more than that.

Disjunctivism in one main form is a response to the argument from illusion. The doctrine is to the effect that while there may be no difference whatever in consciousness between your seeing a leopard and your really hallucinating one, this does not show that on both occasions your consciousness is to be characterized in terms of sense data or the like. Your consciousness across such occasions, can be either one sort of thing or another. This consciousness, so to speak, is disjunctive.

Actually seeing a leopard is to be understood somehow along the lines of direct realism or what was once called naive realism. That is, seeing a leopard is to be understood as your somehow being in direct touch with a leopard, or, yet more obscurely, as the fact that the physical leopard can be said *partly to constitute* the experience. The story with the hallucination, whether or not precisely sense data are mentioned, is entirely different.

This either-or nature of some consciousness, I take it, is what is conveyed by Noordhof's saying in his second paragraph that there are perceptual experiences, where the world appears to the subject of experience, and there are perceptual experiences, in my view wonderfully unhelpfully so called, that involve mere appearance. Notice that with the first sort of thing there are, so to speak, two elements, whatever is said of phenomenology. There is the world and there is the appearing of the world. In the second sort of thing there is only the second element.

At the start of his section on disjunctivism, Noordhof remarks that what Radical Externalism takes perceptual consciousness to be, *a* world, is what disjunctivists take to be a necessary condition for true perceptual consciousness. That is at least misleading. A world of the first kind, so far as I know, is no part at all of disjunctivism, which has to do in part with exactly the physical world. That is as definite as what was noted above, that Radical Externalism supposes a world of perceptual consciousness *not* to be the physical world.

To which can be added that it is not only disjunctivism that makes the physical world a necessary condition for perceptual consciousness. So in quite a different way does Radical Externalism — a world of perceptual consciousness is dependent partly on the unperceived physical world. The physical world is somehow constitutive of it.

Noordhof supposes in the early paragraphs of his first section that disjunctivism does better than Radical Externalism in capturing the phenomenology of our perceptual consciousness — disjunctivism does better in saying what we are *given* in consciousness. This rating, however, is based on a misapprehension — that it has ever been a proposition of Radical Externalism that what is given to me when I see a leopard is in part that the experience is dependent on my neural properties. In fact that would surely be remarkable speculation. It puts a cause within an effect. On the contrary, that what is given to me is in a way no more than a leopard, as you have heard already, is fundamental to Radical Externalism.

It is true that Radical Externalism takes what we are calling the phenomenology of perceptual consciousness seriously. But, as you have heard already, it does not suppose for a moment that in order to have a decent theory of consciousness we need not or cannot attend to anything else. It does not suppose there is no other deciding point, nothing else determinative. Reflection about consciousness, not to mention an overwhelming fact of common sense and neuroscience, supplies to us the proposition of a dependence of my perceptual consciousness on my brain. To repeat, Radical Externalism really cannot be supposed to take what we are given when we are perceptually conscious to be itself *determinative* of a theory of perceptual consciousness. Remember those various criteria for a successful theory.

Nor, of course, to pause for a moment, is the neural dependency proposition, or the proposition of dependency on the physical world, merely thrown in. Actually paying attention to your consciousness, engaging in mental realism, gives you the idea that what it is for you to be conscious is for something somehow to exist. You can go on to explain that idea, come to a clear proposition, partly by way of the dependency propositions. Both are essential to, indeed parts of, the proposition that a certain state of affairs exists — which proposition is the theory's answer to what is the case when we are perceptually conscious.

So, might it be productive to develop an alternative disjunctivist theory as against Radical Externalism? Are we prompted to that by a lower rating of Radical Externalism with respect to the phenomenology? Certainly not in my view. It gets the highest rating. It seems to me no reason has been given for trying to develop an alternative theory.

Further, a theory to the effect that a subject is perceptually conscious if and only if there exists a world *for the subject* sounds like a theory that is circular in being about something you can call a mental world. It is impossible, isn't it, to take a subject to be other than a *conscious* subject? Certainly my book, including the cited p. 130, does not commit me to such a circularity. In quotations, say the quotation that '*for me* a world exists', beware the quoter's italics!

Nor would it be a good idea to persist with a misleading if tentative line or two of mine, open to being misunderstood as to the effect that a world of perceptual consciousness is *dependent on a subject* rather than on a brain. (Read instead the other lines that conceive of a subject naturalistically — in fact, at bottom, neurally [2004, p. 143].) Here too, talk of a traditional non-neural subject produces circularity in an analysis of consciousness — to me wonderfully underdescribed by Noordhof as something 'not ... sufficiently illuminating' (p. 111). A good circularity, as I understand one, is about as illuminating as a coal-hole.

This dismissal is rather too swift for Noordhof. He supposes that light can be shed in such an account — which, incidentally, seems to have nothing essential to do with disjunctivism. The light is owed to the account's including *two* theories of consciousness.

> ... the first characterizes what must be the case for there to be consciousness and the second characterizes the way in which this is done. ... what there must be for perceptual consciousness to be present is *a process of awareness* which makes a portion of the subject, or the neurally independent spatiotemporal world, *for the subject* (p. 111).

Not a lot can be said by me of this since what is said initially of the two theories is unclear to me, and the second sentence of the quoted passage is defeating. There is no keystroke error or the like in the sentence, and so what it comes to, in form, is indeed that *something makes something for the subject*. If there is grammar there, there is not much else for me. Still, I do indeed press the objection that it is not enlightening to explain consciousness by way of a seemingly unexplained process of awareness.

Moving forward quickly, past the idea that to dismiss a circularity as useless in analysis is merely be a *sceptic*, I come to the question of whether Radical Externalism's own development of the idea of consciousness is circular. Or, at any rate the question of whether it is involved in a defeatist strategy for philosophy of leaving science to explain something. The answer, for Noordhof, is yes. In explanation of this, he says the crucial difference between Radical Externalism and the account made up of two theories is that Radical Externalism makes the existence of a world dependent on the neural properties of a particular person. Indeed it does.

What takes me aback, and does not make me confident in writing this reply, is the conclusion drawn from that premise — which conclusion would certainly make Radical Externalism circular. The conclusion is the proposition that Radical Externalism, at least in some important respect or bit or other, is no different from the explanation of perceptual consciousness given by sense datum theorists. What Radical Externalism comes to, very briefly, is that to be perceptually conscious is to experience sense data.

The proposition just doesn't follow from the premise that Radical Externalism makes perceptual consciousness dependent on neural facts. Or, I'm inclined to guess, it doesn't follow unless the respect or other in which it does follow is not very important.

To linger a little longer here, *of course* a sense datum theory of consciousness is likely to make consciousness neurally dependent. Has there been any half-serious theory of consciousness since 1900, say, that hasn't done so? But that is not the main response that is needed here. It is that Radical Externalism explains what it is for your to be perceptually conscious as the existence of a state of affairs outside of you. Could anything be more remote from the theory of sense data? The latter is indeed a theory of a somehow mental world, an inner world.

You, reader, may well do better with these thoughts against Radical Externalism than I am doing. Also with the later thought that Radical Externalism is committed to the possibility of consciousness without a traditional subject, which most certainly it is — whatever is put in the place of that idea that demands some attention.

Here I do grant that there is room for some industry, but of course industry consistent with what the theory has to say of perceptual, reflective and affective consciousness. Let me remark only that the *uniqueness* assigned to a conscious subject can be regarded as partly a matter of the uniqueness of a world of perceptual consciousness and the uniqueness of related facts of reflective and affective consciousness.

Added to the embarrassments for Radical Externalism so far enumerated is the somehow related one that it makes perceptual consciousness into external things that might exist in a different world, a world with different laws, even if there were no subjects or neural properties in it. Let me stick to neural processes or the like

— forget about subjects — and happily accept that something like that is conceivable. So what? It's *this* world that we're in, the only one there is, of which we have different conceptions. And it's this world of which we are analysing something in it, which thing is perceptual consciousness.

I leave it to others better informed with respect to the idea of *intrinsic* properties of human subjects to look into the rest of Noordhof's section on disjunctivism. I do allow that this may be time well spent. It will have to deal with the idea, however, that colour is a sensory property that is *not* dependent on the existence of neural properties or the like. That, I take it, will be as much of a surprise to neuroscience now as it would have been to Locke, Berkeley and Hume. Kant too? Maybe there is more misunderstanding between us here.

To come on to the short section on representationalism, this doctrine was introduced as being supported by the fact that no such phenomenological items as sense data or qualia of a kind are given to us in perceptual consciousness. Rather, what we are given is such as to

> reveal the representational character of phenomenology. ...there are no phenomenal differences without representational differences, that is, differences in what is represented about the world (p. 109).

I need more instruction here, but less so when we get on to something related, which is the supposed intentionality or relation of aboutness within perceptual consciousness.

It has been one of my complaints about this that we are given no representation, sign or such-like in perceptual consciousness — just the leopard — and hence we are not given a term of a supposed relation. It is not just sense data that are missing from perceptual consciousness. Another complaint, noted by Noordhof, is that what we are supposed to get here is a kind of relation, clarified with reflective consciousness as against perceptual consciousness consciousness, such that the other term of the supposed relation, the thing represented, can be missing. No fountain of youth.

To the second complaint, Noordhof replies, maybe truly, that some representations have meanings that are dependent on the existence of what they represent — demonstratives and indexical terms like 'this' and 'that'. Well, for a start, that they have a meaning dependent on the existence of a referent does not give us the proposition that it is a matter of a certain relation, precisely a supposed relation that also holds in cases where there is *no* referent.

But anyway, none of this is about perceptual consciousness. Certainly Radical Externalism *has* a relation of representation or intentionality in what it says of reflective consciousness. Nor, I take it, does Noordhof's use of Russell's Theory of Descriptions help out with perceptual consciousness.

Noordhof has questions about the fundamental relation of representation allowed by me with respect to reflective consciousness. However, I am unsure of the relevance of this to what presumably remains our subject, which is perceptual consciousness. As for my complaints about the supposed relation of intentionality within perceptual consciousness, certainly they do not apply with respect to the fundamental relation of representation supposed by me with reflective consciousness — that something is a representation of something if, for a start, it shares some effects with that thing.

With respect to this idea of representation, there is again a want of understanding between us. I hurry to *assert* what it seems I am expected to deny, that it is precisely effects of a thing that at least enter into determining what it represents. I readily allow that Radical Externalism has so far contained no worked-out account of reflective consciousness and hence representation. Maybe it has a good or promising idea in it of what a representation is, certainly better than the idea that it is an effect of what is represented.

The short section on mental efficacy rightly reports that my being conscious of this room, taken as a certain spatiotemporal state of affairs, can evidently be supposed to be causally efficacious with respect to my behaviour. That is, to take up Noordhof's terminology, perceptual spatiotemporal objects can be taken as in no danger of making Radical Externalism into an epiphenomenalism. However, there is said to be trouble for this complacency when we remember that there is also the physical world — objective spatiotemporal objects as against perceptual spatiotemporal objects.

The trouble is discerned when it is remembered, as it was by Stephen Law (p. 66), that it can be asked of such an account of a mental event as Davidson's whether it is the mental or the physical properties of the event that are causally effective. The supposed trouble is more easily discerned, of course, when you help yourself to the proposition that a perceptual spatiotemporal object *is* the related objective spatiotemporal object. You come nearly to the trouble when you ask if it is the object's being spatiotemporal or the object's being perceptual that is doing the work. You *get* to the trouble — epiphenomenalism — when you suppose it has to be the object's being spatiotemporal rather than its being perceptual that is doing the work.

The short reply to this is that there are two objects in question, both spatiotemporal, and it is the one that is in a world of perceptual consciousness that is doing the work — which it can do in virtue of being spatiotemporal. There are two objects in question because, for a good start, they have *different* properties. Your perceptual spatiotemporal object, owed to where you stand, is different from the related objective spatiotemporal object, which latter thing is precisely *not* owed just to where you stand, etc.

Whatever else is to be said, whatever development of Radical Externalism is needed with respect to relations between kinds of objects and worlds, there seems to be no objection to it here. It is exactly not like Davidson's Anomalous Monism in the relevant respect. There is nothing whatever in it that puts any obstacle in the way of perceptual consciousness having efficacy.

Finally here, it needs remembering that what is wrong with certain theories of consciousness is that they make psychophysical relations impossible, in particular make it impossible to see how thoughts and feelings can cause actions. This epiphenomenalism is enough for disaster. The disaster is *not* that they do not give a full account of how thoughts and feelings cause particular actions rather than others — or the flaring of sunspots. Radical Externalism, whatever you may want to add to it, is not an epiphenomenalism.

The section on reflective consciousness and representation starts in a way that may mislead a reader. It does not only *appear* that I do not reject something, but rather accept it. That thing, in a brisk sentence, is an account of reflective consciousness that gives a place to a certain relation. I plainly and categorically assert that (p. 9). As Noordhof indeed remarks, Radical Externalism is motivated in part by another matter of phenomenology — what you can call differential phenomenology. There is a big general difference of consciousness between seeing green and doing philosophy, and between each of them and wanting something to eat.

Partly for this reason, representation is made no part of the story with perceptual consciousness, but all or the basis of the general story with reflective consciousness. There is no surprise in this and no reason to suspect that the first story casts doubt on the second. As for the relation, it is a fact that a representation or symbol is related to what it represents, at least, in that it has some of the effects of the thing represented or symbolized. That is wholly different from the usual stuff about intentionality (Honderich, 2004, pp. 159–81).

I am glad this may be of use to representationalists, whatever they are, and hope it will lead them in the direction of a clear and argued theory of the nature of consciousness, maybe one not a long way from here.

The first of Noordhof's concluding remarks, to the effect that he is defending the philosophical equivalent of Kuhn's normal science against a proposed paradigm shift, supposes a little confidently that there is now a paradigm in the philosophy of mind. There certainly isn't a Newton. Maybe something that can have the name of being normal philosophy will persist. Indeed it must be likely that it will. But clearly there is overwhelming disbelief with respect to devout physicalism and also to spiritualism when it is actually thought about. Maybe it is the role of Radical Externalism just to make more likely *some* departure from a lot of the philosophy and science of mind that we have.

Noordhof ends with hallucinations, and gives further expression to the demand for concession from me. Having already made the concession and other responses (above, pp. 24–5, 39–40, 56–9, 93), let me add only that he is right to point to a problem in my taking a brain in a vat to be a case of reflective consciousness or something of the sort. Whatever is to be said here will have to be in line with the proposition that all that there is to consciousness itself is what is *given*. I did see that, but now see it with more of a sense of thinking that needs to be done by someone. I reject, as you know, that the stuff about phenomenology is near to constituting *the grounds* for Radical Externalism.

It is good if surprising to have Noordhof's acceptance, if that is what it is, of the strategy of stating a number of success conditions for a theory of consciousness. Also his granting that Radical Externalism meets one of them, the one having to do with what seems to be the case or what is given to us when we are perceptually conscious. I await his account of how disjunctivism and representationalism satisfies all of the success conditions.

### References

Honderich, T. (2004), *On Consciousness* (Edinburgh: Edinburgh University Press).

Ingmar Persson

# *Consciousness as Existence as a Form of Neutral Monism*

I shall here raise and attempt to answer — given the constraints of space, rather dogmatically — some fundamental questions as regards the fertile and far-reaching doctrine Ted Honderich has in the past called Consciousness as Existence. I shall understand this doctrine more narrowly than he presumably does, as simply and solely the claim that 'what it is to be conscious in any way is for something to exist in a certain way' (Honderich, 2006, p. 8).[1] To exemplify by the form of consciousness we both take as primary, perceptual consciousness, the perceiving of a page is '*for the page to be there*' (p. 5). That is to say, your perceptual consciousness of some object is somehow reducible to (the existence of) this object. There is no 'container or vehicle' of this object (p. 5); thus, it may be somewhat misleading to call the object a 'content'.

A bit more precisely expressed, I shall take Consciousness as Existence to be the claim:

> (CE) A full description of what it is intrinsically like to be in the state of perceiving (or being perceptually conscious of) some objects consists in a description of these objects, of there being such and such things in such and such spatial relations to each other.

Since a phenomenological description of an experience is reasonably a description of what the experience is intrinsically like, this claim is likely to belong to the department of phenomenology of experience or consciousness. The claim is to the effect that no mental 'act' or relation of perceiving or being conscious is an intrinsic feature of such consciousness. Nor is any 'subject' performing such acts an intrinsic feature of it. I hold the view, though I do not know to what extent Honderich agrees, that a state of consciousness intrinsically features

---

[1] In this commentary all page references are to this target paper unless stated otherwise.

the subject only as one object among other objects perceived, more specifically, as a body standing in spatial relations to other objects perceived. (One's body is however perceived in a special way, from the inside.) The mode of perception is revealed by the qualities of the objects, e.g., in the case of visual perception the objects are coloured, in the case of tactile perception, they feature thermal qualities, and so on.

Honderich may use Consciousness as Existence as a label not just for CE (assuming that he accepts the specifics of my formulation), but for a set of claims of which CE is a central one. I shall not follow him in this use, for I shall suggest that CE be set in a framework which probably differs from his in some respects. (We may take his term 'Radical Externalism' to designate his framework.) The framework I favour is that of a form of neutral monism.[2] The rationale for the adjective 'neutral' is that the notion of being or existence employed by CE is assumed to be neutral between the mental and the physical. This notion must be taken as primitive and indefinable, and understood through experience (along with many properties experienced, e.g., colours).

It goes without saying that this assumption about the notion of existence figuring in CE is controversial and in need of much more defence than it can receive here. The basic idea is that a description of yourself (i.e., your body) as standing in certain spatial relations to surrounding objects is primary in relation to a description of you as *perceiving* yourself to be standing in these spatial relations to these objects. Now, as long as you have not acquired the knack of producing the latter sort of description, you do not have the concept of something *really* being there, since this presupposes a contrast to what is merely apparently there. You employ a notion of existence or things being there which does not discriminate between things which are merely perceived or apparent and which are really or physically there. This indiscriminate sense is the one my neutral monism take as basic.

I shall now present the fundamental tenets of this neutral monism by means of replies to four questions. In doing so I shall also attempt to relate my replies to Honderich's Radical Externalism. The first two questions concern my neutral monism's entitlement to be called a monism. To earn this title it must define the physical and the mental in terms of its neutral or indiscriminate notion of existence.

---

[2] I first advanced this framework in *The Primacy of Perception* (1985). The picture I paint in broad strokes in this paper is essentially a summary of the view I put forward in this book.

## First Question

What is the relation between the notion of existence used in CE and real physical existence? As already implied, my suggestion is that this notion of existence be employed to define physical existence. I suggest that physical existence be defined as *independent* existence — existence which is independent of the existence of other things, such as states of the observers' bodies and external objects affecting these states. Thus, if, according to a description of what is perceived by a subject S, there is an F in region R, then there is a real physical F in R if there being an F in R cannot be explained in terms of there being something else in R which has certain effects upon the body of S. It may be that, according to this conception, the only things that have real physical existence are the elementary particles of science, but I do not see this as an objection. The crucial point is that *something* must have this form of existence — otherwise there is nothing which can figure in the explanans of perceptual objects.

Honderich describes his Radical Externalism as being 'closer to realism than phenomenalism' (p. 7). It seems reasonable to take realism with respect to the physical world to consist in this world's existing independently of minds and their states. If so, my neutral monism is a realist view of the physical world. On the other hand, it is like phenomenalism in that it takes the physical to be definable in terms of the objects of perceptual states. But phenomenalism confuses the neutral ontological status of these objects with the status of the states of which they are objects. These states are doubtless mental. This brings us to the question what that means.

## Second Question

What makes perceptual consciousness a *mental* state when it intrinsically consists in a state of objects' existing (in a neutral sense)? I answer: this state is something whose existence is *dependent* — more specifically, dependent upon states in the observer's body and things external to this body (all of which must be taken to enjoy independent existence). Suppose, for instance, that I see something white and rectangular in front of me, i.e., there is something white and rectangular in front of me. The existence of this white rectangular thing in front of me can be causally explained in terms of light-rays of certain wavelengths hitting visual receptors of my body. Hence, it is a form of existence which is dependent upon the existence of something reflecting these light-rays and of visual receptors and other relevant parts of my body. This account seems to be in line with Honderich's view of the perceptual as 'being dependent on a scientific or noumenal world underneath and also dependent on you neurally' (p. 6).

Strictly speaking, a qualification should however be inserted. What is causally explained is the fact that my brain enters a certain state. This neural state is nomologically correlated with my mental state of perceiving something white and rectangular in the sense given by Honderich's 'Correlation Hypothesis' (2004, p. 23). There can be no identity between these states, since they enjoy different kinds of existence. So far as I can see, at least some of these correlation laws must be brute, inexplicable facts, since nothing — neither anything physical nor anything mental — can provide the link between neural and mental states.

With the help of a neutral sense of existence we have then defined physical existence as independent existence and the mental as dependent existence. The *concepts* of the physical and the mental come out as inter-dependent, then. But it is important to notice that there is no *ontological* inter-dependence. In contrast to Berkeleyan idealism, my neutral monism does not make the physical ontologically dependent upon the mental (and in contrast to phenomenalism, it does not reduce it to the possible existence of something mental). On the other hand, it makes the mental ontologically dependent upon the physical. I believe this gets our intuitive ontological priorities right. It also concords with the widely accepted point that mental states can only be individuated — i.e., numerically distinguished from qualitatively indistinguishable ones — by reference to the physical. In other words, mental states are, by necessity, states of subjects that are physical; this follows from their definitive dependency. This rules out substance dualism and renders property or attribute dualism the only dualist alternative.

A merit of this view is that it gives us a conceptual guarantee that there is a physical reality of *some* kind. What this kind is is an empirical matter and, so far as I can find, we could be seriously mistaken in thinking that there is a physical world of the extension common sense and science assume. Conceivably, my mental states could be dependent upon nothing but my body which may be utterly different from what I imagine. Honderich probably disagrees for he writes:

> According to Radical Externalism, there isn't a sufficient neural condition for perceptual consciousness (p. 8; cf. 2004, pp. 212–13).

Certainly, we could by stipulation make it part of the concept of perceptual consciousness that it has a cause that is external to the subject's body. This may disqualify hallucinations as perceptual consciousness. However, I do not see the point of this trick, for sceptics could rephrase their challenge thus: how do you know that you have perceptual consciousness rather than hallucinations?

As will transpire in the response to the *Fourth Question*, the dependency of mental states also entails that they borrow their causal efficacy from the physical states undergirding them.

## Third Question

What is the difference between perceptual consciousness and reflective consciousness? All Honderich that has to say about reflective consciousness — that is, thinking — seems to boil down to that it is 'for certain representations to occur' (2004, p. 195). This is right, but it does not take us very far. We want to know about these representations whether they are linguistic, images, or of some other kind. We also want to know what it is that makes them, but not perceptual objects, representative (or 'designative'). As regards the first of these questions, my reply is that the representations in terms of which we think cannot ultimately be linguistic or symbolic in any way which takes what they represent to be fixed, not at all by their intrinsic character, but wholly by something external to them (by conventions, etc.).

Laurence BonJour puts well the chief objection to such a linguistic or symbolic conception of thought:

> According to that conception, *all* that is present in my mind (or brain) when I think contentful thoughts is symbols of the appropriate sorts; these symbols are meaningful or contentful by virtue of standing in relations of some sort to something lying outside the mind in which they stand, but this meaning or content is represented in the mind only by the symbols themselves, not by any further content-bearing element or feature. Thus, merely having such thought-symbols present in my mind (or brain) in itself gives me no awareness of their content, and there is apparently nothing else that the symbolic theory can appeal to in order to account in general for such awareness. Therefore the acceptance of the symbolic conception seems to lead inexorably to the conclusion that I have no awareness of the content of my thought, no internal grasp or understanding at all of what I am thinking. But this is surely an absurd result ... (1998, p. 169).

BonJour concludes:

> Instead, at least some of the elements of thought must be *intrinsically* meaningful or contentful, must have the particular content that they do simply by virtue of their intrinsic, non-relational character (1998, p. 180).

There seems to be only one means by which we can achieve this: by taking the representation itself to instantiate the property which it represents. This move would abolish the 'distance' between the representation and the property represented, and so the need for the mind to 'reach out' for the latter — but, unfortunately, it does so at the price of making it hard to tell them apart. BonJour distinguishes between two ways of discriminating between these items: 'make sense of two distinct instantiation relations' and postulate two 'distinct, though presumably intimately related universals' (1998, p. 183). BonJour favours the second alternative, whereas I shall here try to develop sketchily the first one.

I shall do so by reviving a traditional empiricist idea which BonJour spurns: that of a representative medium of images. Plausibly, an image of redness, triangularity, etc. itself instantiates redness, triangularity and so on. So, images seem to fulfil one requirement of being capable of representing something in virtue of their intrinsic nature, by sharing a feature with what is represented. But BonJour denies that they meet another requirement:

> an image does not represent anything by itself, but rather needs at least to be supplemented by a content directing that it be interpreted in the right way (1998, p. 182n).

That is, we are confronted with the following question: what is it about an image of red that makes it represent redness? It is not enough to reply: the fact that it instantiates redness. For a perceptual object which is red also instantiates redness, but it does not represent (or designate) redness. My answer, which is a variation of a traditional idea, is that an image of red represents the redness of perceptual objects for the reason that it belongs to a class of entities whose members are in general 'derived' from perceptual objects of the appropriate colour. Thus, put in a nutshell, my claim is that images are representative of perceptual objects because their existence is derivative from or dependent upon these objects, and they represent those kinds of objects from which they could be derived by virtue of the fact that they are (most) similar to them (and that they belong to a class of entities whose existence is derivative). It is the second feature which makes the representativeness of images partly 'intrinsic' to their nature, for they represent something to which they are similar in an intrinsic respect.

We can now state the counterpart of CE with respect to reflective consciousness. Reflective consciousness consists in the existence of objects whose existence is a matter of *second-order* of dependence,

dependence upon the objects of perceptual consciousness which, as we have seen, themselves are dependent. It is this order of dependence rather than some difference as regards some intrinsic feature — like the comparative faintness of which Hume speaks — that distinguishes images from perceptual objects. This dependency accounts for the asymmetry of the relation of representation which contrasts with the symmetry of the relation of similarity which is the other characteristic of the representativeness of images.

As is well known, the idea of thinking in a medium of images faces many challenges: e.g., how can thinking in such a medium be propositional (i.e., of a subject–predicate structure) and abstract? I do not pretend to know the answer to all these questions, but sometimes the difficulties seem to me to be exaggerated. For instance, it has been said that an image must be too specific or determinate to represent unambiguously cats rather than black cats, striped cats, etc. But a drawing can be very sketchy and indeterminate and can as a result be seen as a drawing of a cat rather than as a drawing of a black cat, etc. Moreover, if this is correct, we can see the beginnings of an account of how propositional thinking in images could be possible. For thinking that a cat is black could then be something like having an indeterminate image of a cat and then superimposing an image of blackness upon it. All the same, it must be admitted that it is a daunting task to make comprehensible how it is possible to think abstract thoughts — including, e.g., the thought that it is possible to think abstract thoughts in an imagistic medium — in an imagistic medium. On the other hand, it is not to be expected that this be readily comprehensible as long as language-learning to a considerable extent is shrouded in mystery.

Honderich lists affective consciousness alongside perceptual and reflective consciousness. It comprises such phenomena as desires, intentions and emotions. But going by what he says about affective consciousness (2004, p. 201), it seems composed of elements of perceptual and reflective consciousness and, so, it does not seem to deserve a place among the fundamental forms of consciousness. Anyway, this is the stance towards them that I adopt; hence, I shall leave affective consciousness on the side.[3] The analysis of this sort of consciousness would bring up the topic of mental causation, i.e., of mental states or events as causes. But this topic is also raised by my treatment of reflective consciousness as involving the existence of entities that are 'derivative' from perceptual objects; so, it is about time to turn to it.

---

[3] For my analysis of desire and emotion, see Persson (2005), chaps. 4 and 5.

## Fourth Question

Is CE compatible with mental states being causes, of other mental states and physical states, like bodily movements? It does not seem so, for it is mental states rather than their objects or contents which are most naturally construed as causes, but CE regards mental states as intrinsically being nothing over and above their objects.[4] My claim is that explanations which refer to something mental are not themselves causal, but that they presuppose underlying causal mechanisms. For instance, your perceiving some object enables you to retain a (representative) image of it because there is a *similarity* between the object and the image. Likewise, seeing a cloud leads you to visualize an armadillo because there is a similarity between the shape of the cloud and that of an armadillo. Your thinking that if p then q and p straight-away leads you to think that q because the former content *logically entails* the latter. It might be thought that when the outcome is something non-mental, like a bodily movement, the relation it has to its mental antecedent, e.g., an intention, must be causal. But this is not so: an intention to bring about p explains your bringing about what you *think* is p, not directly what is in fact p; so, the link to behaviour is 'content-mediated'.[5] Explanations in terms of mental entities, then, are apparently 'contentual' rather than causal.

Although these and other mental explanations are not causal, they do however presuppose that the mental phenomena which figure in the explanans are somehow grounded in, correlated with, something that is causally efficacious. As remarked, the mental is a dependent form of existence, and for mental explanations such as the above to be true that which the mental explanans is correlated with must be a cause of the correlate of the explanandum. More specifically, there must be appropriate causal connections between the neural correlates of mental states.

Is this a disreputable form of epiphenomenalism? Quite often it is implied that any view which refuses to assign a causal role to mental states falls prey to this criticism. It is argued that if we hold that (1) mental states are distinct from physical states, (2) the physical world is causally closed, so that everything in it which has a sufficient cause has a sufficient physical cause, and (3) there is no large-scale overdetermination in the physical world, then we are committed to

---

[4] In opposition to this, Honderich regards it as a virtue of 'perceptual consciousness as existence' that it allows 'for comprehensible causal relations' (2004, p. 154). Needless to say, psycho-neural correlation is not a causal relation, since it is symmetric, while causation is asymmetric.

[5] I say a bit more about this in Persson (2005), chaps. 4, 13 and 31.

epiphenomenalism. If this argument is right, I must concede that I am an epiphenomenalist.

It is however less clear that I am an epiphenomenalist in Honderich's terminology. He speaks of a 'conviction that consciousness is efficacious' which makes epiphenomenalism 'impossible to believe'. This conviction is not to the effect that 'mental events *cause* other mental events and action'. It is rather to the effect that 'mental events are *ineliminable parts of the explanations* of later mental events and actions' (2004, p. 37). So, it would appear that he takes epiphenomenalism to be the denial of this claim. But in this sense I am not a epiphenomenalist: my view is that explanations in which something mental forms an ineliminable part of the explanans can be true, but that their truth requires in the strictest sense a physical undergirding which is causal.[6]

Honderich claims that the conviction that consciousness is efficacious 'has the character of a datum' (2004, p. 37). I now want to argue that we do not *experience* mental events as causing anything, so my rendition of mental explanations, whether or not it be called epiphenomenalist, does not fly in the face of everyday experience. Contrary to Hume, I think that we do have perceptual experiences of singular causal connections. I have such an experience when I try to push that heavy sofa into the corner and eventually succeed. This is an experience of my body's being in contact with surfaces that initially offer resistance to it, but that eventually give way so that my body's movement is transferred to the sofa. In this case, I experience causation when I am acting, but this is not necessary. I can also experience causation when I am being acted upon, for instance, when you, some heavy inanimate object or the wind, moves my body independently of my will, or when something makes me hot or cold. Hume made the mistake of concentrating on vision, but vision, like hearing, does not provide any experience of causation, but only of successions of events.

Once it becomes clear what an experience of causation is like, it is readily seen that we do not experience mental events as causes of what they explain. When I think that q because I thought that if p then q and

---

[6] I am however unhappy with Honderich's 'Union Theory' which views a 'psychoneural pair' as analogous to a liquid's getting hotter and expanding (2004, p. 64). For in the latter case 'unification' is achieved by the fact that it is the same microscopic state of affairs, the increasing movement in a certain set of molecules, that underlies both of them. I am disinclined to speak of a 'union' in the case of the psychoneural pair, since we have here different forms of existence, one independent and the other dependent. However, Honderich himself may have left the Union theory behind as incompatible with the doctrine of consciousness as existence (2004, p. 213).

p the moment before, I surely do not experience the latter as causing the former thought. What I experience is nothing like what I experience when your push causes me to move; it is simply a succession of objects. What I am aware of is not even in the right category to be a cause: what I am aware of is the content of my thoughts, if p then q and p, not my *thinking* that if p then q and p, but it is the latter, if anything mental, which is a cause. Immediately after having thought that if p then q and p, I can think that I have had this thought, but it would be absurd to hold that I could then be aware of this thought having exercised a causal influence of which I was unaware when I had the thought. I was then instead aware of thinking that q because q is entailed by if p then q and p. This is both the mental explanation and the rational justification of my thinking that q but, I claim, it can be the explanation only if there is a physical underlay which is causal.

I have argued that in a mental explanation of the form 'X because M', where 'M' is some mental event and 'X' is some other mental event or an action, the 'because' is not causal, but that there must be some physical underpinning of M and X which exhibits requisite causal relations for the explanation to be true. It would be too strict, however, to require that the physical correlate of M must be a cause of X (or its physical correlate). This is often true, but not always, and it is important to look at the exceptions, for this would diminish the temptation to think that the 'because' of a mental explanation must nonetheless be causal.

Consider a simple omission, such as refraining from moving your hand and letting it remain where it is on some horizontal plane. Here you decide not to move your hand and, as a result, you do not move it. The result, your hand remaining motionless, is the same as it could have been if you had made no decision at all, but had, say, lost consciousness. But there is an evident difference: in the first situation when you decide not to move your hand, your hand's remaining motionless is controlled by your decision, while this cannot be the case in the second situation in which you make no decision. This is the difference which justifies our saying that you *let* your hand remain where it is in the first situation, but not in the second.

In this respect, of the result being controlled by your decision, of its occurring because of your decision, the first situation is like an intentional action, e.g., of your moving your hand: just as the movement of your hand is intentional because it occurs because of your intention, so your hand's remaining where it is is intentional because it occurs because of your intention. But when you act intentionally, it is easy to slip into thinking of your intention as a *cause* of your movement, for your mental state is here correlated with states of your brain which do indeed cause your hand to move by sending electric impulses down your efferent pathways to your hand. When you let your hand remain motionless, however, it is harder to think of the upshot, your hand remaining where it is, as being caused by your intention not to move it. For, as we have seen, the upshot is here the same as it could have been if you had formed no intention at all, i.e., the same as it could have been if you evidently had not been in any mental state whose neural correlate exercises an influence over your hand.

Thus, it is wrong to take the claim that something intentional occurs 'because of' an intention to imply that, at least, the physical correlate of the intention must have caused the intentional thing. For when you intend not to move your hand, the correlate does not cause your hand to remain motionless, since this result is the same as what would have happened had these events been absent. This is quite different from the situation in which you intend to move your hand, for here the correlate of the intention does cause your hand to move: here your hand would not have moved if your intention and its correlate had been absent. Certainly, there are occasional cases of overdetermination in which, say, a twitch would have caused your hand to move even if your decision had not. But such cases are exceptions, whereas when you let your body remain where it is, the rule is that the outcome is the same as it would have been had you made no decision.

I take this to be further evidence that we do not experience our decisions or intentions as causes when we act. For we take them to control our bodies in the same way whether we act or refrain from acting. But the latter case shows that intentional control is not essentially causal, for there is not at any level any causing of an instance of letting something happen. Of course, when we perform bodily acts we normally cause some change in the physical world, but that is another matter than mental antecedents being causally operative in producing bodily movements.

This concludes my exposition of how CE could be worked out in a framework of a neutral monism. I have tried to indicate where my framework conflicts with Honderich's, but the points of disagreement may be more numerous than I suspect. Nevertheless, put against the background of state of the art in the philosophy of mind, it is the overall similarity between our approaches that is most striking. I have therefore found it very stimulating and fruitful to compare our views, and I am grateful for having been offered the opportunity to do so.

## References

BonJour, L. (1998), *In Defense of Pure Reason* (Cambridge: Cambridge University Press).
Honderich, T. (2004), *On Consciousness* (Edinburgh: Edinburgh University Press).
Honderich, T. (2006), 'Radical externalism', *Journal of Consciousness Studies*, **13** (7–8), pp. 3–13. [This issue]
Persson, I. (1985), *The Primacy of Perception: Towards a Neutral Monism* (Lund: Gleerup).
Persson, I. (2005), *The Retreat of Reason: A Dilemma in the Philosophy of Life* (Oxford: Clarendon Press).

## REPLY TO PERSSON BY HONDERICH

The philosophy of neutral monism was espoused in different ways by William James, Ernst Mach and Bertrand Russell. Its central idea, according to reports, is that what exists is a single kind of primal stuff, not in itself either physical or mental, but stuff that has in it or about it at least the possibility, indeed something more than the possibility, of both physical and mental aspects, attributes or characters. A little differently, neutral monism is said to be the doctrine that nature consists in primitive elements, events, neutral experiences, pure experiences, experiences, or sensibilia, these being neutral between the physical and the mental, but events or whatever that can be combined or organized into the one sort of thing or the other.

Here is Russell's summary.

> Neutral Monism — as opposed to idealistic monism and materialistic monism — is the theory that the things commonly regarded as mental and the things commonly regarded as physical do not differ in respect of any intrinsic property possessed by the one set and not by the other, but different only in respect of arrangement and context. The theory may be illustrated by comparison with a postal directory, in which the same names appear twice over, once in alphabetical and once in geographical order (Russell, 1956, p. 139).

The simple comparison may be misleading. So may another of Russell's remarks about something that may have influenced him, that matter had been shown to be less material by recent physics and that mind had been shown to be less mental by recent psychology, particularly behaviourism.

It may be better to regard historical neutral monism — Hume is sometimes conscripted into it — as related impulses rather than an idea. They face considerable difficulties. One is the basic obscurity in the impulse to regard what exists both as one stuff and somehow two stuffs, or on the way to two stuffs. If this is avoided by taking what exists as itself consisting in what is neither physical or mental, but only raw material for the later production or logical construction of the physical and the mental, then the primal stuff is indeed mysterious. In what way does it exist?

Are there similarities between Radical Externalism and historical neutral monism? There are. The latter doctrine, so to speak, registers two sides of a reality. And it is part of Radical Externalism that there is a bottom reality to which we bring our conceptualizing activities. That reality is spoken of, certainly not in a developed way, in terms of Kant's noumenal world and the like — what there was before our arrival on the scene and what there is there now wholly independent of us and is likely to be forever. It is that of which our conception of the physical world in its two parts or levels is true, and it is that of which the concepts of worlds of perceptual consciousness is true.

Two things need to be distinguished there, however. One similarity between Radical Externalism and historical neutral monism is in fact trivial. Registering sides or parts of reality is no distinctive feature of these two things. They have endless counterparts in science, philosophy, religion, politics, economics and so on down. In a multitude of ways, all or more likely some of ur-reality is attended to, selected, concentrated on. There is a distinctive and hence larger similarity, though, between the two things. This is simply that they are in the same line of life, giving an account of consciousness or the mind and relating it to the rest of what exists, and that they do this, in so far as a general or covering characterization is possible, by registering two sides of a reality.

The distinctive similarity, however, seems overwhelmed by differences between the two things. Traditional neutral monism gives no further characterization of consciousness than what you have heard. Or rather, as it may be better to say again, it has within it impulses of entirely different kinds. It can be no surprise that despite Russell's separating it from idealistic monism and materialistic monism, it *has* been taken to have in it what makes it an antecedent of the mind-brain identity theory in the form of devout physicalism. It can be no surprise, either, given that it has the imprint of James on it, and is said to be about a fundamental reality that consists some kind or other of experiences, that it can be taken to fall towards if not into spiritualism.

Those are great differences between traditional neutral monism and Radical Externalism. They can be described in another way as important — and which reminds us that they are numerous. There are no counterparts whatever in the neutral monism of the past to Radical Externalism's adequacy criteria for for theories of consciousness, its insistence on what is given in consciousness, worlds of perceptual consciousness, its externalism as against neuralism, reflective consciousness as representation in a certain sense, its character of near-physicalism, and its assumption of a reality beyond our ken that did or could have preceded any beginning of consciousness whatever and could or will persist in the absence of any remaining taint of consciousness.

Come now to Ingmar Persson's intriguing and challenging piece on his own neutral monism and on Radical Externalism. He takes the latter theory as the claim that what it is to be conscious in any way is for something to exist in a certain specified way. That is true but of course incomplete.

That it is incomplete, by the way, is a principal reason for speaking of the theory as Radical Externalism rather than Consciousness as Existence. The theory is not merely that what it is to be conscious is for something to exist in a certain way, of course. It is for something to exist outside your head in the case of perceptual consciousness and for things to exist there and in your head in the case of reflective consciousness, and to exist in both places in the case of affective consciousness.

Persson proceeds in his piece by way of a certain sentence.

> (CE) A full description of what it is intrinsically like to be in the state of perceiving (or being perceptually conscious of) some objects consists in a description of these objects, of there being such and such things in such and such spatial relations to each other (p. 128).

That sentence may be taken as an understanding of part of Radical Externalism or Consciousness as Existence if the sentence is taken in a certain way, as expressing the following statement ordinarily understood.

- ($CE^1$) To be perceptually conscious of some objects is for the objects to have a place in space and time in a certain way.

That can be enlarged into something else by specifying further what the existence comes to beyond the spatiotemporality — the objects have perceived properties and have both a neural and another dependency.

We get to Persson's neutral monism, if I may abstract from some of his terminology, of which my grasp is unsure, by putting a quite different understanding on the sentence CE. As he says, he considers what you get if you take the notion of existence employed in CE to be neutral between the mental and the physical (p. 129). As a result of that large change, and a couple of others, if I am right, his neutral monism is to be taken as conveying the following statement.

- (CE$^2$) To be perceptually conscious of some objects is for those objects, and also a human body or the like, to exist or be related spatially in a primitive and indefinable sense that is neutral between mental and physical existence.

That proposition is a best summary of Persson's form of neutral monism in my understanding of it. Certainly it is a contentful doctrine that makes brief summary uncertain.

Its similarity to Radical Externalism, you can first suppose, is that both theories escape cranialism — they do not make perceptual consciousness a cranial fact but rather take it to consist in an outside state of affairs. They are alike in supposing there is a bottom-level reality. Further, they do not suppose that consciousness has in it a subject, container, act or relation to anything. Maybe as in the case of Radical Externalism, all such supposed facts, or some of them, become such facts of consciousness itself as its subjectivity in the sense of individuality or uniqueness, and also facts of the explanation of consciousness as distinct from its own nature.

But the extent to which this neutral monism is different from Radical Externalism — the difference between CE$^1$ and CE$^2$ is greater than the similarity. We can look at this matter and others in terms of Persson's four questions, of which the first is that of the relation between *neutral* existence and *physical* existence.

To say something or other exists neutrally, I take it, is to say that it exists in such a way that it may also be physical or mental. To say that it may be physical, we learn, is to say that it may have an existence that is *independent* of the existence of other things, such as states of observers' bodies or external causes of such states. Maybe this independent existence is had only by elementary particles.

What is closest in Radical Externalism to Persson's thinking of independent existence is not the physical world as conceived in Radical Externalism and indeed elsewhere. The perceived part of the physical world *does* indeed have a dependence on the states of the bodies of observers generally. Something's being coloured has a dependence on us. So too, evidently, is the other level of the physical world, the theorized world of fundamental science, what there is as registered in our physical theories. What is therefore closest in Radical Externalism to things of independent existence is what we have been speaking of in terms of a noumenal world.

The difference between Radical Externalism and the neutral monism, say between CE$^1$ and CE$^2$, in terms of neutral existence and independent existence, is therefore considerable or great. For a start, neutral monism makes immediate use of its idea of neutral existence, whatever is to be said of it, in characterizing perceptual consciousness. As to objection or question with respect to neutral monism, let me say only that something will be said soon of the primitiveness or indefinability of the 'is' of independent existence.

The second question is said to be what it is that makes perceptual consciousness a mental state. The answer is that the existence of the objects in which your being perceptually conscious consists is an existence *dependent* on states of the observer's body and also causes of those states — light rays and so forth.

Here, arguably, there is some degree of similarity to Radical Externalism. Both accounts conceive of perceptual consciousness in terms of things outside the head that are dependent somehow or other on things inside the head. As in comparison with historical neutral monism, much more of those things is said in Radical Externalism, I take it — in terms of how they serve to satisfy the theory-constraints of the reality of consciousness, what is given in consciousness, and so on. But that in itself does not put in question the seemingly arguable degree of similarity.

Something else does reduce the similarity very dramatically, however, maybe remove the argument.

The state of affairs that is your being perceptually conscious, according to the neutral monism, say the state of affairs when you see this page, is said, strictly speaking, to be dependent on causes external to the observer by way of a certain connection.

> Strictly speaking, a qualification should however be inserted. What is causally explained is that my brain enters a certain state. This neural state is nomologically correlated with my mental state ... in the sense given by Honderich's 'Correlation Hypothesis' [2004, p. 23] (p. 131).

So the state of affairs of your being perceptually conscious, according to neutral monism, is correlated with your neural activity in the way specified by the Correlation Hypothesis, a fundamental part of a theory of mind and brain supplanted in my own thinking by the theory of Radical Externalism. What is fundamental to the Correlation Hypothesis, in brief, is that brain states are nomically sufficient for or necessitate conscious states, the conscious states thus being necessary to the brain states. What is relevant now is the neural sufficiency.

To come to the point, Persson's theory has it that your brain states are sufficient for the existence of objects outside your head. He reiterates this, I take it, when he compares his view with a quoted line of mine denying neural sufficiency for perceptual consciousness. It must seem that the theory has gone badly wrong. Is it really being asserted that what is in your head is sufficient for the existence of objects outside your head? Well, something has not gone badly wrong in a way that first comes to mind.

To return to $CE^2$, what it asserts is that what it is for you to be perceptually conscious is for things outside your head to exist *in a primitive and indefinable sense*. We have added to this that the existence, whatever it is, is guaranteed by your neurally. This allows us to speak of the things having mental existence. But it remains the case that the theory has not gone badly wrong in a certain way — it is not as if it is being claimed that *physical* things outside your head have their physical existence guaranteed by your brain.

That *does* leave us, however, with a large problem, now necessarily more a focus of attention than when we first contemplated $CE^2$. In *what* sense do things neutrally exist? We are told, you will remember, that this sense in which things exist is primitive and indefinable. That seems to bring us perilously close to the idea that we are being given a theory of perceptual consciousness to the effect that perceptual consciousness is indefinable, that references to it must taken as primitive. We seem to be a long way from, indeed out of sight of, Radical Externalism and from $CE^1$.

Something else comes to mind. Do we actually have an externalism in this neutral monism, an escape from cranialism with respect to perceptual consciousness? In this theory, perceptual consciousness consists in objects that exist in a way that is left obscure. Someone tough-minded is going to say light is not shed in such a way as definitely to give us an externalism by the reference in CE to descriptions of objects in spatial relations. Someone tough-minded might wonder if Persson has had fully in mind, in thinking of a comparison with Radical Externalism, that it does have as its basis a literal and plain proposition about things outside the head.

Will we learn more from the answers to Persson's other questions, of which the third is that of the difference between perceptual consciousness and reflective consciousness?

He remarks, with reason, that what has so far been said in Radical Externalism of your thinking of something, maybe your departed brother, is that this consists in the occurrence of representations, these being items in a world of perceptual consciousness or in your head that have effects that were also some effects of your brother.

Of these representations, he reports BonJour's view that they cannot ultimately be a matter of something external to them, such relations to other things as conventions of language. Is the gist of this that when some marks or sounds stand for something, the supposed convention or the like cannot be *certain* properties of the marks or sounds? And hence that at least some representations are representative on account of intrinsic or non-relational facts? Well, not enough is said to make this line of thought explicit.

At any rate, we come to Persson's view of images, from which he hopes to advance to an account of representations generally. An image represents a thing, we have it, in virtue of being like it, say in colour, and also being in a way derived from such things. A possible counter-example comes to mind. It is not clear why, as a result of the given definition of an image, that black kittens do not represent their black mother. He allows at least that even if his view of images is persuasive, we still seem to be a considerable way from an account of abstract thought, that to try to give an account of it is a daunting task.

I shall not embark on an attempt to make sense of representation, indeed of the large subject of *meaning*. The question to which Radical Externalism is an answer is this: What is it for someone or something to be conscious? That general questions calls for, or first calls for, a general answer. That answer must have to do with general kinds of things. The level of generality can be taken as set by the history of the question.

Radical Externalism gives such an answer when it claims that what it is for your to think of your departed brother is for certain things to exist in your world of perceptual consciousness or in your brain — things having a general character known to us all but evidently in need of an adequate analysis. It is the claim of Radical Externalism that you have an answer to its question without the further analysis. It is worth remembering that good and great answers to questions in science, philosophy and the rest are at least typically answers such that more analysis of them can be asked.

Leaving aside Persson's reluctance to rank affective consciousness with perceptual and reflective consciousness, for which reluctance there may be something to be said, I come to his fourth question. Does Radical Externalism really allow for what we all believe, that consciousness is efficacious, say that our thoughts and desires are essential to the explanations of our actions?

Persson remarks that what we take to be causal is in an ordinary sense the perceptual consciousness rather than the content or object of the consciousness. Well, as you will anticipate, the pieces of philosophy inserted into what we ordinarily say are pieces of philosophy rejected by Radical Externalism. In place of taking your awareness itself to be a mental state in your head related to a physical object, it takes your awareness to consist in an object in a world of perceptual consciousness. Persson gives no reason for thinking that the thing cannot be causal.

As for the idea that logical relations explain beliefs, with these things certainly being taken as events or occurrences rather than abstract objects, this is difficult for me to contemplate. When someone blunders, and from *if p then q*, and *p*, comes to believe other than *q*, I suppose his belief had a cause. Is it possible to say so and suppose that his belief that *q*, if he comes to that, would have no cause?

Is epiphenomenalism escaped if you suppose that some kind of a neural correlate of a belief somehow conceived was causal with respect to an action? That, as it seems to me, is on the way to the proposition that beliefs make no difference, which does indeed seem to me to fly in the way of experience and all reasonable theory (Honderich, 1988, pp. 154–63). Of course the matter is complicated.

We are also wide apart on the subject of causation, which cannot get much discussion here. Persson's argument is that causal connection is *experienced*, that we do not experience our perceptions causing our actions, and hence that they do not do so. Whatever else is to be said, it does not take bravery to deny the initial general proposition. Suppose I exert myself, do some pushing, and a sofa is afterwards in a corner. Do I know the exertion *caused* the sofa to be in the corner? Not if counterparts of the exertion in counterpart situations are not followed by sofas in corners. Ergo I do not experience causation in the relevant sense.

Now to revert too quickly but necessarily to where we began, that was the question of whether Radical Externalism is a form of Persson's neutral monism. You will anticipate that my answer is no. The similarities between Radical Externalism and this neutral monism (p. 142), and also between Radical Externalism and historical neutral monism (p. 139), are indeed overwhelmed by differences between them. The points of disagreement are to me not only numerous but fundamental. You will know that I remain inclined to one of these theories.

## References

Honderich, Ted (1988), *A Theory of Determinism: The Mind, Neuroscience and Life Hopes* (Oxford: Oxford University Press).

Russell, Bertrand (1956), *Logic & Knowledge Essays 1901–1950*, ed. Robert C. Marsh (London: George Allen & Unwin).

Stephen Priest

# *Radical Internalism*

Honderich claims that for a person to be perceptually conscious is for a world to exist. I decide what this means, and whether it could be true, in the opening section *Consciousness and Existence*. In *Honderich's Phenomenology*, I show that Honderich's theory is essentially anticipated in the ideas and *Ideas* of Husserl. In the third section, *Radical Interiority*, I argue that although phenomenology putatively eschews ontology of mind, and Honderich construes his position as near-physicalism, Honderich's insights are only truths because we are spiritual substances.

## Consciousness and Existence

Honderich says

> What it is for you to be perceptually conscious now is for a world somehow to exist, a certain changing totality of things (2000, p. 67).

Much rests on 'perceptual' here, otherwise it is doubtful that this biconditional holds.

For example, there is no contradiction in the supposition that there are conscious states but no things. Bodily sensations, some moods and pervasive states of anxiety or euphoria are, in some sense, conscious states but are not things. Nor do they necessarily 'take' objects, so do not necessarily take things as objects. Globally, there logically and metaphysically could be a pure consciousness utterly devoid of contents, for example, the emptiness of mind on certain Buddhist views.[1] If this kind of Buddhism is true then it is psychologically or

---

[1] In referring to *anatta* (Sanskrit *anatman*) it is arguably necessary to give up talk of consciousness, *viññāna*. For *anatta*, see Rahula: 1967 pp. 26 (fn. 2), 52–3, 55–7, 63 (fn.1), 64, 66, 77 and for *viññāna* pp. 23 ff., 53, 65. Alexander Norman has suggested to me, rightly I think, that *anatman* is not a 'state'. Norman says the emptiness of *objects* is a property (roughly, their being essentially constituted by their relations and having no intrinsic essence). I maintain that the emptiness of *consciousness* is the infinite interiority of the soul (*malgré* the etymology of *anatman*). [footnote continued overleaf]

phenomenologically false that things or contents are necessary for consciousness. *A fortiori*, it is false that any world is necessary for consciousness.[2]

Conversely, there is no incoherence in the commonsense realist view that there could be a world without consciousness. Unless Berkeley's view, or similar, is correct the existence of a world does not entail the existence of consciousness and the fact, if it is a fact, that it is not possible to conceive a world without conceiving it as an actual or possible object of consciousness does not entail that it could not exist without consciousness, consciousness of it, or that particular conception of it. So, it is coherent to suppose that something's being an object is not sufficient for 'a world somehow to exist', except either in a highly abstract or metaphysical sense of 'world' (in which, say, $w$ is a possible world in which at least one intentional object exists) or in the phenomenological sense that even an object cannot be presented except in a subjective field or phenomenological space.[3]

If 'perceptual consciousness' means 'intentional consciousness' then it is analytic that if there is perceptual consciousness then there is at least one intentional object. However, this conditional tautology holds whatever the substantial facts of the philosophy of mind.

Suppose the use of 'what it is for' implies that $x$'s being perceptually conscious is identical with the existence of a world. Honderich's expression

> The conception of your perceptual consciousness as a certain totality of existing things ... (2000, p. 71)

---

St. John of the Cross says that if the soul (*alma*) reflects from (only) a natural point of view (*naturalmente*) '[...] it never continues in one state; for all is ascending and descending'. (St. John of the Cross, 1916, p. 164) On both of these Buddhist and the Christian views, an utterly changeless inner space is where my experiences happen.

[2] It is a consequence of these doctrines that (*pace* Brentano *et al.*) intentionality is not necessary for consciousness. I do not pursue this here because Honderich is unsympathetic to doctrines of intentionality.

[3] Suppose by 'a world' is meant 'a world that is an actual or possible object of consciousness'. Being a possible object of consciousness does not entail being an object of consciousness, so does not entail that consciousness exists nor, *a fortiori*, that perceptual consciousness exists. It does not follow that $x$ is perceptually conscious if and only if a world exists because it does not follow that $x$ is perceptually conscious if a world exists. If a world is an actual object of consciousness it does follow that consciousness exists but it does not follow from the existence of that world, or the consciousness it entails, that perceptual consciousness exists. It is consistent to suppose that a world is an object of consciousness only because it is an object of thought and not because it is an object of perception. It follows that the existence of a world that is an actual object of consciousness is not sufficient for the existence of perceptual consciousness. If by 'a world' is meant 'a world that is the object of a perceptual consciousness' then the thesis is analytic and, again, not substantive.

implies that the relation is identity if and only if '$x$ exists as $y$' implies '$x$ is $y$'. What kind of identity is this? Is it necessary or contingent, type or token? Is it known *a priori* or *a posteriori*? If it is false that '$x$ is perceptually conscious' is true if and only if 'a world exists is true' then the sense of '$x$ is perceptually conscious' is not the sense of 'a world exists'. Do '$x$ is perceptually conscious' and 'a world exists' differ in sense but not extension? Clearly not, because they differ in truth conditions.

Suppose the use of 'what it is for' implies that $x$'s being perceptually conscious is *constituted by* the existence of a world. Then the relation between perceptual consciousness and the existence of a world is *is made up of*. If it makes sense to talk of perceptual consciousness as constituted, then *prima facie* candidates for constituents are phenomenological constituents and neurological constituents. On some phenomenologies, perceptual consciousness is a whole that has a subject, a *noesis*, and noematic content, as parts. On some materialisms, perceptual consciousness exists only because a certain brain process exists rather as some water, macroscopically described, exists because some $H_2O$ exists. It is not plausible that perceptual consciousness should be constituted by the existence of a world, if a world is that towards which perceptual consciousness is directed, or has as contents.

Suppose 'what it is for $x$ to be perceptually conscious is for a world to exist' is true if and only if being perceptually conscious may be *reduced to* the existence of a world. This is not what Honderich means because it is inconsistent with the reality of consciousness; a tenet that he thinks any plausible theory of consciousness has to observe. Nevertheless, as an unintended entailment it is plausible. Consciousness of a set of objects might be ontologically nothing over and above the obtaining of those objects *qua* phenomenological objects. If there is pain there might be no feeling of the pain 'over and above' the phenomenological pain. If there is phenomenological red, there might be no consciousness of phenomenological red 'over and above' the obtaining of phenomenological red. Phenomenological red is, then, the end of the story not the beginning of a story about consciousness. Neurology, then, ends in phenomenology but consciousness does not begin with phenomenology. Where, pre-theoretically, I think of my own consciousness there seems to be nothing. However, this consciousness is not nothing but no-thing-ness.

What is the world which exists if and only if perceptual consciousness exists? Where is it? Honderich claims:

> What it is for you to be aware of your surroundings is for, in a certain sense, there to be certain things with various properties in space and time (2000, p. 67).

Suppose existing in space-time is a sufficient condition for being physical; it follows that a subjective world is physical and, if there is only one actual space–time, then a subjective world is in the only actual space–time. Nevertheless Honderich says

> Your world of perceptual consciousness is exactly not the physical world (2000, p. 72).

A subjective world is

> ... a constituent ... of the physical world (2000, p. 73).

Even so, Honderich says

> No world of perceptual consciousness is identical in its contents with the perceived part of the physical world — or of course the other part (2000, p. 72).

Although a subjective world at a time is not identical with a perceived part of the world at that time, I take it that a perceived part of the world is a part of a subjective world. Honderich says about his subjective world 'mine now consists in things in this room and outside the window' (2000, p. 67). These are perceived parts of the world and parts of a subjective world so if the perceived parts of the world are not identical with a subjective world they must be identical with a part of a subjective world. If perceptual consciousness is to be explained reductively, in terms of subjective worlds, then perceptual consciousness and the perceived part of the world that is its object are nothing 'over and above' part of a subjective world. If a subjective world is not exhausted by a perceived part of the physical world, what else does it consist in?

Honderich says 'a person is certainly part of it' (2000, p. 67) so a subjective world is at least both a perceived part of the physical world and a person, plausibly; the perceiver, or subject of perceptual consciousness. Because, like Sartre, Honderich thinks that it is

> inconsistent to speak of something as within or a part of consciousness and also hidden (2000, p. 68),

the subject can only feature in a subjective world as an appearance. Redescribed as a subjective world, perceptual consciousness has only the parts it seems to have.[4]

Honderich thinks the existence of a subjective world is

> ... no more than a kind of claim as to the existence of things, not exactly standard physical things (2000, p. 67).

When he says

> what it is ... is a totality of different things in space and time (2000, pp. 72–3)

'different things' had better not commit Honderich to a set of physical things numerically distinct from and extra to the totality of physical objects in space-time. This would be inconsistent with his thesis that perceived parts of physical things are parts of a subjective world and it is not clear where in space-time extra entities could be located.

Honderich says about a subjective world:

> It is prior to and a constituent ... of the physical world (2000, p. 73).

What does 'prior to' mean here? Suppose $a$ is prior to $b$ if and only if $a$ is a necessary condition for $b$. Then $a$ may be ontologically prior to $b$, logically prior to $b$ or epistemologically prior to $b$. There is no reason why the world, in Honderich's sense, should be ontologically prior to the physical world. Some sound argument for strong idealism would be required to show that the physical world only exists if some portion of it tied to consciousness exists.

If a portion of the physical world were logically prior to the physical world then it would be contradictory to hold that the physical world could exist without that portion of it. The claim would have to be shown to entail some contradiction, by *reductio ad absurdum* (or similar). *Prima facie* there is no such contradiction, so no reason to suppose any perceived part of the physical world is logically prior to the physical world.

If a portion of the physical world dependent on perceptual consciousness is epistemologically prior to the physical world then it is not possible to have knowledge of the physical world without having knowledge of that portion of it. This entails a kind of empiricism: No knowledge of a physical world is possible unless there is knowledge of some part of it that is perceived. There could in principle be perception of part of the physical world without that perception being

---

[4] See Priest (2000). Part of Sartre's repudiation of the unconscious rests the impossibility of consciousness hiding anything from itself. I maintain that consciousness is ordinarily hidden from itself by its own contents.

necessary or sufficient for knowledge of that part. (Suppose, for example, that perceptual acquaintance with $x$ is neither necessary nor sufficient for propositional knowledge of $x$.) It requires some argument for empiricism to show that the perception of the physical world is necessary for knowledge of it. Suppose, on the contrary, that some being knows about the physical world by the exercise of *intuitive intellect* (that is, has the faculty Kant says we lack) but has no empirical faculties.

Honderich claims that for there to be perceptual consciousness is for a world to exist. What does 'exist' mean here? Honderich seeks a middle way between 'A perceives $x$' and '$x$ exists' where '$x$ exists' is consistent with 'A does not perceive $x$'. 'A perceives $x$' does nothing to analyse 'perceptual consciousness' in perspicacious terms or explain what perceptual consciousness is. '$x$ exists' is consistent with there being no perceptual consciousness. Honderich rules out '*to exist for you*'. The work of explaining perceptual consciousness is done by the concept of a subjective world rather than any special analysis of 'exists'.

Honderich needs to say more about the structure and content of a subjective world to show how perceptual consciousness could be explained in terms of it. As things stand, the concept is left at an intuitive level: My subjective world includes the word processor, thoughts about Honderich's work, the tops of my hands, parts of the keyboard etc. Is there a causal relation running from subject to subjective world (but not to the whole objective world in space–time even though to part of it)? What is the phenomenology of subjective worlds? Does a subjective world have an inside but no outside, a lived interiority but no physical exteriority? Could it then be physical? Is a subjective world uniquely tagged to an individual, or an individual at a time, or could we exchange subjective worlds, say by exchanging physical positions?

## Honderich's Phenomenology

Honderich says

... for me a world exists (1998, p. 140).

A major motivation for Husserl's phenomenology (paradigmatically in *Ideas* I) is answering the question How is the world possible? He means: How can there be a world for me?

Following Kant (in the *Critique of Pure Reason*) Husserl draws a distinction between transcendental idealism (*transzendentale Idealismus*) and transcendental realism (*transzendentale Realismus*).

Transcendental realism is the thesis that the world (of physical objects) exists independently of the human conscious subject. Transcendental idealism can be understood in two main ways: (a) Essential features of the physical world are bestowed upon it by the consciousness of the subject, and (b) The conscious subject has to be capable of various constituting 'acts' to detect the physical world (for there to 'be a world' for that subject). (a) entails that if there is a world there is a subject. (b) entails that if there is knowledge of a world there is a subject. Reading (a) is strongly or ontologically idealist. Reading (b) is weakly or non-ontologically idealist. Reading Husserl in way (b) is consistent with Honderich's physical realism. Reading Husserl in way (a) is not. Husserl himself oscillates between these positions but the less crude reading of him is (b).

Honderich thinks

> ... *all* of my consciousness now...consists in the existence of a world (1998, p. 140).

He and Husserl share the insight that consciousness may be presented (to itself) as though it could be all there is. This is a phenomenological fact that makes solipsism thinkable. Husserl exploits this fact to draw the crucial distinction between the world of the natural attitude and the world of *epoché*. The world of the natural attitude is the commonsensical world we ordinarily believe in before we engage in phenomenology. It contains physical objects and other people. It is always 'already there' in a completely taken for granted way, and the *epoché* is the act of putting the world of the natural attitude in brackets or parentheses. It is methodological agnosticism about the world of the natural attitude. So, if *p* is any proposition of the natural attitude, after the *epoché*, *p* might be either true or false. The phenomenological agnosticism adopted by the inquirer is: *p* is neither believed nor disbelieved, which does not entail any denial of the existence of the external world. It is neither believing nor disbelieving in the world of commonsense. All scientific, metaphysical and theological beliefs are suspended (or 'dislocated'). Husserl thinks these are premised on the natural attitude.

The result of Husserl's *epoché* is Honderich's

> my perceptual consciousness now consists in the existence of a world (1998, p. 140).

Husserl calls this 'the world (or 'field') of transcendental subjectivity'. 'Transcendental' in this context means 'condition for the possibility of experience'. 'Subjective' means 'pertaining to that which thinks or experiences' and 'mine'. 'Subjective' gives semantic contrast to 'objective' in claiming that the world of the natural attitude is objective.

Having drawn this distinction, Husserl shows how the world of the natural attitude is 'constituted' by acts of consciousness. He thinks the (objective) world is an achievement of consciousness. We should not read this as ontological idealism. He is trying to describe how the world can be a world for me.

Like Sartre, Honderich maintains that it is

> ... a falsehood ... that we can attach sense to talk of a reality-behind with respect to consciousness itself (1998, p. 142).

Honderich and Husserl share the view that while objects in the external world admit of an appearance/reality distinction (because they may be presented veridically or non-veridically to consciousness) consciousness does not admit of an appearance/reality distinction in the ways in which it is presented to itself. (Of course this view is consistent with consciousness being neurologically grounded, acts of consciousness being individuated through intended objects in the external world, and so on). Husserl means that after the *epoché* a conscious state's obtaining and its having a phenomenology are the same thing. Honderich agrees with Husserl about the appearance/reality distinction:

> that is not a distinction within consciousness. The distinction presupposes consciousness (1998, p. 142).

This is part of what Husserl means by the absolute being of consciousness in *Ideas I*.[5] Absolute being does not admit of an appearance reality distinction. After the *epoché*, appearance is treated as reality.

Husserl also agrees with Honderich's Cartesian claim that

> There isn't any other experiential access to it [consciousness] than the single one we've all got (1998, p. 143).

Indeed, his whole method of phenomenological 'description' is premised on this assumption. Husserl does not call this access 'introspection'. Introspection may only occur in the pre-phenomenological world of the natural attitude.

There are two differences between Honderich and Husserl on intentionality. Honderich says:

> The theories ... having to do with aboutness or intentionality, cannot be regarded as successful (1998, p. 143).

---

[5] See Priest (1999). Husserl is a fundamental ontologist *malgré lui*.

One difference is that Husserl thinks that intentionality is the essence of consciousness. Husserlian phenomenology is strongly essentialist. Husserl devotes many pages to discovering the essence of consciousness, the essence of perception, the essence of a physical object and so on. Despite the subjectivism of the *epoche* he is a strong realist about essences. (The later existentialism of Sartre *et al.* is a conscious reaction against Husserl's essentialism). The other difference is Husserl does not think the claim that intentionality is the essence of consciousness is a theoretical claim. He thinks that the intentional structures of consciousness survive the *epoche* and may be described, read off consciousness. Honderich says

> We would not get anything useful by ... taking perceptual consciousness to consist in awareness of subjective things — representations, sense-data, or the like (1998, p. 144).

Husserl too does not think the world after the *epoché* a world of psychological impressions or sense data. The *epoché* is a 'phenomenological reduction' in which the world is reduced to the appearance of it. Appearances, or 'phenomena' are not mental or physical. Husserl tries to remain agnostic about philosophical theories of perception in doing phenomenology.

> ... each of us ... distinguish[es] herself or himself ... from all else (1998, p. 145).

Each of us distinguishes two portions of what is, the portion that I am and the remainder that I am not. There can be no *physicalist* explanation of this distinction. The distinction obtains, so physicalism is false.[6]

Honderich thinks

> In the absence of the subject, there would not exist anything of the world whose existence is what perceptual consciousness consists in (1998, p. 145).

Husserl thinks the world of transcendental subjectivity (in a way, Honderich's consciousness as existence) presupposes a subject. He calls the subject after the *epoché* 'the transcendental ego' 'I pole', or 'pure ego'. This is the phenomenologically reduced subject. It is not a strange, extra, metaphysical entity, and certainly not a Cartesian soul.

---

[6] Each of us divides what is into two mutually exclusive and jointly exhaustive parts: the part that one is and the remainder that one is not. That this distinction obtains is a metaphysical mystery, a presupposition of the ordinary intelligibility of the world as well as philosophical questions, conspicuously the problem of other minds. As so often, naturalistic philosophy barely contains the equipment to pose the problem, let alone address it.

One's ordinary conception of oneself as a psycho-physical whole human being with an empirical identity is suspended by the *epoché*. One's ordinary self-conception is part of the natural attitude. However, in a very abstract sense I survive the *epoché*. I still remain the source of a subjective point of view, not on the objective world any more, but on reduced phenomenological (*noematic*) contents. We may think of the transcendental ego as abstracted from our empirical self-conception (even though it is a concrete object of post-*epoché* description).

Honderich says

> ... there is but one world (1998, p. 146).

Husserl is not concerned with ontological multiplication either. Honderich says

> The world in which my present perceptual consciousness seems to consist is surely spatial. ... So with time (1998, p. 148).

Husserl thinks there is a phenomenology of spatio-temporal relations, which may be described. Phenomenological spatio-temporal relations are not objective spatio-temporal relations (which are described scientifically). He thinks that objective science is grounded or founded phenomenologically. (Merleau-Ponty says in *Phenomenology of Perception* that unless we could do things like hike across a landscape we could not have cartography or geography.)[7]

Like Husserl, Honderich, does not think there are two sets of things, phenomenological things and objective things. Things may be described phenomenologically or objectively and, like Honderich, he thinks the phenomenology makes objectivity possible for us. Honderich says

> If something didn't look different from different points of view, it wouldn't be a chair (1998, p. 151).

Husserl thinks it is part of the essence of a physical object to be presented through profiles, or perspectives (*Abschattungen*). This demarcates physical objects sharply from emotions or moods for example.[8] There can be a house for me because I can be visually presented with

---

[7] Husserl's main discussions of the phenomenology of time and space are in the 1905 *Lectures on the Phenomenology of Internal Time Consciousness* and in *Ding und Raum* [*Thing and Space*] (1907).

[8] Daniel Came has drawn my attention to Nietzsche's view that all cognition is necessarily perspectival, in that there is no manner of apprehending an object of consciousness that is not shaped by subjective factors. Whether or not this quasi-Kantianism is true, physical objects, but not affective contents, present *Abschattungen*.

the front, this side, the back and so on. I can touch it and it is solid. The house is constructed as a whole object though my experiences of it. Because of this, when I see it I take it to be a whole even though I do not see the whole of it at any one time. This is an achievement of consciousness. (The transcendental imagination reads the preconceptions about it having a back, an inside, etc. into the present perception of it.) Husserl is trying to explain how there can be a house for me (or anyone) not how there can be a house.

Honderich talks about 'a real point of view' (1998, p. 153). Merleau-Ponty thinks that only a physical being can have a subjective point of view. (I can only see from where my head is. I can only be where my body is, etc.) These ideas about physical subjectivity are anticipated by Husserl in the second volume of *Ideas* but I do not pursue this here.

Honderich's 'subjective world' now appears a thoroughly phenomenological concept. Honderich is reducing perceptual consciousness to its contents, construing these contents realistically not idealistically, and implying that they have sufficient unity to be called 'a world'.

## Radical Interiority

Is Radical Externalism true? By adopting a phenomenological view, Honderich has adopted a Cartesian *methodological* standpoint. The existence with which he identifies consciousness is what is presented to a subject from their own first person singular point of view. Admittedly, this is a huge improvement on the anonymous or wholly third-person materialisms of the industrial age. It is a phenomenology of the screen age, a virtual mentalism for the epoch and the *epoché* of virtual reality.

However, in the conjunction of eight theses, Honderich is unknowingly committed to radical *internalism*:

(1) consciousness is something we *have* (Honderich, 2006, p. 4).[9]

This is right, if it means experiences are undergone and are logically private (by acquaintance) and inalienable. It at least entails the truth that we cannot have each other's token experiences. Floggings with the cat o' nine tails and haircuts are of course public and physical but they can only be 'had' in the sense of *undergone* if they entail having experiences.

(2) I know there is past, present and future (p. 4).

---

[9] In this section all page references are to this target article.

Honderich provides no explanation of the existence of past, present and future. The tripartite temporal taxonomy has no physicalist or scientific or empirical explanation (never has, never will). Any explanation that is not empirical or scientific is metaphysical or theological so if the existence of past, present, and future can be explained, it can only be explained metaphysically or theologically.

Empirically, I am presented to myself as 'between' the past and the future but it is phenomenologically misleading to think of oneself as located 'in' time. This might not be wrong at a historical or abstract level but it is a judgement *made on* the phenomenological facts, not a *given* fact. Existentially, you are the becoming past of the future. Why you should have the enormous cosmic privilege of being the demarcation between the past and the future is a mystery. It only admits of a theological explanation.

(3)   [I know] that representations represent (p. 4).

We have no scientific or empirical idea of what presence is. Derrida is wrong in his view that Western Metaphysics (whatever that is) has overtly or covertly privileged the metaphysics of presence. On the contrary, presence is suppressed by science. Science is a subject without a subject. (I leave aside the obvious construal of 'representations represent' as analytic.)

(4)   Consciousness is present to me, immediate, in no way a matter of inference (p. 5).

This might not be quite right as a claim about the contents of consciousness. There might be no unmediated content (for roughly the reasons amassed by Vico and Kant). Consciousness is an emptiness, a space, a phenomenological zone or field in which the world is presented. This is presented immediately. However, it is only presented immediately when devoid of content. The contents of consciousness hide consciousness from itself.

(5)   The most useful form of the proposition that consciousness is something we have is this: with respect to consciousness, *there is no difference between appearance and reality.* With consciousness, what there seems to be is what there is. What there seems to be is all there is (p. 5).

This is right if consciousness is the void or emptiness of the Buddhists or the infinite interiority of the soul. That zone of absolute interiority that I am is given as the one-ness it is.

It is not right, if a claim about the content of consciousness. Then the claim is: if $p$ is a first person singular psychological ascription then if $p$ is believed then $p$ is true. Although widely endorsed, this incorrigibility thesis is false. Suppose J.J.C. Smart wires me up so that those parts of my neurology that operate when and only when I believe I am in pain are operating. I scream and writhe appropriately. I believe I am in pain. However, I am not in pain. Therefore, consciousness admits of an appearance/reality distinction (and *pace* Wittgenstein, I can believe I am in pain and this belief can be false)[10]

> (6) It wasn't as if what seemed to be had, or given and or on hand, like the page, included something else as well. There wasn't something such that the rest of what was on hand was a *content* — there was not a container or vehicle. There wasn't any sign at all of this item raised up into being by ordinary philosophical talk of the contents of consciousness. There wasn't 'the mind' or 'the self', which still turns up in advanced philosophy that does not remember Hume's service in reminding us that we are aware of no such thing. ... There wasn't a relationship of intentionality, aboutness or directedness in your consciousness of the page (p. 5).

This is not right, even though very widely believed. Hume missed just about everything that really matters in introspection: the eternal present, absolute interiority, the presence of consciousness as an inside without an outside, the *me-ness* of my psychological interiority, the infinite inner space of the soul. Of course none of this is given as 'something else', as an extra discriminable item available within introspection. It is the subjective space where it all takes place.

Phenomenologically, the point about intentionality is right: the content of conscious is given without the consciousness of that content being given. (This means much of Husserlian phenomenology needs rethinking.)

> (7) *your world of perceptual consciousness* is things being in space and time, with such further properties as colour, and being dependent on a scientific or noumenal world underneath and also dependent on you neurally (p. 6).

Does consciousness depend on the neurological? On one level, the answer to this is *completely obvious*: 'Yes'. It needs no training in science to know that damage to the brain impairs the capacity to think. (That this knowledge is ancient is obvious from accounts of ancient warfare.) Indeed, this dependence is as obvious to Descartes, Berkeley, Hegel and the British Idealists as it is to Honderich: as obvious as

---

[10] Here I assume, for sake of argument, that there are neurological conditions sufficient for pain. Benedikt Göcke has suggested to me that felt pain is the cause of one's screaming, not the belief that one is in pain. Nevertheless, in the scenario, I believe I am in pain but I am not in pain and that is sufficient for the incorrigibility claim to fail.

blindness being caused by destruction of the eyes. It is wrong to think that dualism and idealism have been refuted by science.

However, what is the strength of this dependence? We only know that the neurological is *necessary* for thought and experience, we do not know that it is sufficient. We only know that the neurological is empirically necessary for thought and experience, we do not know that it is logically or metaphysically necessary. Because we know the operations of the brain are necessary for thinking we know, as a matter of logic, that thinking is sufficient for the operations of the brain. (This is the solution to the problem of mental causation. It follows from what we *do* know about the dependence of the mental on the physical that the mental causes the physical. If we take a probabilistic view of the physical causation of the neurological, the problem of overdetermination is avoided.)

Logically and metaphysically, consciousness does not depend on the brain. There is an infinite number of possible worlds in which your consciousness does not depend on your brain. There is no contradiction in talking of consciousness without the brain. Indeed, in talking of a *world of your own consciousness*, Honderich is more than half way to the insight that he is a spiritual substance. Consciousness is given *as existence* because it is a substance. Consciousness is given as *a world* because it is an inside without an outside. Honderich's claim that consciousness depends upon a noumenal world is right. If the existence of consciousness is explicable it is only explicable theologically. Science only explains exteriority: The prospects for a science of consciousness are nil.

(8)  The particular state of affairs in question, and your ongoing world of perceptual consciousness, are different from but also like other states of affairs and worlds (p. 6).

My subjective interiority is numerically distinct from yours but, at certain phenomenological levels, they are qualitatively similar. This is right but a crucial metaphysical issue is missed here. My consciousness is numerically distinct from Honderich's, Honderich's from Jonathan Lowe's and so on. That a consciousness is numerically distinct from any other is not a sufficient condition of its being mine. That some consciousness is one's own is an extra fact about that consciousness, not captured in any mental or physical description of it. There is a huge gulf between philosophers who can see the problem of being someone and those who cannot.[11] That you are one of these human beings (or at least very closely associated with it) is a necessary condition for your describing what is present to consciousness in the way Honderich or Husserl does. You do not inhabit your consciousness as one item amongst others. You perhaps pervade your consciousness, or if consciousness is understood as the soul, you are it.

(9) A world of perceptual consciousness is not the physical world (p. 6).

This is right. It is a private mental world, an absolute interiority, a substance.

If we conjoin the implications of Honderich's nine theses we obtain: (1) consciousness is private and inalienable, (2) Past, present and future are real, (3) The eternal now exists, (4) Consciousness is immediate, (5) Pure consciousness admits of no appearance reality distinction, (6) Hume missed everything important in introspection, (7) Consciousness depends on nothing or the *noumenal*, (8) Your absolute interiority is uniquely and mysteriously yours, (9) the world of consciousness is not the physical world. These properties of consciousness are properties of one another. They collectively entitle us to give up talk of 'consciousness' and replace this term by 'soul' or 'spiritual substance'.

## The Sense of Existence

Honderich says: 'a clear sense has been given or at least gestured at with respect to talk of existence.' (this journal) Does the 'consciousness as existence' doctrine entail: 'to be is to be perceived'? Materialists and idealists unwittingly face the embarrassing possibility that their philosophies are one and the same. Although idealism seems madness, or exotic wish-fulfilment, to materialists and although materialism seems a denial of thought to idealists, materialism entails: 'The mental is physical' and idealism entails 'The physical is mental'. Of course, physicalism entails the existence of a physical reality that is not mental, and idealism entails the existence of a mental reality that is not physical. Nevertheless, it is hard to see how the mental can be physical unless the physical is mental and hard to see how the physical

---

[11] See Nagel (1986) esp. the section 'Being Someone' and Priest (2000). Within anonymous or generalised thinking it is barely registered that someone is oneself. However, that you are this human being, or pervade it, or are centred on it, or view the world from it, is existentially shocking and empirically inexplicable. It only admits of a metaphysical or theological explanation. Inability to see the problem of being someone is symptomatic of physicalism and naturalism.

can be mental unless the mental is physical. At the crucial point of *identification* physicalism and idealism collapse into one another.

'What is existence?' cannot be answered by saying '$x$ exists if and only if $x$ is physical' or '$x$ exists if and only if $x$ is mental' or indeed, '$x$ exists if and only if $x$ is $F$'. Being is not being something. Being rather than not being is not the same as being something or other. It is not the same as it, or what it consists in, even if anything that is is something or other. This problem remains unsolved despite the efforts from Parmenides to Heidegger (from the beginning to the 'end' of philosophy.) I cannot pursue this here but my suggestion is: *Being is that which nothing lacks*, which should be taken in both senses.

## Internalist Questions

When Honderich writes, as noted in the beginning,

> What it is for you to be perceptually conscious now is for a world somehow to exist, *a certain changing totality of things* (2000, p. 67; my italics)

he needs to ask: What remains the same? Absolute interiority, the eternal now, *me-ness*, and subjective space have never changed and remain the same. The terms 'you', 'conscious' and 'now' of Honderich's claim denote the inside of the soul in which the kaleidoscope of Honderich's world changes.

Honderich's theory of consciousness needs to be enriched to explain the reality of the present, why someone is him, why there is a subjective interiority of his own being, why the contents of consciousness are presented as existence: as though they could be all there is. To answer these questions, Honderich will have to cut the thick mooring ropes that tie him to scientific materialism and realise he is a spiritual substance. After all, 'Descartes didn't make it up.'[12]

## References

Barnes, Jonathan (ed. 1987), *Early Greek Philosophy* (London: Penguin Books).
Flew, Antony and Priest, Stephen (ed. 2002), *A Dictionary of Philosophy* (London: Macmillan).
Heidegger, Martin (1986), *Sein und Zeit* (Tübingen: Max Niemeyer Verlag).
Honderich, T. (1998), 'Consciousness as existence', in *Current Issues in the Philosophy of Mind*, ed. A. O'Hear, Royal Institute of Philosophy Lectures 1996–7.
Honderich, T. (2000a), 'Consciousness and inner tubes', *Journal of Consciousness Studies*, **7** (7) pp. 51–62.

---

[12] I am grateful to Corine Besson, Daniel Came, Benedikt Göcke, Peter Hunter, Michael Inwood and Alexander Norman for useful discussion of the issues raised in this paper.

Honderich, T. (2000b), 'Consciousness as existence again', in *Proceedings of the Twentieth World Congress of Philosophy, Vol. 9: Philosophy of Mind*, ed. B. Elevitch (Bowling Green: Philosophy Documentation Center) and in *Theoria* June 2000.
Honderich, T. (2001), 'Consciousness as existence and the end of intentionality', in *Philosophy at the New Millenium*, ed. A. O'Hear, Royal Institute of Philosophy Lectures 2000–1 (Cambridge).
Honderich, T. (2004a), 'Consciousness as existence, devout physicalism, spiritualism', *Mind and Matter*, **2** (1), pp. 85–104.
Honderich, T. (2004b), *On Consciousness* (Edinburgh: Edinburgh University Press).
Honderich, T. (ed. 2005), *The Oxford Companion to Philosophy* Second Edition (Oxford: Oxford University Press).
Honderich, T. (2006), 'Radical externalism', *Journal of Consciousness Studies*, **13** (7–8), pp. 3–13. [This issue]
Husserl, Edmund (1931), *Ideas: General Introduction to Pure Phenomenology*, trans. W.R.B. Gibson (New York: Allen & Unwin; Macmillan).
Husserl, Edmund (1960a), *The Paris Lectures* trans. D. Cairns (The Hague: M. Nijhoff).
Husserl, Edmund (1960b), *Cartesian Meditations: an Introduction to Phenomenology* trans. D. Cairns (The Hague: M. Nijhoff).
Husserl, Edmund (1964), *The Phenomenology of Internal Time-Consciousness*, trans. J.S. Churchill (Bloomington, IN: Indiana University Press).
Husserl, Edmund (1969), *Formal and Transcendental Logic*, trans. D. Cairns (The Hague: M. Nijhoff.)
Husserl, Edmund (1970a), *The Crisis of European Sciences and Transcendental Phenomenology; An Introduction to Phenomenological Philosophy*, trans. D. Carr (Evanston, IL: Northwestern University Press).
Husserl, Edmund (1970b), *The Idea of Phenomenology*, trans. G. Nakhinikian (The Hague: M. Nijhoff).
Husserl, Edmund (1970c), *Logical Investigations*, 2 vols. trans. J.N. Findlay (London: Routledge; Amherst, NY: Humanity Books, 2000).
Husserl, Edmund (1973), *Experience and Judgment; Investigations in a Genealogy of Logic*, trans. K. Ameriks (Evanston, IL: Northwestern University Press).
Husserl, Edmund (1973 – present), *Husserliana: Gesammelte Werke* (The Hague: M. Nijhoff, Dordrecht: Kluwer, and New York: Springer).
Husserl, Edmund (1980), *Ideas Pertaining to a Pure Phenomenology and to a Phenomenological Philosophy, Third Book*, trans. W. E. Pohl (The Hague: M. Nijhoff).
Husserl, Edmund (1982), *Ideas Pertaining to a Pure Phenomenology and to a Phenomenological Philosophy, First Book*, trans. F. Kersten (The Hague: M. Nijhoff.)
Husserl, Edmund (1989), *Ideas Pertaining to a Pure Phenomenology and to a Phenomenological Philosophy, Second Book*, trans. R. R. a. A. Schuwer (The Hague: M. Nijhoff).
Husserl, Edmund (1991), *On the Phenomenology of the Consciousness of Internal Time (1893-1917)*, trans. J.B. Borough (Dordrecht & Boston, MA: Kluwer Academic Publishers).
Husserl, Edmund (1997), *Thing and Space: Lectures of 1907*, trans. R. Rojcewicz (Dordrecht: Kluwer Academic Publishers).
John of the Cross, Saint (1916), *The Dark Night of the Soul*, trans. F. Zimmerman (London: Thomas Baker).
Kant, Immanuel (1979), *Immanuel Kant's Critique of Pure Reason*, trans. Norman Kemp Smith (London: Macmillan).

Kant, Immanuel (1980), *Kritik der reinen Vernunft* (Stuttgart: Philipp Reclam.)
Merleau-Ponty, M. (1962), *Phenomenology of Perception* (London: Routledge and Kegan Paul).
Nagel, Thomas (1986), *The View From Nowhere* (Oxford and New York: Oxford University Press).
Priest, Stephen (1992), *Theories of the Mind* (London: Penguin; New York and Boston, MA: Houghton Mifflin).
Priest, Stephen (1999), 'Husserl's concept of being: From phenomenology to metaphysics', in *German Philosophy Since Kant*, ed. Anthony O'Hear, *Royal Institute of Philosophy Supplement*, **44**, pp. 209–22 (Cambridge University Press).
Priest, Stephen (2000), *The Subject in Question: Sartre's Critique of Husserl in 'The Transcendence of the Ego'* (London: Routledge).
Priest, Stephen (2003), *Merleau-Ponty* (London: Routledge).
Priest, Stephen (ed. 2000), *Jean-Paul Sartre: Basic Writings* (London: Routledge).
Rahula, Walpola (1967), *What the Buddha Taught* (Bedford: Gordon Fraser).

## REPLY TO PRIEST BY HONDERICH

Stephen Priest begins his autonomous, striking and informative paper by contemplating that if perceptual consciousness is very widely understood, wonderfully widely, so as to include your moods and your Buddhist empty-mindedness and so on, then it is doubtful that what it is for you to be perceptually conscious is for a world, a totality of things, somehow to exist. There is a quick reply, that Radical Externalism's subject of perceptual consciousness is the standard one, which includes your consciousness in seeing that yellow wall over there, but not entirely free-floating anxiety or the Buddhist state. There is no need for me to mention doubts as to entirely thing-free anxiety or the perfect emptiness of the spiritual achievement.

Priest means to add, I take it, that if perceptual consciousness is very widely understood, there could indeed be no consciousness of a kind but nevertheless a totality of things. The reply is that what is being maintained is that if someone is perceptually conscious in the standard way, there is *a* way in which a totality of things exists. This is not Berkeley, who took another kind of existence of things, an ordinary physical existence, to have consciousness as a necessary condition — as well as a sufficient one.

To speak differently, Radical Externalism does not assert doubtful conditionals with *some* kinds of consciousness in the antecent and *some* worlds in the consequence, but rather denies these conditionals. And it does not take to be coherent and true, but rather denies, some conditionals with *some* world in the antecedent and *some* kinds of consciousness in the consequent. So far as it asserts any condition of this sort, it has to do only with perceptual consciousness and a world of perceptual consciousness.

Are we to understand that these predictable retorts making it true that perceptual consciousness is a matter of a world rest too much on a certain conception of perceptual consciousness? Is it somehow the case, so to speak, that the chosen conception makes vulnerable the premise of the conditional 'if perceptual consciousness, then a world'? No reason for thinking so is given. None is given, in particular, in the remarks on objects of consciousness and phenomenological space.

Something related may occur to you at this point, of course. It is that there is a subject-matter asking for some attention if you say consciousness divides into three parts, kinds, sides, elements or whatever, the first being perceptual consciousness. This trinity is certainly also a kind of mysterious unity — typically we are all of seeing, thinking of and having an attitude to a thing. But I take it that this does not put the tripartite categorization of consciousness, standard in much psychology and elsewhere, into serious doubt. Still, it may be a good thing that Priest is not pressing me about it, anyway officially.

I pass by the thought about 'intentional consciousness', which stuff may not guarantee any world but is no supposition of mine, to the welter of queries about what can be meant by saying x's being perceptually conscious is identical with the existence of a world. Priest makes a meal of many courses, if a short meal, of asking the nature of the fundamental biconditional that if and only if someone is perceptually conscious, a world in a way exists.

I pass by an unlikely course or two, and note that his general question is one that can be asked of any piece of philosophical analysis. say of truth, time, knowledge, meaning, what is right, or democracy. Or rather, you can ask which of several possible kinds of philosophical analysis is underway. I find it easy to give a decent answer, but not easy to say more. The answer is that Radical Externalism is not engaged in asserting a simple logically necessary biconditional about what we ordinarily understand by someone's being perceptually conscious.

As remarked at the end of my piece at the beginning of these discussions, Radical Externalism is not conceptual analysis, or anyway ordinary conceptual analysis. It begins with our conceptual commitments — or rather, it begins with essential criteria for a tolerable account of consciousness, including the presumably empirical criterion of psychophysical causation. Do the criteria logically entail Radical Externalism? The modality is evidently not that simple. My uncertainty about the kinds of analysis and argument here — logical, metaphysical and so on — gets in the way of audacity on my part. But there seems to me no great difference between this sort of philosophy and common theories in science. I take it you can satisfy yourself about the theory of evolution without engaging in a lot of meta-theory. So too with consciousness.

As for the idea that consciousness is *constituted* by or made up of neurological events, Radical Externalism does not rule this out as a candidate answer, as seems to be implied, but gives reason, having to do with criteria of adequacy, for the idea's being false, admittedly obviously false. So with the other candidate answers. The only possible argument on Priest's part here, I take it, will be consideration of or replies to the mentioned reasons. They do not include, by the way, the more than implausible idea that consciousness consists in a part of itself, its included target or content.

Is there some general difficulty about what it is to take something to be constituted by or made up of something else — as when someone says time is a matter of only the temporal relations of precedence etc and not the supposed temporal properties of pastness etc? Even given my lack of industry in the analysis of philosophical analysis or theorizing, I am content to say that being perceptually conscious is constituted by the existence of a world and not by a brain process or some seemingly spiritual trinity of the the phenomenologists.

Is Radical Externalism in trouble because it *reduces* what it is to be perceptually conscious to the existence of a world? Well, you can think talk of reductionism, a charge or complaint of reductionism, always needs questioning. Some reductionism is good: the reduction of X to Y when there is nothing more to X than to Y. Some is bad: when there is more to X than to Y. The theory we are talking about, if you want to call it a reductionism, replies that it is a good one. Very certainly the theory maintains that to reduce perceptual consciousness to the existence of a world, in its way, is definitely to satisfy the reality-criterion for a theory of consciousness. Nothing does it much better, and the challenge or even superiority of devout physicalism comes to nothing because of its failure with other criteria.

Leaving aside some of Priest's comments of interest on phenomenological objects, there is his report that

> Where, pre-theoretically, I think of my own consciousness there seems to be nothing. However, this consciousness is not nothing but no-thing-ness (p. 149).

That is best considered later, when we come to Priest's own positive view, positive indeed, as against his objections to Radical Externalism.

The next objections have to do with your world of perceptual consciousness now, or mine, and the physical world — with relations between them. Stephen says that for Radical Externalism a world of perceptual consciousness is indeed not the physical world or a part of it, but a world of perceptual consciousness *is* a constituent of the physical world — which sounds bad. In fact contradiction. It will be useful to quote some lines of mine of which parts are in turn concentrated on by him.

> No world of perceptual consciousness is identical in its contents with the perceived part of the physical world — or of course the other part. Your world of perceptual consciousness is exactly not the physical world. What it is, to repeat, is a totality of different things in space and time. It is prior to and a constituent or the like of the physical world.
>
> In short, the fundamental fact of subjectivity is the existence of subjective worlds, no less distinct from the physical world for being spatio-temporal and propertied (1990, pp. 72–3).

By way of a preliminary remark, you will note that a world of perceptual consciousness, like a thing in it, is 'a constituent *or the like*' (my emphasis) of the physical world or a thing in it. And you will remember, I hope, about the theory, that existing in space-time is *not* a sufficient condition for being physical. A world of perceptual consciousness also exists in space-time.

To come nearer the main point, I admit, without a sense of defeat or indeed much discomfiture, that Radical Externalism is not a developed theory with respect to what can be called conceptual schemes and what they are about. That is not to say that the root idea about worlds of perceptual consciousness and the physical world is intolerably vague.

What it comes to is that what there is, the one world barely conceived at all by us, is first and fundamentally given to us or experienced by us in our worlds of perceptual consciousness. Out of this experience we individually and collectively arrive at a world impersonally conceived, the physical world. For a start, it is *not* what there is from only the place where my head is. This is exactly and all that is meant by speaking of a world of perceptual consciousness being 'prior to and a constituent of the like' of the physical world. So there is no contradiction or the like in Radical Externalism.

The general line of thought about our experience and our progress to the physical world is familiar in various forms in the history of epistemology, the philosophy of science, and critical or unspeculative metaphysics, not to mention psychology and more of science itself. From the line of thought, or in the line of thought, as against what Priest supposes, we have it that the perceived part of the physical world is *not* a part of a subjective world. Also, the things in my world of consciousness at the moment, perfectly properly identified as in this room and outside the window, are *not* the admittedly related things in the physical world. Further, the question of what a subjective world is exhausted by or consists in is indeed given an answer by the given line of thought.

Priest presses various questions, too many for me to run through, several of which seem to have mistaken presuppositions or to depend on inexplicit assumptions — questions to which the general line of thought indicates answers or to which consistent answers can be given. Let me just assert some propositions here.

- A person is part of the rough idea or has been part of the story, after a shakey start, only in the minimal sense, not making for circularity, that a world of perceptual consciousness depends on a human being or the like neurally.
- Whatever agreement there may be between Radical Externalism and Sartre, this is no matter of any appearance of a subject within consciousness.
- Yes, there is a plain if not doctrinaire kind of empiricism in Radical Externalism. It is at odds, I guess, with the idea that you could know about the physical world in its two parts only by an exercise of '*intuitive intellect*' (p. 152).
- Yes, what it is for a world of perceptual consciousness to exist *is* explained — and becomes uncertain, I think, only if mistaken assumptions are made, say about what the physical world is taken to be.
- No, the concept of a subjective world is not something independent of a certain conception of existence. Quite the contrary.

Still, I admit there are questions of interest and importance that can be raised about the theory, with answers that would or will enrich it. This is consistent, I take it, with the judgement that the theory as it stands is clear enough to be judged true or anyway arguable. The questions of interest need to be looked into carefully, of course, not so casually, if I may be teacherly, as in Priest's case when he includes in his world of *perceptual* consciousness thoughts about Radical Externalism, and when he supposes that it is part of the theory that his world has an 'inside' or 'a lived interiority'. That would be news to me, bad news, to which we shall return.

The second section of Priest's paper has to do with the idea, welcome enough if true, that Radical Externalism is somehow akin to or indeed anticipated in the thinking of Husserl, the founder of the philosophy of phenomenology. Something like this was remarked to me once by the admirable and authoritative Dagfinn Follesdal.

Sad to say, I have not had the benefit of having read Husserl. But it seems to me we do not get off to a good start in finding kinship by seeing that the physical world as conceived in Radical Externalism might be contemplated in terms not of a tradition of philosophical realism but in terms of one or the other of two kinds of philosophical idealism — two answers to the question of 'How can there be a world for me?'

It needs to be remembered that the physical world for Radical Externalism is neither in part the work of nor detected by any person in particular, let alone a subject in a traditional sense. And it is not a matter of our joined consciousnesses in some traditional sense, our conscious lives as talked of and dignified in the tradition of dualism that is spiritualism. It also needs to be remembered that for Radical Externalism there is also the wholly independent world underneath and prior to the physical world in both of its parts — which independent world brings Radical Externalism into line with realism rather than either of the idealisms.

Is the next idea of kinship more promising? It has to do with what may be the best known piece of Husserl's philosophy. This, I take it, is a step in philosophizing — the *epoché* or suspension of belief — in fact suspension of both belief and disbelief — with respect to what may include more than what is called the world of the natural attitude, which world has in it physical objects and people. Let us confine ourselves to this suspension of belief and disbelief in connection with perceptual consciousness. What you get by this step, I uncertainly take it, is some awareness of what you do not take to be either physical or mental.

Does Priest conjecture that what you have, the result, when you look out the window and perform the *epoché*, is your world of perceptual consciousness? I am not sure about this, and not much helped by the proposition shared with Sartre that all of your consciousness is given to you.

A first reaction to such a conjecture is that your being perceptually conscious, that state of affairs as described by Radical Externalism, is pretty close to the last thing that could be exactly your suspending belief and disbelief in the suggested way. The existence of a state of affairs outside your head is certainly *not* this piece of strategy in philosophizing. What the step comes to, I take it, to avoid some rhetoric, is thinking of your ordinary sense experience without somehow thinking of it as either of external things or of sense-data or the like. That is definitely not what being perceptually conscious comes to for Radical Externalism. As for the step or strategy itself, by the way, is that not something *all* philosophers of perception have engaged in? They pose a question about something they identify.

Is Priest's idea, rather, that it is peculiarly the *epoche* that leads to the conception of perceptual consciousness as a world? Well, I take it that Radical Externalism is the result of contemplating your perceptual consciousness as it is given to you, as certainly without subtraction as without addition. That is what has been called mental realism by me. Is the epoche close to this? Could be.

By way of another comparison, note that Husserl's strategy is one that proceeds *from* the physical world *to* something else that is not physical. What is maintained in Radical Externalism is that in general we proceed from what are not exactly physical, worlds of perceptual consciousness, to the physical world and other worlds also more independent of us.

Does all that leave intact another connection between Radical Externalism and Husserl?

A world of perceptual consciousness, the state of affairs that is your being perceptually conscious, has features or a character that make it reasonable to take it as what it is said to be — what constitutes you being perceptually *conscious*. It is subjective in a clear sense or rather senses. It is also given to us. But, as certainly, it *approximates to* what in fact it is not, a *physical* state of affairs. There is every reason to call Radical Externalism a near-physicalism, which does indeed gesture at its central strength.

Well, there is a kind of similarity between (1) our giving an account of consciousness that is neither devout physicalism nor something that leaves out subjectivity and fails to satisfy some other criteria for an adequate theory, and (2) maintaining with Husserl that it is possible to get into a state where you suspend belief and disbelief in a certain way — of which we can say the additional thing that it is an agnostic state such that what are called its contents are taken as neither mental nor physical. That does not make for a similarity that counts for much against the previous facts that a world of perceptual consciousness is exactly not the philosopher's strategy that is the *epoché*, that the conception of such a world is not tied to any uniquely Husserlian procedure, and that the two philosophies under consideration proceed in opposed directions.

There is much more in Priest's paper than can have close attention here. This second section, which we are considering, was to show what would not be unwelcome, that Radical Externalism is a theory essentially anticipated by Husserl. Let me just assert or anyway float some propositions bearing on what would no doubt be a pedigree worth having.

(a) It is reassuring to learn that Husserl, and also Sartre, have had the view, or something like it, that with consciousness what you have is all of what there is, that it doesn't include a reality-behind.

(b) With respect to intentionality, aboutness or directedness, said to be the essence of consciousness for Husserl, it is certainly not the essence of consciousness for Radical Externalism. On that theory, there is no such relation *in* perceptual consciousness — whatever explanation there is of this consciousness that connects it with other things. The relation of representation that is basic to reflective consciousness is remote from the ideas of Brentano and perhaps from those of Husserl.

(c) It seems evident that Husserl has and depends on an ideal or image of a subject, self, ego or the like that has no counterpart whatever in Radical Externalism.

(d) It seems he does not go in for ontological extravagance, which is good to hear, but rather agrees that 'in the primary and most ordinary sense of the word, there is but one world', of which, or of some of which, we have different conceptions (1998, p. 146).

(e) Husserl not only has it, with the rest of us, that things exist under different conceptualizations, but seems to join many parties already mentioned with respect to the matter of the physical world. In Priest's account of him, 'The house is constructed as a whole object through my experiences of it' (p. 157).

(f) Despite recommending the strategy of the *epoche* or suspension of belief and disbelief to us, Husserl seems far from being with Radical Externalism in reducing consciousness to what others call its contents. There is always the subject in there, and intentionality, and more — as you will be hearing.

(g) To revert to a point already made, or near to it, Husserl and presumably the ancient Greek sceptics, and in a way Descartes, are one in taking a certain means to arriving at truth — a method of doubting what can be doubted. But is is possible to think they are together with *all* decent philosophers — all of whom are different from the credulous, the fantasists, the merely literary as distinct from the pursuers of truth in art, and so on. Husserl, Greek sceptics and Descartes are also in the given way together with all decent scientists.

What separates the philosophers in question one from another, and so with the scientists, is *what* they believe can be doubted and *what* they believe cannot be doubted. This is where to look for similarity between Radical Externalism and Husserl. There is an awful lot of difference between the two about what cannot be doubted. It begins with what cannot be doubted about what it is, as we say, for you to be conscious of the room you are in. Husserl does *not* say or contemplate, or come anyway near saying or contemplating, that it is for the room to exist in the way specified by Radical Externalism.

Given (a) to (g) and the considerations that preceded them, is Radical Externalism close to Husserl? Is Radical Externalism 'a thoroughly phenomenological concept'? I sure have to say no to those summaries.

Turning now to the last three sections of Priest's paper, you will know, reader, that your chance of now reading anything like a full reply to them by me is small. Another whole philosophy and way of philosophy is gestured at, audaciously and enlighteningly, too much for quick understanding and developed objection.

What the three sections come to, by way of an overview, is that chosen propositions or theses of Radical Externalism in fact issue, with some help, in what is given the name of being Radical *Internalism*. That is a doctrine of the nature of consciousness that tries to characterize it by way of ideas of interiority, no-thing-ness as against nothing, a mysterious demarcation between past and future, presence, the subject or self, emptiness or void, a space, a phenomenological zone or field, oneness, the eternal now or present, an inside without an outside, a subjective space, a spiritual substance, a soul, being, metaphysics and theology.

Or, to be more careful, what the last three sections of Priest's paper come to in an overview is that chosen *sentences* of Radical Externalism, taken or maybe freely understood as certain propositions, theses or perhaps images, issue in Radical Internalism, the doctrine of those many terms and notions. Certainly it is a grand exemplar of what I have called spiritualism.

Let me end this response by glancing at items in Priest's sequence and then making a couple of general observations or confessions about Radical Internalism.

That (1, 8) my consciousness is something all of which I *have* is not the proposition that it is private and inalienable in a mysterious sense. None of conceptual possibility and impossibility, logic, natural laws or anything deeper is what gets in the way of something — so arranging what is in two heads and outside of them so that I have and know I have exactly your perceptual consciousness at a time. What gets in the way of your having, so to speak, my experience of that wall's colour, is practical difficulties. That not even this entirely trivial access to another's consciousness is likely to be achieved in fact, however, is fundamental to our actual existence, and a part of or connected to the fact of subjectivity.

There does (2) seem to be an insuperable objection to the usual cautious or empirical policy of reducing the temporal properties of past, present and future to the temporal relations of being before, simultaneous with, or after (Honderich, 1977). Priest's leap from this premise to a proposition of Radical Internalism is breathtaking.

That (4) my consciousness can about as well be said to be something all of which is present to me is not intended as the proposition that if $p$ is a first person singular psychological ascription, then if $p$ is believed, $p$ is true. Nor, of course, is it the proposition, antithetical to Radical Externalism, that when I am aware of the pen in my hand, I am aware of rather more — an emptiness, a space, a phenomenological zone or field in which the pen is presented. For Radical Externalism all that exists in addition to the pen, rather, is a surrounding world.

That (6) Priest agrees about the need to transfer labourers out of intentionality industry or anyway the intentionality-in-perception industry, is heartening. That he says this means much of Husserlian phenomenology needs rethinking is surprising but to me reassuring.

More generally, Radical Internalism as indicated in his paper is presumably a spiritualism, indeed a declarative spiritualism. Consciousness is neither physical nor near-physical. It is something else, somewhere else. The doctrine, certainly until more is learned of it, must fail absolutely to satisfy the criterion of an adequate theory of consciousness that it does not make impossible what is actual, which is ordinary causal connection between mind and body, consciousness and the rest of what there is. There is also the reality criterion.

Again more generally, I am among those many philosophers, certainly a majority among those who are being paid for their work in universities in the English language, who by their philosophizing indicate that they cannot take Logical Positivism to have been a disaster, certainly not a disaster in its effects. That is, they have a scepticism about the extent to which metaphysical utterances have truth-values — the doubt exaggerated into the piece of provocation that they may not be meaningful at all.

It is my own view that the Verification Principle of Meaning, notoriously incapable of general proof, is best taken as a cautious generaliation *owed to* reactions to or reflections on particular metaphysical and other utterances rather than a principle to be *brought to bear* on kinds of utterances (Honderich, 2004). But, to come to the point, I have some doubt about at least some of Priest's sentences. *What* is it, with respect to the nature of consciousness, if we put aside banalities, to have the enormous cosmic privilege of being the demarcation between the past the future.

That is one general impulse about Radical Internalism. It is also possible to feel another. It is true that Descartes didn't make up spiritualism. It is true that what can seem to be the excess of Priest's metaphysics of consciousness can also seem to require attention from us, to derive from all our lives. My inclination is to try to make more sense of it, so to speak, in terms of reflective and affective consciousness — or rather what can be represented and felt in them.

Perceptions of an emptiness or void, a spiritual substance and whatever else, are not to be located within an analysis of consciousness, but rather in larger thinking and feeling about our lives. You might test this by having a look at Priest's books *The Subject in Question: Sartre's Critique of Husserl in 'The Transcendence of the Ego'* and *Jean-Paul Sartre: Basic Writings*. The truth about consciousness itself, however, can be Radical Externalism. I don't think it is to be found in Radical Internalism.

## References

Honderich, T. (1977), 'Temporal relations and temporal qualities', in *Time and Philosophy* (French translation *Le Temps et Les Philosophies*), ed. Paul Ricoeur (UNESCO).

Honderich, T. (2004), 'Introduction to the collection', *A.J. Ayer: Writings on Philosophy* (London: Palgrave Macmillan).

Priest, Stephen (2000), *The Subject in Question: Sartre's Critique of Husserl in 'The Transcendence of the Ego'* (London: Routledge).

Priest, Stephen (ed. 2001), *Jean-Paul Sartre: Basic Writings* (London: Routledge).

# Barry C. Smith

# *Consciousness*
## *An Inner View of the Outer World*

Right now my conscious experience is directed at part of the world. It takes in some aspects of things around me and not others. Some bits of the world occupy my attention, other worldly goings on condition or colour the character of my current perceptual experience. I take in buildings in view through the window, the clothes in the corner of the room, the colour of the walls, the plate with breads, the coffee mugs, the smell of fresh laundry, the muffled sounds of someone in the kitchen, the sounds from the street: a sequence of things that in turn capture my attention moment to moment. And all the while, thoughts occur to me, modulating my conscious awareness. I have no doubt that the world and my place in it, together with my recent past history, explains the particular form my consciousness takes right now. But what shape does that explanation take? Things out there, beyond the boundaries of my skin, enter into the conscious events I undergo. The inner is in this way shaped and determined by those outer things that impress themselves on the mind. What is it, though, for consciousness of this kind to go on at all?

To say that consciousness is, in certain crucial respects, dependent on the world and one's place in it, is not enough to say all that needs to be said about consciousness. There is a contribution I make to these events, there are the inner aspects of consciousness. Right now I feel the faint early signs of a headache, still off-shore but likely to take up more and more of my attention. There is the awareness I have — not always but there right now — that the things I see or hear are being seen or heard by me now. I know that these things are there, that they occur anyway whether I see or hear them at all. But no one else is having this very experience of them. As I look at the corner of the room, or out of the window at the buildings beyond, I am aware that no one else enjoys this view right now, this particular perspective on the world. They could have done, or will do, perhaps, but right now they are not enjoying what I currently experience: only I am presently seeing things from here. There is an awareness of the world from this point of view and an awareness of my sole experience of enjoying it. I am aware of my consciousness as a unique event, of it being mine. Equally, I can tell that no one else is seeing the way the room looks from the opposite corner. They could have been but they are not. A chance for a certain conscious experience has not been taken by anyone. No consciousness of the room from that perspective is being enjoyed right now because there is no one there. There would have to be someone standing in that place, awake and aware, attending to the room and not lost in thought, for there to be such a conscious episode. We know that occupying that space and being a certain kind of minded animal, or brain active creature, is necessary for such a conscious episode to take place. Despite knowing this we seem to know nothing else about what makes such a unique episode available to someone, and appreciable by them for what it is.

Returning to my current experience, I am aware of the independent existence of what I am seeing from my seeing of it: I am aware of the transient nature of my conscious seeings. I stare momentarily at a farmhouse through the window of a train and it then disappears from sight. My experience is one thing: the briefly perceptible farmhouse another. I can also interrupt my conscious awareness of the carriage around me by closing my eyes.

There is also a certain range or reach to my consciousness: it extends outwards and all around me (save perhaps for the space just at the back of my head). It takes in certain things at a certain distance from me. What lies outside my current conscious reach can only be thought about, not heard or felt, smelled, touched or seen. Sometimes the extent of my conscious reach expands when I attend to the noise of the street or the distant sound of a taxi. Sometimes it contracts when I'm lost in thought or pre-occupied with worries not related to the here and now. The mind's eye can turn inward and I can temporarily lose my consciousness of the world. When ill or in a fever the world can shrink to very local concerns with the body. Recovery is sometimes signalled by noticing how far one's conscious awareness now reaches out.

The full extent of the world that occupies my attention when I am awake and alert is what I call my cognitive surround. My current cognitive surround is fairly extensive: it takes in what is happening (heard) in the next room. This cognitive environment (to borrow a term from Sperber and Wilson [1986] ) as created by my current conscious awareness centres on me and radiates out from this centre. It is a consciously experienced world that is not solely located in my cranium: it is not, nor does it feel like, the goings on in an internal, private realm. Instead, it is a way the world is presented to me right now, and a way of my being in the world. It is not shared with another, although we can have overlapping cognitive environments, but we can share aspects of our conscious surroundings. Others can enter my immediate cognitive environment by speaking to me and grabbing my attention. Their words re-configure my experience in certain speech-directed ways. I cannot but hear the sounds uttered as meaningful: as someone saying such and such, and my experience is changed by what they say. The conscious mind is very easily violated by others' words: they get right through to us, entering our minds uninvited.

This interplay between inner and outer, described above, shows the way consciousness depends on both the subject's physical *and* internal environment. The world and the people in it have a part to play in shaping our consciousnesses. But the world is not enough. For it is not just *what* we are aware of but also the fact of our *being aware* of it (even our awareness of being aware), that we seek to explain.

Within conscious experience we can be aware of the difference between what we experience and our having that experience. Consciousness — or at any rate the consciousness human beings enjoy — makes this difference immediately available to us for reflection, and it is this feature that is characteristic of the consciousness we care about and deem worthy of philosophical attention. And yet it is this feature of consciousness that seems to go missing in Ted Honderich's radically externalist account of consciousness.[1]

Despite offering a novel and usefully externalist perspective on consciousness, as well as many important criticisms of other accounts, Honderich's own position doesn't quite scratch the itch it creates. He begins with a person seeing a page, and he asks what 'exactly your consciousness of the page' consist in. (Actually, he asks 'What did your consciousness *seem* to consist in?'). We are told,

> *It was for the page to be there.* What your consciousness seemed to consist in was nothing other or more than that (p. 5).

But this is a very minimal account of a conscious experience — especially of one we have been invited to attend to. Is what it was like for you to be conscious of the page really no more than Honderich says it is? Although useful attempts are made to put it in other words, the

---

[1] Honderich (2006). In this commentary all page references are to this target paper unless stated otherwise.

doctrine of Radical Externalism about consciousness remains a little elusive. Honderich goes on to say:

> the state of affairs that was *the page's being there*, a state of affairs outside your head, is one of the several most fundamental propositions of the Radical Externalism that is our subject (p. 6).

By itself this is a sensible corrective to Cartesian individualism about the mental: a welcome feature of Radical Externalism. But we need more. Honderich seeks to oblige:

> More fully, to be perceptually conscious is only for an extra-cranial state of affairs to exist — for there to be a spatio-temporal set of things with a dependence on another extra-cranial state of affairs and also on what is in a particular cranium. The page's being there, and more generally *your world of perceptual consciousness* is things being in space and time, with such further properties as colour, and being dependent on a scientific or noumenal world underneath and also dependent on you neurally (p. 6).

And again:

> The Radical Externalism being contemplated here in one of its three parts is indeed the general proposition that what it is to be perceptually conscious is for a world in a way to exist — i.e. for things to be in space and time with certain properties and for them to have certain necessary conditions (p. 7).

The key locution, and one Honderich has used in other writings to do a lot of the work, is: 'consciousness is *for a world in a way to exist*'. What world? What way? Exist how? We need all of these questions answered if we are to feel comfortable that Radical Externalism is telling us something about conscious visual experience. For things to be in space and time is for there to be real things, parts of the actual world. But their existence is not enough for consciousness. Many parts of the world right now exist with no one being conscious of them. In some cases, the world we are conscious of, populated as it seems to us with certain objects, does not exist in that way. (More of that in a moment.) If the world (or the part of it) I am conscious of exists, and therefore plays a role in my having the conscious experience I am now having, we can agree to that condition. But what else is needed to get at my being conscious of my surroundings? It is not just for that world, or that part of the world to exist — it is for it, in a way, to exist. What way? Its existing in a way I am consciously aware of? No. Honderich rightly criticises accounts that resort to talk of *awareness*, or of things being perceptually available to *me* since they offer no explanatory advance but merely presuppose the elusive phenomenon we are trying to explain. And yet, we will be obliged to use these terms until we have enough insights from elsewhere, or other terms, to enable us to see that we don't need to make appeal to them anymore and now do understand what those terms either presuppose or gesture at.

But we are far from there as things stand. The world, or the selective perspective on it our conscious experience affords us, requires something to exist, but in what way that will make our consciousness of it intelligible enough to dispense with talk of awareness or how things appear to us? As far as Honderich's focus on the world is concerned, are we talking about the perceived *world*, or are we talking about the *perceiving* of a world? Surely the topic of consciousness is mainly concerned with the latter.

Let us now tackle the theme we passed over, that of consciousness sometimes presenting a world of things that appear a certain way even when those things do not exist. In somewhat Johnsonian fashion, Honderich tries to defuse traditional objections to direct perception theories based on illusion or hallucination. Here we have him saying:

> Well, I myself can tell the difference between a state of affairs that is the existence of ordinary things and a state of affairs that is the existence of representations of ordinary things. In our lives as they are, there is a good difference between representations, which can be in various ways wrong, and ordinary things, which can't. Seeing isn't like dreaming — seeing doesn't seem to be like dreaming, which truth is unaffected by your having to get out of the dream to know the fact (p. 7).

That may be, but of course some people can't always tell the difference. The Nobel Prize winning mathematician, John Nash, like many other schizophrenics reported lucid, stable and persisting hallucinations of people confronting him and talking to him. It is clues from something other than their conscious perceptions that tell schizophrenics that the people they see and talk to are not real. In Nash's case he realised that the daughter of the friend he repeatedly encountered was not getting any older and so could not be real. He was unable to banish these persisting hallucinated figures or to stop their words impinging on his consciousness and altering his current experience. He even had to check with others whether the people he apparently confronted were really there. Schizophrenics will often tell you the imaginary people they see are as real to them as you or I. The condition is so distressing for the sufferers precisely because without neuro-pharmachological help they cannot disabuse themselves of the existence of these imagined friends or tormentors.

These cases are more difficult to deal with than the usual cases of hallucination invented by philosophers. Here, we are not dealing with a dream world or simulation of reality produced by a brain in a vat. The experiences these schizophrenic patients undergo involve perceptions of their physical surroundings that really do exist and which they successfully negotiate, where these perceived surroundings are augmented by characters who do not actually exist. The consciousness of such patients is consciousness of a world but one they have added to, and populated with fictions of their conscious minds. Such experiences can only be explained as episodes *in* consciousness and talk of their being *for a world in a way to exist* may make sense, but now the key phrase is being used in a quite different way when it is the real world, or the world populated with the imaginary objects we are talking about. Consciousness is not always about existence and is not always fully captured by talking about what is out there.

Finally, we get to the nub of the problem for Radical Externalism: subjectivity. Honderich tells us:

> For Radical Externalism, perceptual consciousness consists in a state of affairs that not only is partly dependent on one individual, but is also different from related states of affairs dependent on other individuals. It is also different from the state of affairs that is the perceived physical world as well as other states of affairs that are in defined senses objective. If it is a near-physicalism, it does give clear sense to our conviction about subjectivity (p.12).

I don't agree. This statement tells us what subjectivity is not, but it does not give us a clear sense of *what it is*. We are told that consciousness (with its essential subjectivity) depends on one individual. We also know it involves a swathe of the world. Earlier we are told that consciousness depends on that bit of the real world, perceived and scientifically describable, and on what is in the cranium of the individual. We can agree to all of this, but what we urgently need to know is what kind of dependence between these bits of the world produces the easily recognisable subjective experience of an individual? What is that dependence and how does it result in the states of mind we know so well? As yet, we have nothing more to go on.

My response has been largely critical and sceptical of the account Honderich offers us, and unlike Honderich I am offering nothing positive or new on the topic of consciousness, which remains one of the most puzzling in philosophy. Conscious phenomena are so close to us and so familiar and yet the nature of consciousness is so utterly inscrutable. It is a brave philosopher who dares to propose an account of its nature and attempts to satisfy our philosophical qualms that there is no account to be given. Ted Honderich has made such an attempt and should be praised for doing so. He gives us all more material to get to work on.[2]

### References

Honderich, T. (2006), 'Radical externalism', *Journal of Consciousness Studies*, **13** (7–8), pp. 3–13. [This issue]
Sperber, D. and Wilson, D. (1986), *Relevance* (Oxford: Blackwell).

## REPLY TO SMITH BY HONDERICH

Barry Smith's direct, deft and instructive evocation of ordinary experience at the beginning of his paper can take a Radical Externalist aback for at least a while. Yes, it is all too true that some bits of a room I am now in occupy my attention, are bits to which I attend. Can it also be, as Smith says, that some goings-on, maybe actions of another person, somehow condition or colour my current perceptual experience? Certainly thoughts do come to me in the course of my seeing the room. Indeed they are there more often than not in the course of my seeing the room. Does it make sense to say that they modulate my awareness?

You can wonder, as a Radical Externalist, whether or not your wondering was the aim of Smith's evocation of ordinary experience, if a world of perceptual consciousness contains more than items that occupy the attention of the perceiver, items to which he or she attends. The answer, on reflection, has to be yes. This follows from the fact, speaking ordinarily, that I do indeed see and otherwise consciously perceive more than I attend to. The state of affairs in which my perceptual consciousness consists must indeed be all that of which, speaking ordinarily, I am conscious. Does that proposition in itself raise further difficulty? Any such difficulty needs to be produced.

The fact of attention is a further good reason for an admission made before now (above, p. 6). The admission is that to speak of perceptual as against each of reflective and affective consciousness, or of either of those against the other, is to make a forceful separation of a process of which it may even be too simple to say that three currents in it affect one another and intermingle. What is attending to something? Well, it seems persuasive to say that it is to *think* or *feel* about one thing in particular of those you see. In which case, for Radical Externalism and presumably other accounts of consciousness, what we have a specific kind of eliding of perceptual and at least reflective consciousness.

---

[2] My thanks to Ophelia Deroy for invaluable comments.

Is there an embarrassment somewhere here for Radical Externalism? Certainly it gives different accounts of perceptual, reflective and affective consciousness. Certainly the theory is different from the standard general theories of consciousness in the philosophy and science of mind. Both devout physicalism and spiritualism give wholly uniform or homogeneous accounts of all of consciousness. All conscious events are made into neural processes or whatever. The same is true of compromise theories — they do not distinguish between the parts or whatever of consciousness.

It seems to me possible not only to ask for a difficulty actually to be produced here, but also to recover confidence pretty quickly in the meantime. We all do have an indubitable grip on differences, however difficult to analyse, between seeing and the like, thinking and the like, and wanting and the like. I can right now distinguish to myself, without any trouble, seeing the piece of white paper in front of me, wondering about the next sentence to be put on it, and hoping for the best.

Do such goings-on as the actions of another person, maybe actions that have some emotional effect on me, really condition or colour *what I see*, as distinct from what I attend to? Do the thoughts that come to me modulate, modify or control *what I see*? Any philosophical difficulty here will not only have to be articulated but also have to be sufficient to to outweigh the large recommendation of Radical Externalism with respect to the matter in hand. Seeing, thinking and hoping, as their separate occurrences on other occasions do still more to confirm, *are* different. It is a recommendation of a theory to reflect the fact in our conscious lives that we are indeed given different sorts of thing.

A definitely intended objection to Radical Externalism is first indicated when it is said, after Smith's evocation of events in ordinary experience, that 'There is a contribution I make to these events, there are inner aspects of consciousness' (p. 175). The objection is later stated by way of free if not loose use of talk of awareness.

> There is an awareness I have — not always but there right now — that the things I see or hear are being seen or heard by me at the moment. ... There is an awareness of the world from this point of view and an awareness of my sole experience of enjoying it (pp. 175–6).

The second awareness is bound up with activity of mine, perhaps attention above all. My current cognitive surround or cognitive environment is spoken of by Smith, perhaps not carelessly, as 'created by my current conscious awareness' (p. 176). There is an 'interplay between inner and outer' (p. 177). Also:

> Within conscious experience we can be aware of the difference between what we experience and our having that experience. Consciousness — or

at any rate the consciousness human beings enjoy — makes this difference immediately available to us for reflection, and it is this feature that is characteristic of the consciousness we care about and deem worthy of philosophical attention. And yet it is this feature of consciousness that seems to go missing in Ted Honderich's radically externalist account of consciousness (p. 177).

I take it that while Smith allowed at the start that we are not always and indeed not for the most part not aware of being aware, conscious of being perceptually conscious, that is not the end of the story. The fact that we *can* do the thing is what is worthy of philosophical attention. It is, it seems, the big fact or what points to the big fact about perceptual consciousness in general.

This is that *within conscious experience*, whether or not we are aware of it — whether or not we attend to it? — there is a second awareness. The objection to Radical Externalism is not the truism that I can over a couple of seconds or minutes be conscious of the room and then conscious of the prior consciousness. The objection is that being perceptually conscious of the room, in the perfectly ordinarily way, has within it being conscious of that consciousness. This, I take it, is akin to something heard before in philosophy, maybe from Hegel for a start, that all consciousness is self-consciousness.

If something of the sort is true, Radical Externalism about perceptual consciousness — and also the other two sorts of consciousness — is false. The theory in its distinction would be abandoned absolutely by turning it into the theory that your being conscious of the room you are in is for the room in a way to exist *and* for you to conscious of that fact. Also, of course, the thing would have collapsed into useless circularity.

Well, I can but say that there seems to me no reason at all to add into my awareness of the room, however you understand that awareness, say in a a spiritualist or devout physicalist way, an awareness of the awareness. I am just not *doubly aware* whenever I am aware. I am not aware of an inner contribution of mine. That I can be aware of the room, be conscious in that way, is not itself complicated by having *in it* what I can of course be aware of in another sense a moment or two later, be conscious in thinking about the earlier awareness. What reason can there be for departing from the pre-theoretical truism that I can *see* something without *thinking about seeing it?*

The seeming denial of such truisms and related propositions is derived by Smith from his evocation of ordinary experience, but the way of derivation is not made explicit. Further, to suppose that your perceptual consciousness has in it, of its nature, what you sometimes or often do not have, offends against the solid proposition of Radical Externalism that your consciousness is something you have.

Is it an embarrassment for the philosophy of mind, and hence for Radical Externalism, that some disputes rest at bottom on what can seem to be ground-level divergences between individual philosophers, what used to be called introspective reports? Well, they are not disputes that consist in nothing but announcements of contradictory propositions. There is a lot in Radical Externalism that goes against the 'inner contribution' or 'inner aspect' or double-awareness view of perceptual consciousness. There is that strong proposition, indeed the overwhelming proposition, that what is in consciousness is what you *have* — and, as has to be added, given what we have heard or speculated, that you cannot always have what for the most part you do not have.

Smith goes on to allow, in the second stage of his paper, that Radical Externalism is novel and useful, and a corrective to what is called Cartesian individualism. But, he says, it is a minimal and elusive account of consciousness.

> The key locution ... is: 'consciousness is *for a world in a way to exist*'. What world? What way? Exist how? We need all of these questions answered if we are to feel comfortable that Radical Externalism is telling us something about conscious visual experience (p. 178).

He cannot advance his case for obscurity by the truth, which he does appear to assert, that the existence of some or other real world is not enough for consciousness. He needs to attend to a proposition about exactly a world of perceptual consciousness being sufficient for perceptual consciousness. Also, he does have to attend to what is said, at least explicitly, of what and how it is for such a world to exist. It is certainly not as if the use of 'exist' is left undefined.

Smith contributes a clear thought, again one that is unsettling for a while, when he considers the insistence of Radical Externalism that in a theory of consciousness we need explanatory advance, not presupposition of what we are trying to explain, mere circularity. This, of course, he accepts. But he adds the thought that those who seek to understand Radical Externalism can only understand it by taking 'a world exists' in the theory to be 'a world exists for me' or something of that circular sort. Well, I repeat that an explicit and non-circular definition is on the table.

The third stage of Smith's paper takes us back to illusions and hallucinations. His quoting of a paragraph of mine about our being able to tell the difference between an ordinary thing and a representation could give the impression that that was all that was said of hallucinations in Radical Externalism. It was not, and indeed the paragraph was not in the first instance about hallucinations, as a glance at p. 8 will show.

Still, it is reasonable enough to take what was said as a reply to the argument from hallucination as used against Radical Externalism's account of perceptual consciousness. I have to admit that the fact that ordinarily, on almost every occasion in human life, we are able to tell the difference between a thing and a representation, has to have added to it the uncomfortable fact that there are some people, like the unfortunate mathematician, who on occasion can't tell the difference. I also need to admit that our ordinary, nearly universal competence, does not in and by itself defeat the argument from hallucination.

That may leave room for a further thought, about a use of the fact of our nearly universal competence. Some philosopher stands up and cites the poor mathematician in support of the conclusion that all of us, or rather each of us, is isolated in his or her sense-data or whatever. That is, each of us in our perceptual consciousness only has stuff of the order of representations. There is a reply. It is that we can tell the difference between representations and things, and as a result we don't think what the philosopher thinks about our ordinary experience. There must be something wonky about the argument from hallucination.

I have to grant that there is a problem for Radical Externalism with hallucinations, as there is for the valourous response of disjunctivism. There is the problem, as Smith puts it, of fictional as well as real characters turning up in some rare perceptual experience — or some mainly perceptual experience. If there is this problem in Radical Externalism, however, there is also, to my mind, an awful lot of *solution* elsewhere in Radical Externalism.

You can think that philosophy like the world is imperfect, and that the best theory of something is going to have a problem or two in it. That's life, including the life of thinking. If the Radical Externalist turns his mind to interpretations of Quantum Theory, by the way, he can end up so satisfied with his own theory as to be ecstatic. If he turns his mind to theories of consciousness in terms of Quantum Theory, he can be in danger of needing restraint.

The last stage of Smith's paper is about the theory's explanation of subjectivity. The theory's bottom proposition here, if not the only one, is that your world of perceptual consciousness is different from related things, in fact unique — unless you are in a piece of science fiction. I don't agree with Smith that to say that is only to say clearly what the subjectivity is not.

As for the particular kind or kinds of dependence that your world of perceptual consciousness has on several things, I'm just not sure. How urgent is the question? Can't we suppose, for a while anyway, that it is ordinary non-logical or non-conceptual nomic dependence, the genus that has standard causal dependence as its best known species (Honderich, 1988; 1990, Ch. 1)

## References

Honderich, T. (1988), *A Theory of Determinism: The Mind, Neuroscience and Life-Hopes* (Oxford: Oxford University Press).
Honderich, T. (1990), *Mind and Brain* (Oxford: Oxford University Press).

# Paul Snowdon

# *Radical Externalisms*

Professor Honderich presents his account of consciousness boldly and informally, and his presentation merits a response in similar terms. I conceive of this response as simply the first move in a conversation, in the course of which misunderstandings might be removed and, just possibly, criticisms sharpened, and positions modified.

I want to concentrate on two questions that his very interesting paper prompts me to ask. The first question is; what exactly is the thesis about consciousness that Professor Honderich is proposing? The second question is; what are the main reasons he has for his proposal and are they persuasive? Although there are two questions, I shall mix considerations of them together in a way which I hope it is possible to follow.

Honderich divides the phenomenon of consciousness into three sorts, which he calls the perceptual, the reflective and the affective, or as he puts it, somewhat informally, 'seeing, thinking and wanting' (Honderich, 2006, p. 6).[1] In considering what his positive thesis is, however, I want, for most of the time, to ignore the reflective and the affective, and to concentrate, as Honderich himself does, on what he calls the perceptual. The question then is; what is he claiming about that?

Before I try to answer the first question there are two observations I want to make about the threefold division of conscious states that Honderich proposes. (1) In one respect the list is not complete. If by the 'perceptual' Honderich means episodes which are genuinely perceptual, then the list leaves out what might be called non-perceptual sensory episodes. Hallucinations and dreaming are two examples. Many would also include what are sometimes called sensations, for example, migraines, toothaches, itches and aches. Since Honderich's approach to perceptual cases is to think of them as involving *what is*

---

[1] In this commentary all page references are to this target paper unless stated otherwise.

*there*, for example, an actual page, that analysis cannot apply to, for example, hallucinations. He therefore leaves out and offers no analysis of an important category of conscious experience. (2) In the evidently informal list Honderich includes 'wanting'. But although seeing and thinking (in the sense of occurrent thinking) are, or seem to be, types of experience, 'wanting' does not, in general, stand for an experience.[2] Thus, some people can want for twenty years to be millionaires, but there is no feature continuously before their consciousness which amounts to that desire. Again, I can recognize the onset of a form of consciousness, say a perception or a pain, but I have no conception how to recognize the onset of a desire. What kind of experience is it? Honderich's list is, therefore, too broad.

What, though, is the theory? Honderich imagines that one of us, let us call him or her S, is seeing a page. About this occurrence he claims

> ... this fact of consciousness necessarily was what it seemed to be, the state of affairs that was the page's being there ...'(p. 6).

Later he summarizes it by saying

> perceptual consciousness consists in an external state of affairs ... (p. 10).

He also says,

> ... the theory does not take all of consciousness outside the cranium. It does not do so with all of reflective consciousnesses (p. 9).

But this implies it does so for perceptual consciousness.

So, as a first interpretation, let us read him as proposing an identity along these lines; S's seeing the page is identical with the page's being there. Now, the most natural way to understand the claim that something is there, say a statue, is simply that it exists at the place we mean by 'there'. We thus can say; 'This statue has been there for the last fifty years'. Or again, we can say; 'There has never been a lamp post there', and that means that at no time has a lamp post existed at that place. I want to assume then that in the theory talk of something's being there is to be interpreted in this completely normal way. (The theory so understood has the form of a rather unusual psycho-physical identity thesis. The standard form identifies episodes of consciousness with events in the central nervous system of the subject.) I call this thesis Radical Externalism 1.

Radical Externalism 1 cannot, it seems, actually be true. The most obvious problem is that the page's being there, that fact or state of

---

[2] Occurrent thinking as the form of experience that we know is possible because we are able to control certain inner types of experiences, which we might call imagery. How we exercise control is, of course, very hard to say.

affairs, understood as I have indicated it is most naturally understood, does *not contain enough* to amount to, to be the same as, the fact that S is seeing the page. Thus, the page can be there without S existing at all, or if we assume that S exists, without S's being conscious, or without S's being able to see the page, or without S's looking in the right direction, and so on. It is, surely, quite obvious that the episode in S's consciousness which is his seeing the page cannot simply *be* the same as the page's being there (as normally understood).

The identity cannot obtain, but there is nothing wrong, of course, in saying that S's seeing X *involves or requires* X's being there. On anyone's view, that is a requirement, but we no longer have an account of what the perceptual consciousness consists in, but merely the statement of an obvious entailment.

At this point, not withstanding the fact that the identity thesis certainly merits the name 'Radical Externalism' and also seems to fit some of Honderich's remarks, there arises the question whether it actually corresponds to what he is trying to convey, and if it does not, what exactly it is that he is claiming. Having placed these questions on the table, and on the understanding that I shall shortly return to them, I want to voice some more criticisms of the identity thesis, doing so without any commitment to the thought that Honderich's Radical Externalism *is* this identity thesis.

Let us suppose, then, that somebody did propose the identity thesis as an account of the nature of visual perceptual experience (that is, of seeing). What else might be said against this proposal? One problem with saying that S's seeing X simply is X's being there, is that, presumably, it should also be said that S's *hearing* X is X's being there, and that S's *feeling* X is X's being there. In these equivalences there is nothing which says what seeing X as opposed to feeling X or hearing X is. A second problem is this. S sees the page, and, of course, the page is there. But also between S and the page is a collection of oxygen atoms, a collection of carbon-dioxide molecules (and masses of other things), and where the page is there is also a large number of atoms, and sub-atomic particles, and so on. These are all there, but are not seen. The identity theory quite fails to explain why amongst the things there it is the page and not the rest that is seen, since all it says is that to be seen is to be there. Honderich can be read as briefly touching on this point. He says,

> the physical world ... consists in two categories: (1) things taking up space and time and also having other properties as standardly or publicly perceived ..., and (2) things that also take up space and time, [and] are without perceived properties ... (p. 6).

What, we need to ask, does the difference between, on the one had, being there and having perceived properties and, on the other, being there and not having perceived properties, amount to? Clearly it is not a difference in respect of simply being there. Clearly, also, it is no theoretical clarification of what perceiving an object is to be offered the slogan that it is for the object to be there *with perceived properties* (or aspects).

Third, as well as the identity theory not explaining why the objects seen are the ones amongst those there which are seen, it also fails to explain, what we might call, the *way* the seen object is seen. Suppose (scene 1) S sees some water and a straight stick next to it. What is there is water and straight stick. The stick looks straight and next to the water. Next, (scene 2) suppose that S sees a straight stick in water. In scene 2 the stick looks bent, in scene 1 it does not. There is a difference in the perceptual situation which we express in our talk of how the stick looks. In both scenes, however, what is there is a straight stick. Thinking solely in terms of *what is there* does not provide any explanation for the difference it. We have to think of the perceptual occurrence as more complex than simply consisting of what is there.

Looking at these examples achieves two things, I want to suggest. The first is that we have located some of aspects of the phenomenon of perception which account for the existence of the vocabulary that we have to describe it. Thus we distinguish within the class of what is there between the visible and the invisible, within the class of the visible between what we do and do not actually see, and between the ways seen things look. The phenomenon has a complexity which requires the existence of such a vocabulary. The second is that as theorists of what perception is we are forced to recognize that the phenomenon cannot be reduced simply to the being there of what is there. Radical Externalism 1 is an externalism too far!

I want to return now to the question already tabled but postponed; what does Honderich's Radical Externalism claim? If it is to be true, or close to the truth, it had better not be the Identity thesis, which I am calling Radical Externalism 1. There is another reason (besides that of giving Honderich the benefit of the doubt) to think that his Radical Externalism is a different claim. He says,

> the page's being there, and more generally *your world of perceptual consciousness* is things being in space and time, with such further properties as colour, and being dependent on a scientific or noumenal world underneath and also dependent on you neurally (p. 6).

Now, this sentence, crucial as it is, is hard to make sense of, since it seems to say that your world of perceptual consciousness is things being in space and time, or as I have been putting it, things being there, but it is also something dependent on your neural condition. These seem to be joint characterizations that are inconsistent. The problem is that the thing's being there (for example, the page's being there) does *not* depend on your neural condition. However, a consistent reading would that the state of affairs of your being perceptually conscious of some object, say the page, is something that involves the page's being there and is also a state of affairs the obtaining of which depends on how you are neurally.[3]

Let us call this thesis Radical Externalism 2. I want to make a few remarks both about it and about its status as an account of what is being claimed.

(1) Radical Externalism 2 leaves out, in particular, the claim that neurons or neuronal events are *not* components in consciousness. (This claim represents, I think, what Honderich sees as his rejection of standard materialism.) It does this because, apart from the 'things that are there', Radical Externalism 2 says of nothing else that it is, or that it is *not*, involved. It therefore fails to say something that Honderich wants to say. Perhaps, though, it says only things that he does want to say.

(2) Although not including that, Radical Externalism 2 does, it seems to me, (probably) fit two other claims that Honderich wants to make. He insists that Radical Externalism does not reduce to the claim that what is there is, simply, *what we perceive* (or are aware of). Plainly Radical Externalism 2 does *not* reduce to that. It does not do so because its claim that objects are involved in, are constituents of, the conscious occurrence, while possibly not entailing that these things are not objects of awareness certainly claims *more* than that. Second, he stresses that he is opposed to the idea that the occurrence of the perceptual sort of consciousness is something that has a sufficient condition in the subject's brain. That would indeed seem to be correct if the conscious occurrence has external objects as constituents.[4]

(3) I need to say a little more about how I understand the claim that I am calling Radical Externalism 2. It needs to be distinguished from a thesis that no-one would dispute. The indisputable claim is that if a

---

[3] As we might say, the 'is' in 'your world of perceptual consciousness is the thing being in space and time' is the 'is' of 'is in part'.

[4] I discuss some issues connected with the idea of brain states as sufficient conditions for perceptual consciousness in 'Reflections on an Argument from Hallucination', forthcoming in *Philosophical Topics* 2006.

subject S is genuinely perceptually aware of a G then there is a G. For example, if I actually see an ape in front of me then there is an ape in front of me. In this respect seeing an object is like sitting on an object. I cannot do it unless the object is there. However, Radical Externalism 2 is not a thesis about what has to be there for seeing an object to count as occurring. It is, rather, a thesis about what the conscious occurrence, the experience considered in itself, *involves or consists in*. In putting it this way I am of course assuming that we understand this talk of what a conscious occurrence considered in itself consists of. Some claim not to understand it, but I shall simply assume that we do. Now, one view is that the conscious experience itself involved in sighting an object is something that is only causally related to the object and that it happens inside the subject. Radical Externalism 2 denies this and claims instead that the experience considered in itself cannot be separated from the perceived object. Now, this is not a new thesis. It has some claim to be what the defenders of naïve realism in the philosophy of perception were claiming. It also has some claim to be what so-called Appearance theorists mean to say when they affirm that the most basic characterization possible of perceptual experience is that it consists of an object's appearing to the subject. Finally, it is what some current theorists who call themselves disjunctivists seem to be claiming about perceptual experience. I suppose that this confers some degree of respectability on Radical Externalism 2. I am myself sympathetic to this idea, but for me the interest in Professor Honderich's discussion is whether he provides new and strong reasons to believe it. The next remarks turn to that question.

(4) Honderich's fundamental positive argument relies on a principle that he formulates in various ways. One formulation is this; 'With respect to consciousness, *there is no difference between appearance and reality*' (p. 5). The immediately following formulation is; 'with consciousness, what there seems to be is what there is' (p. 5). I want to concentrate on the latter proposition and shall call it the Positive Seems Principle (PSP).[5] He then claims, and this is the second premise in his argument, that when, for example, you see a page it seems that your consciousness consists in the page being there. It therefore follows, given PSP, that in such a case what it *does* consist in is the page's being there.

It seems to me that both premises in this argument are questionable. Whether the second premise is true is a rather delicate issue. The

---

[5] In a semi-formal way PSP can be formulated; $(\forall e)((e$ is an experience & Seems$(F(e))) \rightarrow F(e))$.

delicate issue is this; although about the case that Honderich is envisaging, in which S sees a page, and, as we might add, the page appears to be a page, so there is no question for S about its being anything but a page, we can certainly say that it seems to S that there is a page, and also that it seems to S that that (seen) item is a page, can we with truth also say it *seems* to S *that S's consciousness consists in the page's being there?* A doubt at least can be generated by comparing how such a subject would (probably) react to two questions. Suppose that we asked S; what seems to you to be there in front of you? In the imagined circumstances S would unhesitatingly answer; it seems to me there is a page. Suppose, however, that we asked instead; what does it seem to you that your consciousness consists of? I suggest that such a question would not elicit any quick response in a typical subject, indeed, it would in all likelihood puzzle or silence them. Yet, if it does manifestly seem to them in undergoing the experience that their consciousness consists of the page's being there, why should they hesitate? We might further ask why the question should have such a silencing effect. Moving faster at this point than I am entitled to, I want to suggest that the difficulty is that in undergoing the perceptual experience of seeing the page there is no such item as the subject's consciousness (or the subject's experience) which seems (or appears) some way to the subject. One way to support this suggestion is to ask of the subject's consciousness which supposedly seems some way to the subject where does it seem to be. It surely cannot be said that the consciousness seems to be in the space ahead, where the page seems to be. Nor can it be said that the consciousness seems to be inside. How then can the consciousness seem to consist of something in particular if there is *nowhere* it seems to be so that its constitution can be revealed? Neither the subject's experience nor the subject's consciousness presents itself to the subject in such a way that it can seem to have a certain constitution. Any conceptually sophisticated and mildly reflective subject will, of course, know that he or she is conscious and having an experience, and so count as being aware of their consciousness in that sense, (in the way, I might provocatively add, that someone who has been told about an approaching hurricane is aware of the hurricane), but amongst the items seeming one way or another to the subject in the course of the episode the subject's consciousness itself does not figure.

I have been making a case for denying that the subject's consciousness itself seems to consist of something. However, the case has not been conclusively made, and I do not think that what I have provided would move someone who is strongly convinced that the consciousness does seem to consist of the external object. What, then, of PSP? Here it seems to me the case against is much stronger. Consider the example of a perfect hallucination of a gigantic pink rat. Clearly this is an episode of consciousness in which it seems to the subject that there is a pink rat ahead, but where there actually is no such pink rat. We certainly cannot say, then, that with conscious episodes what there seems to be is what there is. Consider also the case of illusions. If you see a Muller-Lyer diagram it seems that there are two lines of unequal length, but in fact there are no such lines. It might be replied that the relevant principle concerns how the consciousness itself seems to be, and so these are not counter-examples. However, this cannot be true either. If when I see a large pink elephant the consciousness seems to me to consist of a pink elephant then when I am having a large pink rat hallucination it will equally seem to me to consist of a large pink rat. Clearly, though, the hallucinatory episode cannot consist of that, there being no pink rat to do the constituting. I conclude that we cannot rely on PSP to support a theory of perceptual consciousness.

(5) I have so far discussed the idea that consciousness must be as it seems. But Honderich seems to subscribe to a further principle as well. He says; 'With consciousness, what there seems to be is what there is. *What there seems to be is all there is*' (p. 5; italics added). The principle that I have in mind is the principle expressed in the last quoted sentence. I do not quite know what it means but one possible reading is; an episode of consciousness only has a property P if it seems in undergoing it to be P. Crucially this implies that if it is not the case that the episode seems to be P then the episode is not P. I call therefore call this the Negative Seems Principle (NSP).[6] I do not know if Professor Honderich thinks this, but I wish to explain why he should not.

Note first that if NSP is true then one property that episodes of consciousness possess is fulfilling NSP. According to NSP such an episode can possess this property only if it seems to. A proponent of NSP must claim therefore that each episode of consciousness seems to fulfill NSP. I suggest that this is obviously false. When I have a pain it does not seem to me that the episode has no other properties beyond those it seems to have. The episode hardly indicates such a metaphysical feature to me. So the condition which NSP imposes for being true of consciousness does not apply to NSP. Second, there are obvious

---

[6] In a semi-formal presentation it says; $(\forall e) ((e \text{ is an experience } \& \text{ not Seems } (F(e))) \rightarrow \text{not } (F(e)))$. Putting PSP and NSP together we get; $(\forall e) (e \text{ is an experience} \rightarrow (F(e) \leftrightarrow \text{Seems } (F(e))))$.

counterexamples. My pain can be improved by taking paracetamol. It does not seem so. The episode of phantom limb pain does not take place in the limb (because there is no limb) but elsewhere. It does not seem to of course. Third, since Honderich believes that dualism is false then if he subscribes to NSP he must believe that each episode seems not to involve a spiritual substance. How odd that dualism should be so popular. Honderich himself seems to think that perceptual consciousness depends on how the subject is neurally. But does it seem so?

We should be sceptical of both PSP and NSP, and not rely on them in developing a theory of consciousness.

I have argued, assuming that Radical Externalism 2 is something that Honderich is claiming, that what I read as his main reason for it is unpersuasive because it relies on PSP, which is not true. I want now to engage with a second interesting theme in his account, which, as I said earlier, Radical Externalism 2 leaves out. This is the theme, revealed early in the paper, that consciousness should be conceived of as not having any 'neurons in it' and as not having 'your visual cortex in it' (both quotations from p. 3). I suspect that Honderich regards these conclusions as a rejection of the currently dominant materialist accounts of consciousness, and as, therefore, of some significance.

I want to argue both that no good reasons are presented for refusing to speak as the materialists do, and that if his reasons, or reasons like them, were good ones the conclusion should be regarded as relatively unimportant to the metaphysics of consciousness.

What are the reasons? What might be his first reason is that if we say that 'your visual cortex [is a] part' of seeing the page then it follows that 'there is more to your seeing the page than your consciousness of it' (p. 3). Now, a problem we face in understanding this argument is to know why saying this is wrong or objectionable. One possible reason might be that it is paradoxical, or close to paradoxical, to say there is more to seeing than being conscious of the page. Honderich himself seems to think that the problem with this consequence is not so much that it is paradoxical as that 'our ordinary assumption is that your visual cortex was no part of your being conscious ...' (p. 3).

The second reading of the argument leaves it with a rather disappointing status. Does it convincingly show that a philosopher's claim is wrong if it is contrary to an ordinary assumption? Honderich, who later emphasizes the revisionary nature of his own theory, can hardly think so.

Can the argument be sustained on the first reading? If Honderich has in mind as his target standard materialists then it is worthwhile pointing out that they do not normally say that the *neuron* itself was part of the sighting; rather, they might claim that the sighting is an event a part of which was a happening in the neuron. Would it follow from this that there is more to a sighting than the consciousness? If it does follow is that paradoxical? According to my brief characterization the materialist thinks that the occurrence of the sighting has as a part the neuronal event. This is like saying that part of my apple is a certain pip, which can hardly imply that there is more to my apple than my apple. It does imply that there is more to *know* about my apple than simply that it is an apple. So the materialist must accept that there is more to know about a sighting than that is it a sighting. Why, though, should we reject a position which implies that? Honderich might reply by appealing to NSP. However, I have already argues against that.

Honderich adds some further observations. The first is that since dualists deny that consciousness involves brain events and we can understand their claim then 'talk of your consciousness has to be understood as not itself talk of your brain' (p. 4). Such early psychophysical identity theorists as Smart and Place explained to us the way through this puzzle. The materialist claim is that the referent of 'my sighting' is that conglomeration of neural events, not that the meaning of 'my sighting' is to be given in neural terms. Rather they offered what they called topic-neutral analyses of mental talk. Honderich adds that people talk of correlations between mind and brain, as if this establishes their separateness. Smart and Place saw through this too. I can ask one person to check whether the man with pink shoes is at a series of parties and another to check whether the person with a yellow tie is, and maybe a perfect correlation is established. Why? It is the same person! You can therefore do what might be described, admittedly in a rather short-hand form of words, as correlating a thing with itself.

Suppose, however, that it is *wrong* to say that my sighting can have other, possibly unknown, events as parts. It would then follow that materialists should not say that sightings have neural events as parts, but also that dualists should not say that sightings have immaterial events as parts. This would merely mean that we need to re-express the issue between them in some suitably conceptually hygienic way. One possible way, or perhaps better, the sketch of one possible way, is this. Call one of us who sees a page S. Suppose we construct a physical replica of S, call this thing SR. We then generate in SR in the same physical circumstances the same physical processes as are going in S. Is it possible for SR to lack consciousness? Materialists might be thought of as those who claim it is not possible, and anti-materialists as those who think it is possible. Posing the issue this way makes no commitment to supposing that sightings can have unknown parts. It does require that episodes of consciousness can have unknown modal properties, but what has ruled that out? Maybe there is a problem with this way of posing the issue. However, we are a long way from having been given reasons for suspecting the traditional issue is beyond formulation.

How does this approach relate to Radical Externalism 2? The answer is that Radical Externalism 2 is not alien to materialism. The issue it raises is (or seems to be) just how extensive are the physical constituents of perceptual experience. There is no conflict.

I have argued that Professor Honderich's anti-materialism is not well supported, and that if Radical Externalism 2 is what he is affirming he provides no strong reason for doing so. The question I want to close with is; is Honderich's Radical Externalism actually version 2? I am strongly inclined to suspect it is not. Two passages in particular indicate this. First, Honderich says,

> A world of perceptual consciousness is not the physical world ... there is not much liberty in speaking of there being page in both a world of perceptual consciousness and in the perceived physical world, and indeed in referring to each as a page (pp. 6–7).

This is not what a Radical Externalist 2 would say. There are not two pages; the perceptual episode involves the actual physically real page. Honderich's picture is evidently different. But what then is it? If the page the existence of which is the perceptual consciousness of the page is a different sort of thing from the physically real page, what sort of thing is it? What sort of existence does it, as opposed to the physical page, have? In particular, can it, the page in consciousness, exist without consciousness? The second passage that attracts my attention is where Honderich describes his theory as 'conceptual revision or even reconstruction — conceptual revolution if you are being grand' (p. 10). This is not what one would say about Radical Externalism 2, which can be seen as a form of naïve realism! What then is the conceptual revolution? I confess then that I have to end with an expression of bafflement. In distancing himself from Radical Externalism 2, as I think he does, Professor Honderich is moving himself to a place I do not properly understand and in relation to which I would welcome more elucidation.

The thought might be voiced that in not properly understanding his conclusion my remarks about Honderich's arguments must also be wrong. But about them I have claimed that they contain false premises and that might be fair even if I have failed to understand the intended conclusions.[7]

## References

Honderich, T. (2006), 'Radical externalism', *Journal of Consciousness Studies*, **13** (7–8), pp. 3–13. [This issue]

# REPLY TO SNOWDON BY HONDERICH

Paul Snowdon's paper is as formidable as any in this collection. Will Radical Externalism survive my thinking about his objections in the course of replying to them? Will the conversation he speaks of beginning be discomfiting for the Radical Externalist?

He begins by wondering if perceptual consciousness, as I understand it, includes what he calls *non-perceptual sensory episodes*, such as hallucinations and dreams, and maybe sensations, migraines, toothaches, itches and aches. He rightly answers his question, partly, when he says that perceptual consciousness for me cannot include hallucinations, whatever my earlier taxonomic intuition may have been as a result of the salient similarity of hallucinations to seeing real things. About the importance of hallucinations and dreams to the subject of consciousness, we do not much agree. I take it a good account of perceptual and other consciousness has to measure up to a lot more than demands having to do with pink rats and bent sticks in water.

We definitely do not agree that Radical Externalism leaves out and offers no analysis of his non-perceptual sensory episodes — it can treat of hallucinations in terms of reflective and affective consciousness. So with dreaming. That both of these things are similar to seeing, that they are with some reason called non-perceptual *sensory* episodes, indicates that reflective consciousness has a little more in it than first comes to mind. It has in it thinking and making mistakes about representations *in* that consciousness rather than what they are about. But our aim in life can't be to make things simpler than they are.

As for the other items on his list, the sensations, migraines and so on, they have not had a lot of attention from me, but I will not be rushing to include them in perceptual consciousness, of which the paradigm is indeed visual consciousness. Affective consciousness is importantly a matter of feelings, and thus is the category that comes to mind for the sensations and the rest.

---

[7] I wish to thank Professor Honderich and the editor of the journal for their invitation to be a respondent to the paper, and for their patience in waiting for my response!

Snowdon also wonders about whether *wanting*, also taken by me to be important in affective consciousness, is rightly put into a third category or type alongside perceptual and reflective consciousness. There seems to me no adequate objection to including it in the fact that a want in the sense of an occurring experience is not, as he of course says, before someone's consciousness continuously. So what if there is another kind of want, so-called, that *is* continuous? That neural disposition is no part of our subject. As for recognizing the onset of a desire, it seems to me I often do, to the minute, and can give you an idea of how I do. But, more important, any problems here do not establish that the category of affective consciousness has too much in it. It doesn't, so far as I can see.

What exactly is Radical Externalism? That is the first of two main questions Snowdon puts in front of us, the other being about an argument for it.

Certainly the theory does not merely imply, as he says, but rather asserts, that some consciousness isn't cranial. Snowdon's first proposal as to what the theory comes to is labelled as Radical Externalism 1. It makes use, so surprisingly, of what he calls the most natural or completely normal idea of something's being there, existing — not an idea of being there or existing *in a way*. His proposal, in my words, is as follows.

- Radical Externalism 1: Someone's being perceptually conscious is identical with external things being in places for certain times.

He says, as you might expect, that what we have here is a *psychophysical* identity thesis, if an unusual one — since saying something is in space and time, as he does, with no more said, does indeed convey that it exists physically, or just that it is physical, part of the physical world. So what we have here, in Radical Externalism 1, is that your being perceptually conscious is for an extra-cranial world to exist, which is to say for part of the physical world to exist.

Snowdon now takes the trouble to assert that it seems that Radical Externalism 1 cannot be true. Indeed it can't, first of all in that a page can be there in this sense without anyone being conscious. End of theory. He not only takes the theory to be false for this good and unavoidable reason, however, but also partly for a different bad reason. It is no good saying that the state of affairs identified with being perceptually conscious in Radical Externalism 1 is under-described because it does not contain all that there is in *seeing the page*, where that is broadly understood to have more in it than somebody's being conscious of the page — say the person's head being oriented in the right direction. You may remember that we settled on the subject of consciousness itself, rather than all of what it is to see something, at the very start (p. 3), and indeed Snowdon himself registers the fact later (pp. 192–5).

But Radical Externalism 1 is absolutely definitely not Radical Externalism. After all, back there at the start, there was that declaration: 'A world of perceptual consciousness is not the physical world' (p. 6). There were the following lines in which a world of perceptual consciousness, things of course in space and time, were distinguished in terms of their particular way or kind of existence. They were then explicitly distinguished despite a similarity — both not being 'mental' — from the perceived part of the physical world (p. 7).

It may be that the misunderstanding that Radical Externalism 1 might be Radical Externalism is my fault — that the real theory was not so sharply sketched as I hoped — despite the sketch including things that Snowdon himself takes as telling against the idea that Radical Externalism is Radical Externalism 1 (pp. 190–1, 195). Could it be, too, that the novelty of the theory is itself a barrier to practiced philosophers of mind? I hope its fate isn't progress from novelty taken as blunder to familiarity taken as nearly as bad. You will learn soon that that fate is discerned, even declared.

Snowdon now offers three further objections to the psycho-physical identity theory that is Radical Externalism 1. Might they also be objections to Radical Externalism in his second understanding of it? We can usefully get that second understanding on the table right now. He depends on a quoted sentence of mine, and we can suppose he takes this theory to be as follows.

- Radical Externalism 2: Someone's being perceptually conscious is identical with things being in space and time external to the person, with such further properties as colour, and being dependent on a scientific or noumenal world underneath and also on the person neurally.

Snowdon contemplates for a passing moment that this is just inconsistent, partly by way of his eliding *being in space and time* with *being there* in the sense of being physical. Better, he contemplates that Radical Externalism 2 is inconsistent because something's being in space and time is *not* dependent on how somebody is neurally. He then thinks again and allows the possibility, as he certainly needs to, that the theory is consistent since it does not assert that the things being in space and time, that particular fact about them, is dependent on the person neurally — it can be something else about them that is neurally dependent.

I am happy enough with Radical Externalism 2 as a statement of Radical Externalism in so far as that theory concerns perceptual consciousness, but feel the need to add a relevant confession.

It is that Radical Externalism has not come complete with a contained theory of space and time. More particularly, it has not got into the question of whether or rather to what extent exactly the spatial and temporal facts of something, a world of perceptual consciousness, are owed to a particular person. It hs not got into the different question, either, of whether and to what extent exactly the spatial and temporal facts of something else, the physical world, are owed to to all of us humans, or some of us engaged in understanding and interacting with that world. It leaves all that to Kant, Newton, Leibniz and successors.

The theory will be better when somebody *does* get into the question of space and time in the context of the theory. That, as you will gather it also seem to me, has not been absolutely essential so far. What has been essential is that there is a distinction between those two human dependencies, which certainly there is — and hence a distinction that leaves clear the conception of things being in space and time in a certain way, a world of perceptual consciousness, as against the physical world or a part of it.

Let us now look at the application, to what I shall just speak of as Radical Externalism rather than Radical Externalism 2, of the three further objections made to the obviously false Radical Externalism 1.

One is that the given general account of perceptual consciousness does not itself supply a distinction between the consciousness in seeing something and the consciousness in hearing something. That is true, and maybe the hearing is harder to deal with than the seeing, but no reason is given for thinking that some consistent detail is impossible in the given general account. As for the consciousness of feeling something, in what seems to be the intended sense, that does not fall here at all, as you have heard.

The second objection to Radical Externalism 1 as it was stated — look back at the statement — is another one fatal to it, close to the first fatal one that was unavoidable. It is that there are lots of spatio-temporal things, here meaning physical things, external to the person, and these in no way enter into the person's consciousness. Say a collection of oxygen atoms between him or her and a page. But there is no objection to the real Radical Externalism here. The collection of oxygen atoms is not dependent neurally on the person and so is not something of which the person is conscious according to the theory.

The third objection, applied to the real Radical Externalism, and in brief, is that it does not given an account of a straight stick's looking bent in water. It is true that Radical Externalism has not much attended to this staple illusion (p. 190). Snowdon does not show it to be true in advance that it cannot do so with tolerable success. It might get some help, I suppose, from whatever turns up at this point in the disjunctive theory of perception, of which Snowdon is a principal owner. We will be coming back to this neighbourhood.

Now come up again to where we were, with Radical Externalism well enough stated, i.e. as Radical Externalism 2, and what Snowdon has to say about it.

Comment (1) would apply only to some poorer statement of the theory — one that leaves it open that your consciousness ordinarily includes the things in space and time that are your neurons. The theory definitely doesn't include that bit of materialism.

Comment (2), which has to do with Radical Externalism's not being circular, doesn't seem to take matters further.

Comment (3) attempts to take matters further, pretty dramatically, and needs more attention. It proceeds, by the way, from Snowdon's assuming, as against other unidentified persons, that we do understand talk of a conscious occurrence sufficiently well in order to carry forward this conversation. That is reassuring, if to my mind a remarkable understatement of our grip on our subject-matter, the central and as good as universally agreed subject-matter of the philosophy of mind.

In comment (3), to come to it, Snowdon speaks of Radical Externalism as denying that conscious perceptual experience happens inside a person and is only causally related to an external object. Radical Externalism, he says,

> claims instead that the experience considered in itself cannot be separated from the perceived object. Now, this is not a new thesis. It has some claim to be what the defenders of naive realism in the philosophy of perception were claiming. It also has some claim to be what so-called Appearance theorists mean to say when they affirm that the most basic characterization possible of perceptual experience is that it consists of an object's appearing to the subject. Finally, it is what some current theorists who call themselves disjunctivists seem to be claiming about perceptual experience (p. 192).

Despite the guarded language, this really comes as really a surprise to me.

Naive realism, which I take it turns up as itself, more or less unaltered since about 1932, as one of the two either-or halves of disjunctivism, the half about perception as against hallucinations, has in my reading of it has always been a little vague. It has been a little vague in characterizing something it takes to be within perceptual consciousness and definitely is *not* what it calls the object of the consciousness — not an external object. Something the same is true of most opposed theories or sorts of theory of perceptual consciousness, with *internal* objects.

I mean that both theories or sorts of theory speak of perceptual consciousness as being (1) awareness, apprehension, sensing, non-inferential connection, perceiving, directedness-at, intentionality, aboutness or whatever with respect to (2) external or internal objects. That these usages are a little vague does not make what they designate other than proper parts of the theories.

The internalist theories in particular are always advanced and characterized as giving a particular account of our awareness or whatever of external objects: that it is an awareness *mediated* or *made indirect* by internal objects — sense-data or whatever. Naive realism has always been advanced and characterized as subtracting or denying the internal object, *not* subtracting *both* such an object and also any relation in consciousness to the remaining external object.

Do you wonder if naive realism's talk of awareness, apprehension, sensing, perceiving, directedness-at or whatever *can* be heard and construed as *not* about anything that is within our consciousness — heard and construed as putting within our consciousness *only* an object, say a physical page? Well, that has never been explicit, and so, at the very least, it is certainly false to say Radical Externalism is old-hat in the sense of having had an explicit antecedent. But that is not what mainly is to be said about the idea that Radical Externalism is just naive realism.

Remember, as cannot conceivably be denied, that naive realism indubitably characterizes perceptual consciousness itself in terms of exactly a *physical* object. It is thereby already different indeed from Radical Externalism — a world away, you could say. Remember too, and I trust conclusively, that naive realism if it *is* taken as reducing its account of an episode of perceptual consciousness to just the existence of a *physical* object, is absurd. Not all physical objects are in somebody's perceptual consciousness. Remember, finally, that it is clear that naive realism can be taken as consistent with devout physicalism — one of the two main things that Radical Externalism, to say the least, is not.

It is impossible for me to think, then, that Radical Externalism can be assigned the fate of really being the thin old broth of naive realism, not even warmed up.

The world being the imperfect place it is, with deadlines in it, I cannot acquaint myself with those who are named Appearance Theorists by Snowdon. I can remark that they do not sound like

Radical Externalists. They are reported as meaning to say that the most basic characterization of perceptual consciousness is that it consists of an object's appearing to the person. I take it the appearing isn't the object, whether or not an appearing requires what it seems to require, which is an appearance. Those are items that it is the very nature of Radical Externalism to leave out.

Still more reminders could be offered of the difference of the thing that is Radical Externalism from naive realism etc., starting with the criteria of adequacy and the subjectivity of worlds of perceptual consciousness and so on. Maybe some of this is in Snowdon's own disjunctivism, but I rather doubt it. In any case, you may hurry to agree that I have already taken a little far my desire to get a hearing rather than an obituary for Radical Externalism, not to mention taken a little far my own *amour-propre*.

What matters more, as Snowdon implies, is what can be said for Radical Externalism as against other theories of consciousness. He turns his attention at this stage (p. 192) to his other main question, the argument for it that was put in at the start of my piece beginning this collection of writings. It is important, if not more fundamental than other things.

The argument in its first premise was that your consciousness itself, all of it, is something you *have*, something clear to you, something present to you, immediate. With respect to consciousness itself, to say the same thing differently, there is no difference between appearance and reality. The second premise of the argument was that your being perceptually conscious of something seems to amount to the thing's somehow existing.

Snowdon first questions the second premise. He says that when you are perceptually conscious of this page, there sure seems to you to be a page there. But you're just puzzled or silenced if, as he should go on to say, somebody puts it to you that what your consciousness seems to you to consist in is some kind of existence of the page.

Well, Snowdon and I disagree about this, and we can leave it to you — maybe you as a better judge for being a typical philosopher, scientist or the like rather than just a typical subject, maybe not good a kind of undistracted thinking. We can also leave it to you to agree or not if somebody else puts it to you that your consciousness seems to you to consist instead in a container of some kind with some content in it, maybe sense-data, or consists in a kind of arrow flying at something. Or a bunch of neurons, or some stuff that isn't anywhere.

Snowdon attempts to explain and therefore to make more likely what he supposes, that you are puzzled or silenced by my prompting that what it seems to you to be conscious of the room is for a room somehow to exist. His explanation of your supposed bafflement consists partly in his assigning to you a reluctance to regard your being conscious of something as an *item* — your being conscious as an item. I agree you probably have *that* reluctance. Being conscious isn't much like a pound of butter.

But do I not rightly do you as much credit in assigning to you a willingness to regard your being conscious as your having a *property*, or there being a *fact* or *state of affairs* pertaining to you? There is nothing in *that* attitude that gets in the way of your agreeing with the Radical Externalist proposal about what your being visually conscious of something seems to consist in.

And, to press on with Snowdon's explanation of your supposedly being puzzled or silenced, do you really suppose, as Snowdon seems to propose, that the state of affairs, say, of your being conscious, is *nowhere*? Isn't any state of affairs where the main thing or things in it are? And does a state of affairs — say a world of perceptual consciousness — have to have exact and settled boundaries in order to be somewhere? In which case many wars, plays on and behind stages and a lot else are nowhere. I agree we have hesitations about consciousness and space, but not enough for Snowdon's purposes. and in fact they can be taken to tell in the direction of Radical Externalism (2004, pp. 184–5)

He allows in sum that he has not made a conclusive case against the second premise in the argument for Radical Externalism — that it seems to us that our perceptual experience consists of there being a certain external state of affairs. It strikes me that he has more reason for this self-doubt about his case than he supposes.

The first premise of the argument for Radical Externalism, now to turn to it, in my quoted lines, was that 'consciousness is something we *have*' (p. 4), that 'with respect to consciousness *there is no difference between appearance and reality.* With consciousness, what there seems to be is what there is' (p. 5). Snowdon is not specific but he first takes this, I gather, as something like the following named thing.

- Positive Seems Principle: What there seems to be in consciousness is what in the natural or normal idea there *is* — if something seems to be, in consciousness, it exists. The seeming is sufficient for the existing.

He also contemplates, I gather, that the the first premise is something else.

- Negative Seems Principle: What there seems to be in consciousness is all there *is* in the natural or normal sense —

if something doesn't seem to be in consciousness, it doesn't exist. The seeming is necessary for the existing.

I'm surprised again. Surprised to hear myself saying so, but it really seems that you find out what the first of those mouthfuls comes to when Snowdon refutes it, to his very proper satisfaction, by citing somebody's hallucination of a gigantic pink rat. The refutation, more particularly, is that there isn't a gigantic pink rat there in the room in front of the poor fellow. There isn't a physical rat there.

That refutation assumes an understanding of the first principle that commits somebody who holds it to the conclusion not only are that there no hallucinations as ordinarily understood, which is bad enough, but no false beliefs in human life either. Also no misdescriptions of things, no mistakes, no self-deceptions and so on. In short, the principle as understood would have us believe that all of what are called contents of consciousness, including all beliefs, are true.

You learn what the second mouthful comes to when Snowdon refutes it by noting, among other things, that it isn't part of what your conscious pain seems to you to be that it can be affected by paracetemol, but it can be. The pain *is* affected. Snowdon also refutes the Negative Seems Principle by noting that if it were true, my passages of thinking about spiritualism, where it seems to me that consciousness doesn't involve a spiritual substance, would in themselves somehow refute the spiritualism.

Well, something has gone awfully wrong. It's a good thing that this is only the first exchange in a longer conversation. Whatever my quoted lines come to, they can't usefully come to this stuff. I take it Snowdon will do me the small compliment, however quick my lines were, of allowing that you have to try to find another way of understanding them. I pay him the compliment of having got to me to try to think some more, making myself more explicit and distinguishing two kinds of givenness.

To leave close consideration of his paper, my past idea and hope in a nutshell was to use a general proposition about our *having* all our consciousness in order to put together a general argument for your perceptual consciousness being some existence of a world, not neurons or an inner theatre of the spirit, and of course to put together the general argument without getting committed to the existence of gigantic pink rats. Also, for success with the argument, if it involved demoting the hallucination to reflective and maybe affective consciousness, essentially demoting it to false belief, there would have to be some way of avoiding demoting perceptual consciousness. That is, there would have be some way of keeping the seeming nature of a piece of perceptual consciousness from falling to the level of the hallucination — being no evidence or indicator of any reality. Some way of keeping a world of perceptual consciousness from collapsing into just belief or whatever in a head. Some way of defending the essence of Radical Externalism.

The idea and hope was preceded by something else, by the way, which is worth spending a minute or two on before we go ahead. It will have a greater role and value depending on how the idea and hope turns out on further reflection. It is that you can actually go some way towards Oscar Wilde's general view that it is only shallow people who do not judge things by their appearances. That is, you can contemplate the general idea that when you have not got a lot to go on with respect to the question of the nature of something, you'll rightly attend to its *apparent* nature — say a plant or an animal unprecedented in your experience.

What about consciousness? Do we have a lot to go on, a lot of information, evidence or the like about *its* nature? Well, we know a lot about its connection with the physical world and hence its beginning, alteration and ending. But although we have a grip on the fact of our consciousness we haven't had much of an analysis of it, if any.

I suspect that what has made devout physicalism the most hopeless cause among reflective persons since the 17th Century and Hobbes, and what drives seemingly devout physicalists to hopeless stratagems of one kind and another, is indeed a need to judge consciousness by its appearance. The need also results, I can suppose, to come to the main point, in support for Radical Externalism's account of perceptual and indeed reflective and affective consciousness.

But return now from a general policy about anything's apparent nature, and hence the nature of consciousness, to what is certainly distinct, the idea and hope relevant only to consciousness. As already remarked, I have felt the need to try to think again about this as a result of Snowdon's piece in particular but also those of Harold Brown, Tim Crane, James Garvey, Jonathan Lowe, Derek Matravers, Paul Noordhof, Stephen Priest and Barry Smith. Must have been a plot.

With respect to all of consciousness — perceptual, reflective and affective — we can surely stick to the point that there is a sense in which it is had by or given to whoever or whatever is in question. It is present, immediate, not a matter of judgement or inference. There is nothing in or to your consciousness itself, no part of it, that is not had by or given to you in this way. There seems to be, maybe must be, some sense in which statements to oneself about one's consciousness itself, as against what it is about, are true. (Priest, you will remember, says otherwise [pp. 158–9] and his argument will have to be dealt with.) Does conviction this have to be qualified a little to allow for *confused* consciousness? I doubt it. The confusion too is *there*.

Certainly what is had or given in this way, to repeat, is not what consciousness may represent, be about. There is no such guarantee with statements about those other things. With respect to a gigantic pink rat of which you are conscious, the rat in your consciousness, you know that he is in there. You don't know that there is a rat out there in front of you.

But that seems to leave something certain. Unless you're in some piece of science fiction, some advanced set-up where you are actually inspecting your own neurons or neural activity or process, those things are no part of your consciousness. The fact that our consciousness is all *had*, and the fact of what is ordinarily had by us, gives us the conclusion that devout physicalism is indeed the mistake it has and is taken or suspected to be by almost everyone. I don't see that this line of reflection has been refuted or that it can be refuted. It works as well against spiritualism.

That is not the end of a story. Consider perceptual consciousness by itself, typified by your being conscious of the room you're in. There is something else going on here, which maybe I half had in mind in the past.

Before you get around to forming beliefs or judgements with perceptual consciousness, there are what we can call *the facts*. We *have* or are *given* them, in a different sense from the one above that pertains to all of consciousness. What is wrong with the coherence theory of truth or anti-realism, at bottom, is not the old argument that you often need to accept another proposition to verify a first one. What is wrong is that the coherence theory supposes you are never out of the ring of propositions, never in touch with the truth-makers. Somehow you are.

To come towards the crux of the matter for this line of inquiry, there *is* a way in which propositions about the facts, *these* facts in perceptual consciousness, are *secure*. If my consciousness of a gigantic pink rat is as much given to me, in the familiar sense, as what I call my consciousness of this room, there is a further sense in which my latter consciousness is different in being *secure*. This second sense in which something is had by you, given to you, is the crucial sense for our present concern.

To come closer to the very crux, there are some statements to be made with perceptual consciousness that are somehow beyond doubt, statements that are necessarily true in some unordinary way. There are some statements here that are different indeed from the one about the rat. They are also different from a vast amount of respectable belief, indeed by far the largest part of our body of belief. It includes most of science and philosophy.

You ask what the somehow necessarily true statements of perceptual consciousness are. The answer is that they are a few very general statements having to do with propertied things in space and time, some or other somehow propertied things. For whatever reason, however deep or shallow, it cannot be that the general report of my perceptual experience as having to do with propertied things in space and time, some or other propertied things, is false.

Now to come to the crux you've no doubt anticipated, it is the proposition that these reflections are well on the way towards what you have been hearing from the beginning, the much less general conclusion that my perceptual consciousness consists in a certain full-fledged or replete world of perceptual consciousness, as does yours.

Certainly the secure facts of perceptual consciousness can't be expressed as being anything like that my perceptual consciousness itself is axons and dendrites in my head or anything like stuff in a spiritual place that isn't anywhere. Those are way past the limits of possibility. So we now have a second ground for disbelief in materialism and spiritualism. Do you whisper that someone logically could have perceptual experience that consisted in pure or unexpressed numbers, or just a glow of God, or the great emptiness? You will anticipate that I want to say no, they couldn't. That wouldn't be perceptual experience.

So — all of consciousness is given in an ordinary sense, which fact goes against materialism and spiritualism. With respect to perceptual consciousness, something is *given* in another sense, which helps with Radical Externalism. The last thing is new in Radical Externalism.

No doubt you will want to hear more about the distinction between the few secure propositions owed to perceptual consciousness and the insecure propositions either owed to it but not general or fundamental or a long way away, including one about the rat. There is a lot to say, but not here. Snowdon rightly speaks of the philosophy of mind as in part being metaphysics of perception. There is no staying out of that. It can't be left to metaphysicians.

Let me just make two remarks. One is that there is a unique order, stability and consistency about the secure propositions, as against pink rat propositions and so much more than them, indeed almost all of our propositions. The other remark is that it may be that our possibility of subject-predicate propositions, those at the bottom of our existence as knowers, requires the secure propositions. Have a look, maybe, at Peter Strawson's fine book *Individuals*.

Snowdon finishes his piece by in effect defending or anyway being tolerant of materialism or devout physicalism, which he surprisingly describes as the 'currently dominant' account of consciousness. Really? Dominant where? Certainly not in the human race, or the reflective human race. Certainly not in the professionally inquiring human world outside of philosophy, definitely including neuroscience as well as the rest of science, where at least an agnosticism plainly rules. Not in philosophy generally. Not in philosophy in the English language either.

And not, arguably, in our English-language philosophy of mind. Almost all current philosophers of mind in our language mix a little mystery into their reasonable commitment to the reality of consciousness, sometimes taking care to stick to cooler metaphors, as in the case of Searle and his lines about levels (Honderich, 2004, pp. 89–90; 2005, pp. 96–117). What you need to mix in, according to Radical Externalism, is the recognition of subjectivity and more that comes with worlds of perceptual consciousness. What you need is that near-physicalism. And to revert to Snowdon's declaration of a dominance of materialism — to which materialism, incidentally, I myself have no emotional resistance owed to religion, high humanism, literary sensitivity, personality or the like — there is also need for another of those doses of psychology or sociology on or of philosophy, this time on the insecurity of our line of life, its hopeful assumption of comrades on every side. Wish I was entirely free of it.

Towards the end of his paper, Snowdon and I seem not to be on the same wavelength. Maybe the main trouble is my inexplicitness back at the start of what he is discussing, my initial paper. What I was up to was no more than fixing a subject-matter for discussion — first using a supplied understanding of perceptual consciousness to fix that subject-matter. To this end I settled on the ordinary understanding of what it is for you to be perceptually conscious, which I did not try to supply but which I confidently persist in thinking does not include in the consciousness your neurons or your retinas. So it evidently is taken as something other than, in fact less than, your *seeing the page* in a natural understanding.

Snowdon gives the impression of thinking that this was a case of begging the question of the nature of consciousness against devout physicalism. My idea is that it wasn't and isn't. The understanding and the fixing of the subject-matter leaves it open that the thing identified in the given way is different than it is assumed to be in the understanding. It could be all neural activity. It could be ghostly stuff. This circumstance of inquiry is one we know all about at the moment in another context, where someone speaks of what he calls *terrorism* and we know what he means and we can still have a fruitful disagreement about its nature and morality, disagreement about what he puts into his definition (2006, p. 83).

I grant, of course, that you can try to beg questions and influence people by your initial identification of a subject-matter, of which advantage you may indeed feel a need, as in the case of sticking neural activity into consciousness. Maybe I was moved a little by that kind of impulse myself. But it wasn't intended to and certainly doesn't settle things. The arguments of Radical Externalism against materialism are rather its failure to satisfy imperative criteria for a decent account of the nature of consciousness.

I am puzzled by particular comments made by Snowdon in this last part of his paper. What he speaks of as my first reason for not including the neurons in the initial identification of consciousness is that then it would follow that there is more to seeing the page than your consciousness of it. Well, I don't follow that diagnosis or interpretation of my motivation or whatever. It was *I* who was speaking of your seeing the page as having more in it than your consciousness. More puzzles follow for me in what Snowdon says. You as reader may sort them out, having the advantage of not being internal to, maybe stuck in, the language and usages of one of two interlocutors.

Let me just add that it is very clear to me that it is possible to avoid what you take to be question-begging and worse by certain stratagems. If somebody wants to run together up and down, as you see it, or male and female, or brain and mind, he can specify some items that will help him. He can get into a good deal of trouble about reference and meaning, of course, particularly if the supposed meaning is Frege's 'mode of presentation of the referent', but no matter. He can keep a question unbegged — but he won't prove up is down that way.

What remains to be said, or rather what can be said now in this imperfect world, is only a word or two on the penultimate paragraph of Snowdon's greatly appreciated paper. The penultimate paragraph isn't right. Radical Externalism *is* Snowdon's Radical Externalism 2, at least as understood by me, and it isn't Naive realism. At the end of our first exchange of conversation, in which I have not replied to everything he had to say, my situation is one of rumination but not great discomfiture.

## References

Honderich, T. (2004), *On Consciousness* (Edinburgh: Edinburgh University Press).
Honderich, T. (2005), *On Determinism and Freedom* (Edinburgh: Edinburgh University Press).
Honderich, T. (2006), *Humanity, Terrorism, Terrorist War: Palestine, 9/11, Iraq, 7/7* ... (London: Continuum).

# *Contributors*

***Ted Honderich*** <t.honderich@ucl.ac.uk>, formerly Grote Professor of the Philosophy of Mind and Logic at University College London, and a visiting professor at Yale and the City University of New York, is now visiting professor at the University of Bath. His books include *A Theory of Determinism: The Mind, Neuroscience and Life-Hopes*, and a philosophical autobiography, *Philosopher: A Kind of Life*. He is editor of *The Oxford Companion to Philosophy*. His book *After the Terror* caused controversy in for its moral defence of Palestinian terrorism against neo-Zionist ethnic cleansing. A related volume, *Humanity, Terrorism, Terrorist War: Palestine, 9/11, Iraq, 7/7*, was published in July 2006.

***Harold Brown*** <hibrown@niu.edu> is Professor of Philosophy Emeritus at Northern Illinois University. He is author of *Perception, Theory, and Commitment: The New Philosophy of Science, Observation and Objectivity, Rationality*, and *Conceptual Systems*. He has published numerous articles, mainly in epistemology and philosophy of science.

***Tim Crane*** <tim.crane@ucl.ac.uk> is a professor of philosophy at UCL, and director of the Institute of Philosophy in the University of London (www.philosophy. sas.ac.uk). He is the author of a number of articles on the philosophy of mind and metaphysics, and of *The Mechanical Mind* (2nd edition Routledge 2003) and *Elements of Mind* (OUP 2001).

***James Garvey*** <j.garvey@royalinstitutephilosophy.org> is Secretary of the Royal Institute of Philosophy and author of some books and articles, mostly on mind and the history of philosophy.

***Stephen Law*** is currently lecturer in Philosophy at Heythrop College, University of London.

Formerly Junior Research Fellow in Philosophy at The Queen's College, Oxford, he has B.Phil and D.Phil degrees from the University of Oxford. Law first entered academia via The City University, London as a mature student. He previously worked as a postman.

**E.J. Lowe** <e.j.lowe@durham.ac.uk> is Professor of Philosophy at the University of Durham, specializing in contemporary metaphysics and the philosophy of mind and action. Amongst other things, he is the author of *Subjects of Experience* (CUP 1996), *The Possibility of Metaphysics* (OUP 1998), *An Introduction to the Philosophy of Mind* (CUP 2000) and *The Four- Category Ontology* (OUP 2006). He is currently writing a book on the philosophy of action entitled *Personal Agency*.

**Derek Matravers** <D.C.Matravers@open.ac.uk> lectures in Philosophy at the Open University, where he is currently Head of Department. He is also a Fellow Commoner of Jesus College, Cambridge. He is the author of numerous articles on aesthetics and ethics. His book, *Art and Emotion*, came out with Oxford University Press in 1998. He is currently working on a book on value, to be published by Acumen.

**Paul Noordhof** <paulnoordhof@clara.co.uk> takes up an Anniversary Professorship of Philosophy at the University of York in October 2006, having been a professor of philosophy at the University of Nottingham. He has been awarded a three-year Major Leverhulme Research Fellowship to conduct research in consciousness and representation, the fruits of which will be published in his book *Cement of the Mind* (under contract with OUP). He has published on these issues in *Analysis*, *Australasian Journal of Philosophy*, *Mind and Language* and *Philosophy and Phenomenological Research*. He is also Reviews Editor of *Mind*.

**Ingmar Persson** <ingmar.persson@phil.gu.se> is professor of practical philosophy, Gothenburg University, Sweden. His fields of research are ethics and the philosophy of mind and action. His principal publication is *The Retreat of Reason: A Dilemma in the Philosophy of Life* (OUP 2005).

**Stephen Priest** is a member of the Faculty of Philosophy in the University of Oxford (10 Merton Street, Oxford OX1 4JJ). He is Senior Research Fellow of Blackfriars Hall, Oxford and a member of Wolfson College, Oxford and Hughes Hall, Cambridge. He is author of *The British Empiricists*, *Theories of the Mind*, *Merleau-Ponty* and *The Subject in Question*. He is editor of *Hegel's Critique of Kant*,

*Jean-Paul Sartre: Basic Writings* and co-editor (with Antony Flew) of *A Dictionary of Philosophy*. He has lectured widely in the United States and Europe and his writing has been translated into Spanish, Russian, Japanese and Korean.

**Barry C Smith** <b.smith@philosophy.bbk.ac.uk> is senior lecturer in the School of Philosophy at Birkbeck College and Deputy Director of the Institute of Philosophy at the University of London. He has written on the philosophy of mind and language and on the emotions. He is joint editor of *Knowing Our Own Minds* (OUP 1998) and *The Oxford Handbook of Philosophy of Language* (OUP 2006).

**Paul Snowdon** <p.snowdon@ucl.ac.uk> has been Grote Professor of Mind and Logic at University College London since 2001. Before that he was a Fellow at Exeter College, Oxford. He has published articles about perception, personal identity and a range of other topics in the philosophy of mind. His first book *Persons, Animals and Ourselves* is due to be published in 2007.

# Index

aboutness
  see intentionality
absences, experienced 53-4
actions and consciousness 181-2
  see also affective consciousness
acts, mental 5-6
affective consciousness 8-9, 36, 134, 198-9
Anomalous Monism, 61, 65-6
anti-realism 208
appearance and reality of consciousness 14-15, 24, 32, 35, 64, 69, 78-80, 87-91, 118, 154, 158-9, 161, 171, 192-5, 204-10
  see also givenness of consciousness; have, consciousness as something we
appearance theorists 203-4
Apkarian 21
Aristotle 20, 45
attention 80, 91, 175-6, 181
awareness of awareness 10, 181
  see also inner and outer
Ayer 8, 38, 59, 89, 156
  see also Logical Positivism

behaviourism 55
being 161
being there 5, 29, 79, 80
  see also existence
Berkeley 29, 37, 39, 44, 81, 91-2, 124, 148, 159, 164
bent stick in water 48, 79, 190, 202
Blair 58
Bonjour 132
brains in vats 8, 48, 50-2, 59, 83-4, 93, 118, 127
Brentano 148, 171

Buddhism 147, 158
Burge 7, 45

Campbell 97, 103
causal efficacy
  see criteria for an adequate theory of consciousness: causal interaction
causal interaction of consciousness and the physical
  see criteria for an adequate theory of consciousness: causal interaction
causation 32, 65-6, 73-5, 136, 146
Chalmers 33
circularity 9, 39, 100, 107-8, 111-12, 122-3, 178-9, 183-4, 191, 202
cognitive environment or surround 176-7, 182-3
coherence theory 208
colour 113, 124
compromise theories of consciousness 182
conceptual analysis 10, 16, 165
conceptual revision, revolution 16-20, 22, 26, 45, 127, 165-6
consciousness, 3, 5, 6, 177 see also
  affective consciousness;
  appearance and reality of consciousness;
  criteria for adequate theory of consciousness;
  givenness of consciousness
  have, consciousness as something we;
  perceptual consciousness;
  reflective consciousness;
  worlds: worlds of perceptual consciousness;
Consciousness as Existence 8, 28

consciousness, most resilient
    proposition about 55, 207, 209
  *see also* criteria for adequate theory
    of consciousness: seeming nature,
    subjectivity
content 5, 8-9, 80, 103, 110, 159, 171,
    204 *see also* medium
content, non-conceptual 7
Correlation Hypothesis 131, 143
  *see also* Union Theory
counter-example 57
cranialism 3, 9, 15-16, 25, 81-3, 142,
    144, 199
criteria for adequate theory of
    consciousness 10-11, 33, 40-1, 127
  causal interaction with physical
    events 12, 20-21, 42, 65, 87
  efficacy 12, 115-16, 125
    *see also* mind-brain relation,
      epiphenomenalism
  on subject 10, 34
  reality, 12, 20-1, 33-4, 44
  seeming nature 10, 55
  subjectivity 9, 42, 62, 64, 69-72,
    91-2, 96, 171, 204

Davidson, 58, 65, 72-3, 125
  *see also* Anomalous Monism
democracy 55
dependencies 6, 9, 24, 29, 37-8, 46-8,
    51, 56-8, 68, 93, 112, 153, 168,
    191, 201
  *see also* mind-brain relations
dependency, right kind of 58
Derrida 158
Descartes 10, 12, 20, 27, 33, 41, 62, 87,
    93-4, 155-7, 159, 162, 171, 174, 178,
    184
desire 28
devout physicalism 10-11, 42, 54-5,
    70, 73-4, 94, 123, 127, 140, 155,
    161, 166, 182, 195-6, 203, 207,
    209-10
  and spiritualism, division of
    philosophies of mind into 28,
    33-5, 72, 93-4, 102
dilemma of subjectivity or causal
    interaction 63-4
directedness *see* intentionality

disjunctivism 26, 29, 31-2, 38, 40, 56,
    109, 111, 117-18, 120-2, 127, 185,
    202, 204
dispositions, mental 5
DNA 19
double awareness 183-4
double vision 48, 99-100, 106-7
dreaming 7, 48, 51-2, 59, 187
dualism 4, 10-11, 20, 33, 41-2, 66, 73-4,
    85, 93-4 *see also* spiritualism

Einstein 18
empiricism 151-2, 168
Empiricism, British 7, 105
emptiness 155, 173, 174
epiphenomenalism 12, 63-8, 74-5, 116,
    125, 136, 146
epoché 153, 155, 157, 169-79
events, nature of 73
existence 6, 7, 36, 45-8, 148-52, 188
  in a way of worlds of perceptual
    consciousness 7, 28-9, 30, 36, 46
  not a predicate 45-6, 56
  sense of 161-2
externalism 7, 29, 32-3, 81-3
  *see also* Radical Externalism

facts, the 208
finger in eye
  *see* double vision
Fodor 9
Follesdal 169
Frege 211
Freud 5, 36
functionalism 55

Galileo 18
Garvey 102, 106
givenness of consciousness 5, 40, 90-1,
    106, 120-1, 127, 205-10
grip on consciousness 55, 202

have, consciousness as something we
    4-5, 8, 24, 64, 71, 78, 85-6, 90-1, 106,
    112, 154, 157, 161, 172-3, 183-4,
    204-10
  *see also* givenness of consciousness,
    appearance and reality

hallucinations, argument from 8, 24-5, 31-3, 39-40, 48, 50-2, 56-9, 83, 118, 120, 127, 179-80, 184-5, 194, 205-6
Hardcastle 21
Hegel 159
Heidegger 162
Helmuth 21
Hobbes 55, 207
Hume 5, 45, 124, 136, 139, 159
Husserl 147, 152-7, 159

idealism 37, 42, 139-40, 152, 159, 161-2
ideas 7
identity theory of mind and brain 34, 140, 189-90, 196, 200
    see also devout physicalism; cf Union Theory
illusions 14, 48
    see also subjective contours; cf hallucinations
illusion, argument from 8, 39-40, 49-52, 60, 83, 89, 93, 107, 120, 184-5, 190
images 133
inner and outer 175, 177, 179, 182-3, 184 see also interiority
inside see interiority
intentionality 5, 31, 35, 37-8, 71-2, 99, 113-16, 148, 155, 159, 171, 173, 203-4
internalism 157-61, 172-4
interiority 152, 158-62, 168

Jackson 44
James 139
Johnson 38

Kant 44, 45, 73, 124, 152, 158, 201
Kuhn 127

Leibniz 20, 73
Locke 20, 81, 89, 124
Logical Positivism 173

Mach 139
Manzotti 8, 13
marriages of devout physicalism, spiritualism 11, 41-2
Martin 29
mass 17

materialism 11, 55, 74, 161-2, 196, 210
    see also devout physicalism
materialism, eliminative 11, 34, 55, 62
McGinn 95, 102
medium 80, 91
mental efficacy
    see criteria for adequate theory of consciousness: efficacy
mentalism see spiritualism
mental realism 71, 121
Merleau-Ponty 156-7
metaphysics 48, 88-9, 174, 209
mind 5, 106,
mind-brain problem insoluble 102
mind-brain relation 4, 8, 31, 47-8, 52, 56, 62-3, 74, 159, 160
monism 4, 42
    qualified materialist 42
moods 147
Moore 50
Muller-Lyer diagram 194

Nagel 38, 44, 161
naive realism see realism, naive
Nash 179, 185
naturalism 54-5, 161
near-physicalism
    see physicalism, near-
negative facts 60
Negative Seems Principle 194, 205
neutral monism 129-31, 139-41, 142
neutral monism, comparison with Radical Empiricism 140-1, 142-6
Newton 17-18, 19, 73, 201
noema 156
non-conceptual content
    see content, non-conceptual
non-existence 48-
non-perceptual sensory episodes 187, 198
Norman 148
nothingness 53
noumenal world see worlds

objective world see worlds
Occam's Razor 8, 49
occasionalism 20, 63
On Consciousness 44

pain 21, 67

Papineau 3
perceptual consciousness 6-8, 36, 39, 58-9, 147-52, 164-5
  apparent, but in fact conceptual 24-5
  worlds of *see* worlds
perceptual, reflective, affective consciousness 6, 36, 53, 104, 165, 175-7, 181-2, 199
phenomenalism 7-8, 40, 83, 130
  *see also* sense-data
phenomenology 28, 31, 49, 89, 110, 118, 121, 128, 149, 155-7, 159, 169-72, 187-8
  *see also* appearance and reality
philosophy of mind, current 10-11, 22, 26, 34-5, 40-2, 44, 55, 63, 72, 78, 93, 210
physical causal closure 67, 75-6
physical world *see* worlds
physicalism 44
  devout *see* devout physicalism
  near 12, 38, 42, 119
physics 17-19, 55
Place 196, 211
Plato 48, 56
point of view 47, 97, 105, 156-7, 176
Positive Seems Principle 192, 205
pre-established harmony 63
presence 158
privacy of consciousness 39, 64, 71, 157, 161, 172
psychoneural relation
  *see* mind-brain relation
psychophysical laws 65-7, 75
Putnam 7, 45

qualia 109, 112, 119-20
Quantum Theory 185

Radical Externalism, general character, judgements on 7-9, 17, 23, 30, 35, 37, 41-5, 61, 63, 70, 77, 101, 109, 117-19, 147, 162, 172, 177-8, 180-1, 200-1
realism 7, 25, 31, 36, 130, 148, 152-3
  direct 83
  naive 59, 109, 120, 192, 202-4
  representational 49, 56, 81

reductionism 166
reflective consciousness 8-9, 24, 58, 113-17, 125-6, 132
reification 78, 85-6, 90, 98, 149, 172, 193, 205
representationalism 109-10, 113-15, 124, 126
representations 7, 9, 31, 48-9, 57, 116-17, 132, 144-5
Ruda 21
Russell 139

Sainsbury 99, 106
Sartre 53, 59, 151, 154, 168, 171, 174
scepticism 48, 84-5, 171-2
science, all consciousness as subject for 12, 87
scientific world *see* worlds
Searle 210
seeing 3, 7, 23-4, 182, 189-90, 199-200, 201, 210-11
seems/is *see* appearance and reality
self *see* subject, self
self-consciousness 182-3
sensations 28, 187, 198
sense-data 7, 8, 30-1, 39, 57, 81, 92, 109, 112, 123, 203
simplicity *see* Occam's Razor
Smart 159, 196, 211
soul 161, 172
space 6, 12, 41, 50, 65, 73, 81-2, 92, 156, 201, 205
special relativity 18
Sperber 176
Spinoza 20
spiritualism 10-12, 33, 41-2, 62, 85, 93, 140, 161-2 *see also* dualism
St. John of the Cross 148
Strawson 28, 35-6, 209-10
subject or self 5, 11, 71-72, 86, 94, 112-13, 122-3, 128-9, 155-6, 158, 160-2, 168, 171, 174
subjective contours 14-16, 23-6
subjective worlds *see* worlds: worlds of perceptual consciousness
subjectivity *see* criteria for adequate theory of consciousness: subjectivity

terrorism 211
Thagard 10
time 73, 156-8, 161, 173-4, 201
to be is to be perceived 37, 81, 92, 161
    *see also* Berkeley
Tonneau 8
transparency 99, 106

unconscious 5
Union Theory of mind and brain 107
ur-world *see* worlds: what there is

Valberg 32
values 9
Verification Principle of Meaning 173
Vico 158

wanting 188, 199
Webber 53
what it is like 5, 69
what there is *see* worlds: what there is
Wilde 207
Wilson 176
Wittgenstein 32-3, 159
world, ur-
    *see* worlds: what there is
worlds 47, 95-9, 102-6, 115-16, 125-6
    mental or 'mental' 47-8, 52, 56, 92,
        98, 122-3, 161
    noumenal 47, 160
    objective 47
    of perceptual consciousness 5-7, 23,
        29, 36, 37, 47, 63-5, 67, 91-3, 96-9,
        119, 161, 167, 178, 188-9
    physical 6-7, 12, 25-6, 30, 38, 167,
        169-71
    relations between 30-1, 38-9, 68,
        75-7, 125-6 *see also* dependencies
    scientific 47
    what there is, ur-world 6, 24, 44,
        169

# *Journal of Consciousness Studies*

**imprint-academic.com/jcs**

'With *JCS*,
Consciousness Studies has arrived'
Susan Greenfield, *Times Higher Educational Supplement*

# Subscription Form (see also: imprint-academic.com/jcs)

Name . . . . . . . . . . . . . . . . . . . . . . . . . . . . . . . . . . . . . . . . . . . . . . . . . . . .

Address * . . . . . . . . . . . . . . . . . . . . . . . . . . . . . . . . . . . . . . . . . . . . . . . . .

. . . . . . . . . . . . . . . . . . . . . . . . . . . . . . . . . . . . . . . . . . . . . . . . . . . . . . . . .

Home phone no . . . . . . . . . . . . . . . . . Email . . . . . . . . . . . . . . . . . . . . . . .
*Credit card customers must supply cardholder registered address*

## ANNUAL SUBSCRIPTION RATES: Vol. 14 (2007)

12 issues. Prices inc. accelerated delivery (UK/USA), rest of world surface.
**Individuals:** $127/£67     **Libraries:** $437/£230     **Students:** $91/£50*
*(full-time student status evidence & course completion date required)
Individuals with UK bank accounts can also subscribe for only £16.50 per quarter by Bankers' Direct Debit. Contact **sandra@imprint.co.uk** for details.

☐ Enrol my library/individual/student subscription ☐ Airmail extra: $52/£26

☐ **Free with new subscription**. Choose one of the following back issues:
☐ *Trusting the Subject, Parts 1 and 2*, ed. Jack & Roepstorff
☐ *Psi Wars: Getting to grips with the paranormal* ed. J. Alcock *et al.*
☐ *The Varieties of Religious Experience: Centenary Essays*, ed. M. Ferrari
☐ *The View from Within: first person approaches*, ed. F.J.Varela & J.Shear
☐ *Between Ourselves: second-person approaches* ed. Evan Thompson
☐ *The Emergence of Consciousness*, ed. Anthony Freeman

### Back Volumes Special Offer
Full set of back volumes 1–13 (1994–2006) @ *80% discount* (online only*).
**Individuals/Students:** $330/£174; **Institutions:** $1136/£598.
* for online **and** print editions add £75 (UK), £175/$332 (ROW).
☐ Please enter my Individual/Institutional discount back volume order.

### Payment Details

☐ Cheque (pay 'Imprint Academic') $ (US bank) or £ Sterling (UK bank)

☐ VISA ☐ MASTERCARD ☐ AMEX ☐ MAESTRO ☐ DELTA ☐ JCB

Card No. . . . . . . . . . . . . . . . . . . . . . . . . . . . . . . . . . . . . . . . . Expiry date . . .

Security code (last 3 digits on back) . . . . . Signed . . . . . . . . . . . . . . . . . . . . .
*Credit cards (except US Amex) charged at £ Sterling rate and converted by your card issuer*

---

☐ **10% introductory discount on Volume 14 for CCDD**
We have been authorized by Barclays Bank to operate a credit card direct debit (CCDD) system, whereby we automatically charge your card at subscription renewal time. We will notify you by post in advance to give you plenty of time to cancel the transaction and your consumer rights are fully protected by your card issuer.
*I authorise Imprint Academic to recharge my card on the annual renewal date.*
Signed . . . . . . . . . . . . . . . . . . . . . . . . . . . . . . . . . . . . . . . . . . . . . . . . . . . .

---

*U.S. Subscriptions Office:* Center for Consciousness Studies, Dept. of Psychology, University of Arizona, PO Box 210068, Tucson AZ 85721-0068
*Rest of World:* Imprint Academic, PO Box 200, Exeter EX5 5YX, UK
Tel: +44 (0)1392 851550   Fax: 851578   sandra@imprint.co.uk